# Experiments & investigations

## ■ How scientists work

Scientists collect and use information in many different ways. A biologist might observe the behaviour of an animal in its environment and then compare these observations with others of the same animal under different conditions. Statistics, a form of mathematics, can help to analyse the results and to discover if the differences observed mean anything.

Studying animal behaviour.

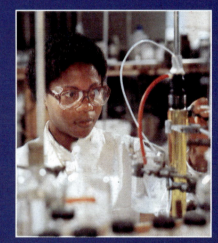

Investigating a group of newly discovered chemicals.

A chemist might try to solve a particular problem. For example, she might be trying to design a new type of antifreeze using a group of newly discovered chemicals. She might have to analyse the chemical properties of all the members of this group before a suitable antifreeze can be produced. The scientist might have to run hundreds of separate tests, each involving the careful control of variables so that the results can be compared fairly. In this case, the scientist would have a good idea what to expect, but would not know exactly what the answers to the questions she was investigating were going to be.

A physicist might be trying to discover exactly what is in the centre of an atom. He might be part of a team of more than a hundred scientists, working in different laboratories in different countries. Each of his experiments might cost millions of pounds and so his team cannot afford to do more than one a year.

An aerial view of the huge loop near Geneva where scientists study atomic structure.

The people on the previous page are all scientists but they all work in different ways. This book does not suggest that scientists work in the same way. Nor does it suggest that one method of working is better than any other. Instead, it suggests a range of methods that can be used in studying science. Some of these methods might also be useful in other situations – at home or in a maths lesson, perhaps.

▸ *Make a list of some of the skills you think a scientist would need.*

## Things to think about

Use practical work to help your learning. Try to explain the results you get from practical work in terms of **models**. Models are systems that can be used to help understand other problems and to predict what might happen in other situations. Using information from many different sources will help you understand your classwork better. Do not be afraid to ask for help, or to ask a friend to explain an idea to you. You may be given the chance to use computers to collect or to handle data, or to write up notes or experiments. Computers are very good at finding patterns in data.

▸ *Write down a list of all the possible sources of information you might use for a project in science.*

Try to apply what you learn to a real-life situation. Do not think of science as just something learned in a classroom. Look for it in your everyday life, but do not think that science can solve all the world's problems. Some problems seem just too difficult for even the greatest of scientists and others are just too expensive to solve.

▸ *Think of some problems that science has yet to solve. Can you think why we have failed to find a solution?*

Just as we study different types of scientific problems in different ways, you might like to write up your notes in different ways. Graphs, tables and diagrams help to explain complicated information. Presentations, models and posters can help to make the information more interesting.

Longman Co-ordinated
**S·C·I·E·N·C·E**

# BIOLOGY

*Terry Parkin*
*John Simpkins*

*with*

*Julie McCarthy*
*Jackie Reffin*

*Series Editor*
*Terry Parkin*

LONGMAN

Addison Wesley Longman Limited
Edinburgh Gate, Harlow, Essex CM20 2JE, England

First published 1996

© Addison Wesley Longman Limited 1996

Designed and produced by Gecko Limited, Bicester, Oxon

Printed in Great Britain by
Scotprint Limited, Musselburgh, Scotland

ISBN 0582 276535

## Acknowledgements

**We are grateful to the following for permission to reproduce copyright material:**

Bayer Diagnostics for the product, Glucostix; the Health Education Authority for an information chart from *A Guide to Healthy Living*; IACR-Rothamsted for two data tables; Ewan MacNaughton for extracts from the article 'Mandela: Let us eat elephant' by Greg Neale from the *Sunday Telegraph* 13.11.94. © The Telegraph Plc, London 1994

**We are also grateful to the following for permission to reproduce photographic materal:**

**Front cover: Alfred Pasieka/Science Photo Library**
Polarised light micrograph of crystals of vitamin B12
**Ace Photo Agency**, pages 63 centre (photo Ben Simmons), 85 left
**Allsport**, page 77 (photo Mike Cooper)
**Dr Deborah Allen**, pages 13 top, 15, 23
**Audi**, page 13 centre
**Biophoto Associates**, pages 32 top, 65 centre, 79 top right, 79 top left, 96 left, centre and right, 143, 218, 243 bottom right
**Bridgeman Art Library/Christies, London**, page 143
**BP**, page 1 top right
**Catherine Blackie**, pages 2, 165 bottom, 228 centre left and centre right
**Anthony Blake Photo Library**, page 45 bottom
**Bubbles Photo Library**, page 232 top right (photo Jenny Woodcock)
**Cern**, page 1 bottom
**Trevor Clifford**, pages 31, 39 top, 51 (all photos), 189,
**Bruce Coleman**, pages 216 top (photo Henneghien), 217 top left, page 224 (photo Jen & Les Bartlett), 232 centre top (photo Jennifer Fry)
**Collections**, pages 83 bottom left, centre and right (photos Anthea Sieveking), 217 top right (photo Barbara West), 221 (photo Alain Le Garsmeur)
**EEV**, page 112
**John Frost**, page 93
**Ronald Grant Archive**, page 19
**Robert Harding Picture Library**, pages 54 bottom (photo Peto Blackwell), 130 (photo Walter Rawlings), 157, page (photo Waltham)
**Michael Holford**, page 18 top
**Holt Studios**, pages 54 top (photo Nigel Cattlin), 183 (photo Nigel Cattlin), 190 (photo Nigel Cattlin), 199 centre left, centre and centre right (all photos Nigel Cattlin)
**Image Bank**, page 13 bottom left (photo Paul Trimmer)
**International Horticulture Research Centre, Littlehampton**, page 184 bottom
**Katz Pictures**, page 205 top left, top right and bottom (all photos Drew Gardner)
**Kanehara & Company**, page 89
**Andrew Lambert**, pages 21, 57, 165 top right and left, 166, 191 bottom, 237 top right, 237 bottom, 240
**Frank Lane Picture Agency**, pages 1 left (photo Phil Ward), 208 centre top (photo WS Clark)
**Lister Hospital (Fertility and Endocrinology Centre)**, page 100
**Longman**, page 193 bottom
**National Medical Slide Bank**, page 40 top, 70 top

**Oxford Scientific Films**, pages 74 centre (photo LSF), 101 (photo David Frazier), 105 left and right (photos Geoff Kidd), 141 right (photo Raymond Blythe), 158 (photo Stan Osolinski), 159 (photo Jal Cooke), 168 left (photo Terry Heathcote), 168 centre (photo Mike Birkhead), 168 right (photo John Gerlach, 173 (photo Michael Fogden), 191 top (photo Jim Clare, Partridge Films Ltd), 199 bottom (photo James Robinson), 202 (photo Souricat), 207 left (photo Daniel J Cox), 207 centre (photo Michael Fogden), 207 right (photo Andy Park), 208 top left (photo Eric Woods), 208 top right (photo RL Manuel), 208 centre right (photo Daniel J Cox), 211 (photo Mike Slater), 214 top (photo Jeff Lepore), 214 centre right (photo Daniel J Cox), 216 centre left (photo Ronald Toms), 217 bottom left (photo Souricat), 17 bottom right (photo Sean Morris), 228 bottom (photo Peter Parks), 229 left (photo Andy Park), 229 centre (photo Michael Fogden), 229 right (photo Barrie Watts)
**Rex Features**, pages 29 (photo DCA), 81 (photo M Powell/Times), 127, 136, 184 top (photo DHT), 216 bottom right (photo Peter Brooker), 232 left
**The Royal Collection copyright Her Majesty Queen Elizabeth II**, page 137
**Royal College of Surgeons of England**, page 149
**Saatchi and Saatchi/Courvoisier** page 85 right
**Science Photo Library**, pages 13 bottom right (photo CNRI), 17 far left (photo Francis Leroy), 17 centre left (photo CNRI), 17 centre right (photo Alfred Pasieka), 17 far right (photo D. Phillips), 18 bottom (photo JC Revy), 32 centre (photo AB Dowsett), 36 top and centre (photos St Mary's Hospital), 36 bottom (photo John Durham), 37 top (photo St Bartholomew's Hospital), 37 bottom (photo CNRI), 38 (photo Professor Molta, Department of Anatomy, University of La Sapienza, Rome), 39 top left (photo Jane Shemilt), 39 bottom (photo BSIP, Beranger), 40 bottom (St Bartholomews Hospital), 45 top (photo Andrew Mcclenaghan), 48 left (photo James Stevenson, 48 right, 55 top (photo BSIP Bajande), 55 centre (photo Dr Beer Gabel/ CNRI), 61 left (photo Martin Dohrn) 61 right (photo Alexander Tsiarao), 63 top (photo Chris Priest and Mark Clarke), 64 (Biophoto Associates), 65 top (photo Hattie Young), 68 top left (photo Chris Priest), 68 top right, 68 centre left (photo Matt Meadows), 68 centre right (photo Schleichkorn) 70 bottom, 71 (photo CNRI) 72 (photo Department of Clinical Radiology, Salisbury District Hospital), 79 bottom left (photo Larry Mulvehill), 79 centre right, 79 bottom right, 82 (photo Manfred Kage) 83 top (photo Don Fawcett), 86 top (photo CNRI), 86 centre (photo Dr Colin Chumbley), 87 (photo Ralph Eagle), 102 (photo Adam Hart-Davis), 113 right (photo David Gifford), 113 left (photo Biophoto Associates), 117, 119 (photo Simon Fraser, Royal Victoria Infirmary, Newcastle-upon-tyne), 120 left (photo Simon Fraser, Royal Victoria Infirmary, Newcastle-upon-tyne), 120 right (photo Simon Fraser), 128 (photo CNRA), 160 top, 160 centre, 106 bottom (photo Dr Jeremy Burgess), 223 (photo Dr Jeremy Burgess), 243 centre left (photo Sinclair Stamners), 243 centre right (photo Eric Grave), 243 bottom left (photo John Walsh)
**Topham/Associated Press**, page 109
**John Walmsley**, pages 45 centre and left, 193 top and centre, 242, 237 top left
**Andy White**, pages 141 top, 147
**Ivy Wilkinson**, page 74 top
**Nigel Wood**, University of Bristol, page 133
**World Health Organization**, page 33

# Contents

# How to use this book

In Chapter One (Experiments and investigations) you will find out how to do experiments and what to think about when planning and carrying out investigations. In Chapter Sixteen (Biology help) you will find general information and hints which you might need for your practical work.

All the other chapters are organised in the same way. The first page of each one is an introduction to the subject which you are going to cover. The second page is designed to remind you what you might have learned before. There are some questions to help test what you remember. The remaining pages cover what you need to know for your exam.

## Experimental science

This book also contains introductions to the practical work which you might do. There are detailed worksheets to help you carry out your experiments. Use the practical summaries if you miss a lesson or need to revise.

The icons show you which skills you will be using;

planning      obtaining evidence

analysing      evaluating

▶ *There are questions marked with an arrow head like this. These are designed to help with your understanding of the text. For example you might be asked a short question to check if you have understood the paragraph you have just read.*

Your teacher will tell you whether you need to cover material which is marked like this.

You will find a summary at the end of each chapter.

Finally, there is a selection of graded questions at the end of each chapter. These are similar to the questions that you might get in your exams. You may be asked to do the questions in class or as homework. Your teacher will tell you which questions to do.

We hope you enjoy using this book.

These boxes contain extra information

▶ *Write down all the ways you can think of for showing data from different experiments.*

▶ *Copy the list of words below and discover their meaning. You might need a dictionary. Two are done for you as examples.*

- *fair test*
- *accurate*
- *reliable*
- *precise*
- *hypothesis*
- *variable*

**Hypothesis** *Based on earlier tests or some background research, this is an idea which can be tested by experiment. Usually, a hypothesis will involve predictions.*

**Variable** *This is a factor that can affect the outcome of an experiment.*

# Experimental work

Scientists spend much of their time collecting and analysing data. To do this effectively they must have a clear idea of exactly what they are trying to discover or test. Following a series of steps is helpful for many people. You might like to use these general headings when planning your practical work.

## Planning

- Be clear about what you are trying to test or discover.
- Can you write it out as a question?
- Can you write it in a more general form as a **hypothesis**?
- Can you support your hypothesis with knowledge that you already have?
- Do you need to do any background research?
- Are you sure that your method is safe?
- Do you know what apparatus is available?
- Which factors need to be controlled?
- Which factors will you measure?
- How will you measure these things?

## Evaluating evidence

- How could your experiment have been improved?
- Are the results fair?
- Can you explain any surprises in the results?
- Would comparing your results with another group help?
- What experiment needs doing next?

## Obtaining evidence

- Is it a **fair test**?
- Will you collect enough data to form a **conclusion**?
- Are you able to use all the apparatus correctly?
- Can you make accurate measurements?
- Do you need to repeat your experiment?

## Analysing evidence

- How are you going to record your raw data?
- Can you show it as a table?
- Can you convert it into bar charts or line graphs?
- Are patterns or trends obvious?
- Can you produce general statements from your data?
- It it possible to produce a conclusion linking your **variables**?

🔺 Things to think about when planning and carrying out experimental work.

# Safety

Remember, you will be doing a great deal of practical work. You, just as much as your teacher, will have to be responsible for your safety, so do not start any practical activity unless you are sure of what you are doing. You should carry out a **risk assessment** for each practical. One simple way of doing this is to write down each step of the practical, highlight any dangers and find a way of reducing your risk. Your teacher may give you a worksheet to help you each time you need to do a risk assessment.

Danger    Biohazard    Flammable    Wear gloves

Corrosive    Toxic    Irritant or harmful    Wear eye protection

🔺 Hazard signs.

# Apparatus

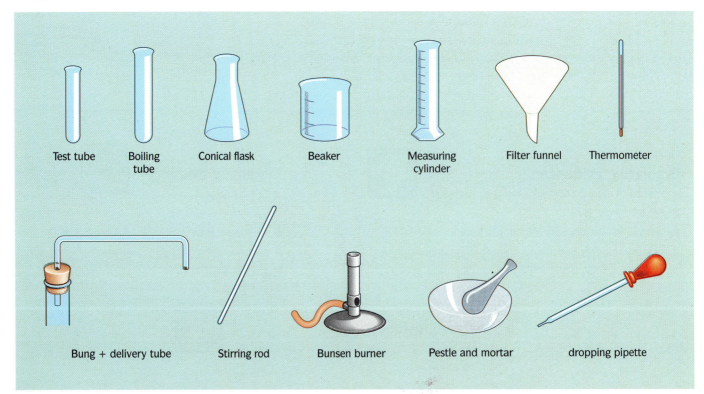

Test tube    Boiling tube    Conical flask    Beaker    Measuring cylinder    Filter funnel    Thermometer

Bung + delivery tube    Stirring rod    Bunsen burner    Pestle and mortar    dropping pipette

🔺 Here are some examples of apparatus that you might use in your investigations.

# Carrying out an investigation

It is often easiest to see how a model works if you can see it in action. Follow through this investigation on transpiration to see how the investigation model on page 3 might be used.

# Investigating transpiration

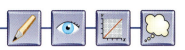

## The task

The first stage in an investigation is to make sure that the task is clear. In this case the task is to investigate how different factors affect the rate of transpiration in leaves.

▶ *Do you understand the task? Identify the key words or phrases in the problem and make sure that you understand each part. In this case, you might refer to textbooks to find out about* transpiration.

You should include any information you discover in your report, either as an introduction or perhaps in the discussion of your results.

▶ *List all the ways you might research this topic in your school, at home or in the local library. In each investigation, you should include a list of all the books or other sources, such as CD-ROMs, you consulted. This will form part of your* **bibliography**.

From your information search you might discover that the rate of transpiration depends on many things: on air movements over the leaf, the temperature, humidity, light levels and even the type of leaf. You might include sketches at this stage.

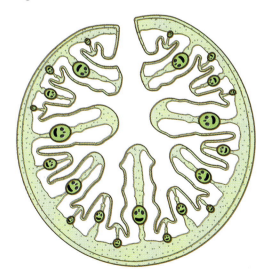

And you have not even started developing the plan yet ... .

However you decide to proceed, it is important that you are clear as to exactly which feature you are testing. For each experiment you do, you should alter only *one* feature of your investigation otherwise you will find it difficult to make it a *fair test*. If you change two or more features in a single experiment, it is impossible to say which is the more important. The features to be controlled, changed and measured are called **variables**. There are three different types of variable.

## Controlled variables

The **controlled variables** are those factors which you intend to keep the same throughout the experiment. The fact that you could change them makes them variables. The fact that you have decided to keep them unchanged makes them controlled.

## Independent variables

You will choose to test one or more factors. In each of your experiments you will focus on one feature. For example, in an investigation of the solubility of salt, you might investigate how changing the rate of stirring affects the rate of dissolving. The variable you choose to investigate is the **independent variable**. You might carry out separate tests on each independent variable to discover how it affects the system you are investigating. It is often possible to show these data on a graph. An independent variable is usually plotted on the x-axis of a graph.

## Dependent variables

This is the variable which you measure during the experiment. For example, the rate of change of temperature or of mass. Of course, the thing you measure might also change during the experiment, but it changes because of the experiment. We call this variable the **dependent variable** and it is usually plotted on the y-axis of a graph.

▶ *Copy these headings down and complete the table for the transpiration investigation.*

| Controlled variables | Independent variable | Dependent variable |
|---|---|---|
| | | |

▶ *Explain which of the independent variables you would investigate.*
▶ *What results would you expect when you investigate this variable? (You are making a prediction.)*
▶ *Is it possible to make a **quantitative** prediction? For example, many reactions double in rate for each 10°C increase in temperature. It is at this stage that your preliminary research might come in useful.*
▶ *Think back to some previous work. Did you do a similar investigation then? If so, perhaps you could base this experiment on your earlier work.*

## The prediction or hypothesis

A **prediction** is not quite the same as a **hypothesis**. The hypothesis has a stronger base of evidence, whereas a prediction is more of an informed guess. A hypothesis might be quantitative and based on previous work, and will form the basis of your subsequent work after the initial prediction has been tested.

▶ *You decide to investigate the effect of air movements and temperature on transpiration. Make a* prediction *for this investigation. Try to link the rate of transpiration with one of your independent variables and phrase it so that the prediction includes quantities of something that you can measure.*

## The plan

Once you have your prediction you now have to prepare a test to see if you were correct. Unless you can take accurate measurements, your experiment might not be very helpful in evaluating your hypothesis. To make a plan you must know what apparatus is available to you and how to use it.

▶ *List the apparatus available in your laboratory. Circle anything you think might be useful in this investigation. Underline any piece of equipment you are unsure of.*

▶ *What should you do if you are unsure about how to use a piece of equipment?*

Professional scientists have to **evaluate** (judge) the degree of risk in any experiment they intend to carry out. This procedure is called a risk assessment. Your teacher may give you a worksheet to help you each time you have to carry out a risk assessment.

DON'T LET THIS HAPPEN TO YOU!

▶ *Perform a risk assessment on an experiment you have done recently.*

## Risk assessment

Here is a sample risk assessment for the transpiration experiment. Can you think of any other risks?

| Hazardous chemical or micro organism being used or made, or hazardous procedure | Nature of the hazard(s) | Sources of information | Method(s) of reducing the risk |
|---|---|---|---|
| Use of scalpel for cutting stem | Very sharp | Observation, Safety warnings | Use scissors |
| Use of fan heater | Front of casing gets hot | Observation | Be careful. Let it cool before touching |
| Use of potometer | Not certain about about how to set up | — | Ask teacher |

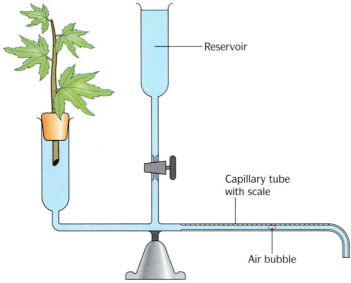

Reservoir

Capillary tube with scale

Air bubble

▲ Potometer.

## Collecting results

An important part of the investigation is thinking about collecting your results before you record them. You need to think about how to record your results (for example, in a table) and how to interpret them (for example, on a graph). If you plan well, you will be able to include the results in the form that you collected them. There will be no need to write them up neatly. In the transpiration experiment you might decide to use 'loss of mass' from a cut leaf as your dependent variable.

▶ *How could you measure the independent variable, the rate of air flow over the leaf?*

▶ **a** *Sketch out a possible plan for this experiment, including a results table. Remember your experiment must be a fair test with the appropriate variables controlled.*

    **b** *Will your experiment produce sufficient data for graphs (at least five points for each dependent variable)?*

    **c** *What units will you be using?*

Unfortunately, experiments do not always work in the way you hoped at the planning stage. Often you have to repeat an experiment and collect more results. This is done for two main reasons. First, it is difficult to say with certainty that a result observed only once is a **valid result**. Repeating the experiment once or even twice helps you to believe that a result is valid. Second, you may have overlooked an important feature of your experiment. Being able to recognise the need to repeat an experiment is an important skill.

## Analysing and presenting evidence

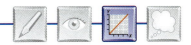

One group of students doing this investigation decided to use ribbon tied at a fixed distance from a hair dryer to give them an estimation of air speed. The faster the air moved over the ribbon, the nearer the ribbon moved to the horizontal. Their results are given in the table below.

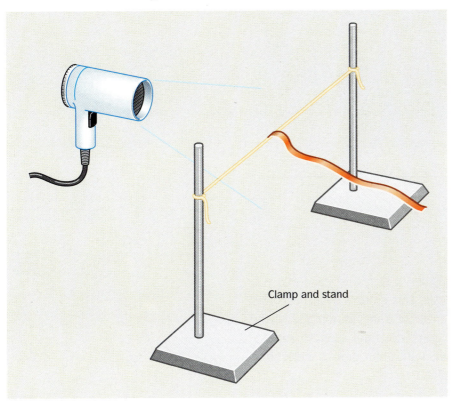

🔺 The group hung a piece of ribbon in front of a cold air blower. With the blower off, the ribbon hung downwards at 0°, and at 90° with the blower full on.

▶ *Study the results that the group collected. Suggest another way they might be presented.*

| Degree elevation of ribbon by blower | Mass (g) of 10 leaves | |
| --- | --- | --- |
| | Start | End |
| A | B | C |
| 90 | 3.90 | 3.59 |
| 60 | 5.19 | 4.84 |
| 45 | 3.44 | 3.14 |
| 0 | 4.18 | 3.81 |

BIOLOGY

Looking at these raw data in the table, it is hard to see a pattern. You need to analyse the data a bit more.

▶ *Work out:*
  **a** *the change in mass (B – C)*
  **b** *the percentage change in mass* $\dfrac{(B-C)}{B\times 100}.$

  *Which is the more useful value?*

▶ *Plot the percentage change on a graph. Have degree elevation as the x-axis and percentage change in mass as the y-axis.*

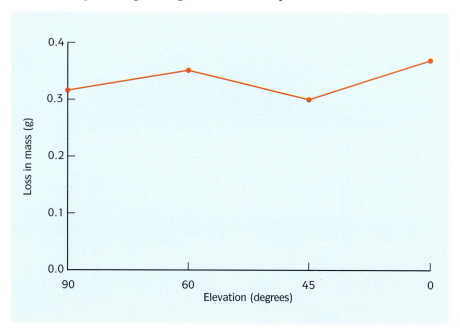

▶ *Can you see a pattern now?*

It is still difficult to make sense of these results. It is at this stage that you need to refer back to your original hypothesis. This group's hypothesis was that 'the faster the air flow, the greater the rate of transpiration and so the greater the loss of mass by the leaf'. The graph does not seem to support that hypothesis. They discussed their results with other groups working in the laboratory. Each group had similar results.

▶ *Can you think of any other experiments you could do which might help you to understand these results?*

# Evaluating evidence

The results of the experiment didn't fit the initial prediction, so the group thought of a new prediction and planned an investigation to test it. They **brainstormed** what might have caused the rate of water loss to have been lowest in the strongest wind.

▶ *Spend a few minutes with a partner brainstorming what might have caused this unexpected result.*

One of the group, Sophia, thought that the leaves were sensitive in some way to the air flow. She had discovered through her background research that the underside of leaves are covered in tiny pores called **stomata**. Stomata are able to open and close and so regulate the flow of water vapour from the leaf. Sophia hypothesised that these stomata would be more likely to be closed when the air movements were the fastest.

▶ *Plan an experiment to test Sophia's hypothesis.*

Sophia placed ten leaves in the blower's airstream and turned it on full. Every 30 seconds she coated the base of the leaf with nail varnish to fix the stomata in position and to give her a **cast** of the leaf surface. From this cast she intended to discover the percentage of open stomata for each time interval. When the nail varnish dried, she peeled it off and examined it at 600 × magnification under a microscope.

▶ *What do you think she saw … ?*

## Conclusions

Sophia will write up her results as a series of linked conclusions. She will also identify the most important variable. You should do this when writing up any investigations. You should also make a comment about your confidence in your findings.

You may be given the opportunity to check the significance of the results of an experiment using statistical tests. You might use similar tests in mathematics. Statistical tests help scientists to decide the amount of importance they should give to a particular result. If you discover through a statistical test that your result would be expected to occur 95 times out of 100 tests, you can have a high degree of confidence in the importance of the result.

The investigation should close with an evaluation of the techniques used. Your results might lead you to suggest further experiments, but you may not be able to find time to carry them out. You might even be able to include a comparison of your results with those of other groups in your class, or occasionally, to a published scientific paper.

Dr Debbie Allen is an engineer, but she does not build bridges or cars. She works on a much smaller scale.

Debbie engineers proteins, producing made-to-measure antibodies.

To engineer proteins Debbie needs to know how cells work. She needs to understand the way in which proteins are made inside cells so that she can make them in the laboratory.

This chapter introduces you to the knowledge needed by an antibody engineer. Make a record as you work your way through it of the key facts needed to make 'made-to-measure' proteins, like the one shown below, on the right.

# Cells

Antibodies protect us from disease. You may read about antibodies in Chapter Three (Health and blood). They have the ability to recognise other proteins. Some companies use antibodies as the basis of different kits to test for disease. They are also vital in the search for a cure for cancer. Protein engineering is big business.

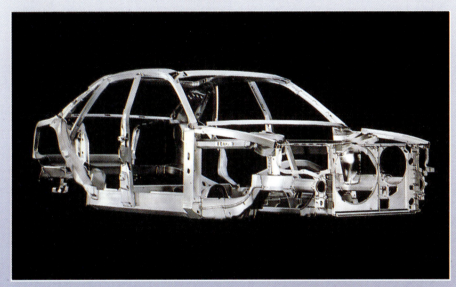

Different scales of engineering.

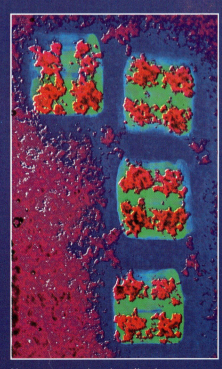

Human monoclonal antibody. Applications of the technology include tests for diseases and targeting of drugs in cancer treatment.

# Review

**Before going any further, read this page and attempt the tasks. Write the answers in your notes.**

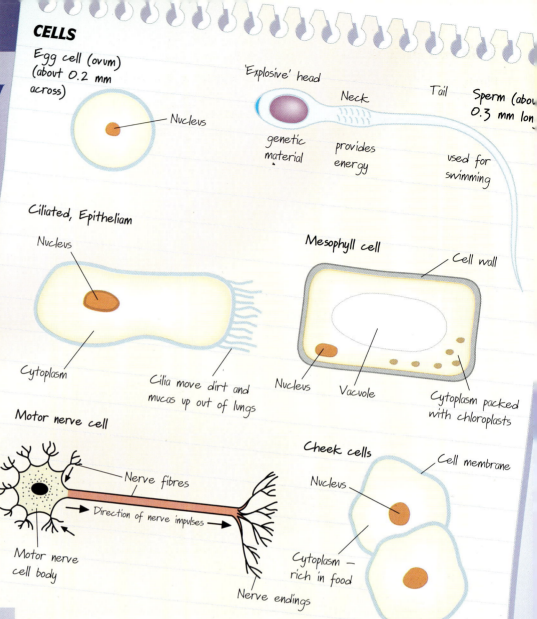

**CELLS**

Egg cell (ovum) (about 0.2 mm across) — Nucleus

'Explosive' head — Neck — Tail — Sperm (abou 0.3 mm lon

genetic material — provides energy — used for swimming

Ciliated, Epitheliam
Nucleus
Cytoplasm
Cilia move dirt and mucas up out of lungs

Mesophyll cell — Cell wall
Nucleus — Vacuole
Cytoplasm packed with chloroplasts

Motor nerve cell
Nerve fibres
Direction of nerve impulses
Motor nerve cell body
Nerve endings

Cheek cells — Cell membrane
Nucleus
Cytoplasm — rich in food

## CHECK TWO

*Look at the cells above and then try these questions.*

**1 a** If you saw these cells down a microscope, and watched them for some time, how would you be able to tell if they were alive or dead?

**b** What characteristics do living things show? Remember that individual living cells carry out all the same processes as larger organisms, even if you can't see them doing it!

**2** Here is a list of some structures you might have studied before. These structures are called organs.

    lungs   root   leaf   testes   ovaries
    flower   intestine   stomach

**a** Draw a table in your notes. It should have the following headings:

| Cell | Organ | Job |
|------|-------|-----|
|      |       |     |

**b** Match the types of cells shown above to the organs listed.

**c** Complete the 'job' column.

**d** Do you know of any other organs and cells? Add them to your table.

**e** Organs often work together in systems. List as many systems as you can. Here are two to start you off:

  *i* reproductive system (testes and ovaries)
  *ii* breathing system (lungs and windpipe).

# Tissues and organs

Plants and animals are made up of millions of cells working together. These cells are organised into **tissues** and **organs**. Tissues are made up of many cells of the same type working together. Tissues combine together to form more complex structures. These are organs.

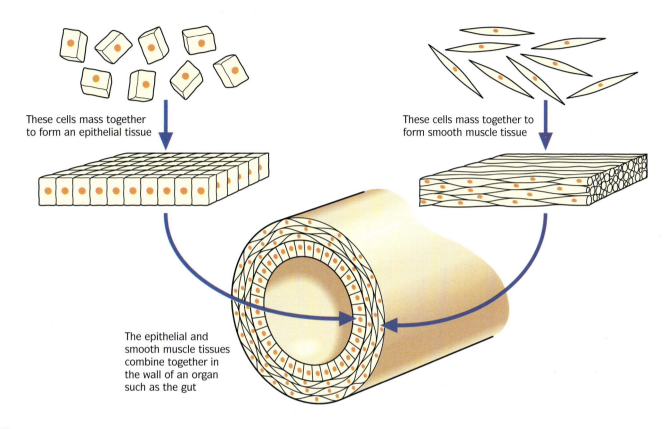

These cells mass together to form an epithelial tissue

These cells mass together to form smooth muscle tissue

The epithelial and smooth muscle tissues combine together in the wall of an organ such as the gut

🔺 Cells, tissues and organs.

# Cell structure

Plant and animal cells have the same basic structure, sharing many features. Just as organisms are made of smaller units (organs), cells contain smaller units called **organelles**. This chapter examines the microscopic structure of the cell. As you work through it, compare the organelles found inside cells with the tissues, organs and organ systems inside your body.

When Robert Hooke first observed cells in cork in 1665 he was already following a form of scientific research described as **atomistic**, that is, understanding how organisms work through studying their components (parts).

▶ *Could you work out how a car works by discovering how each individual part works?*

▶ *What other information would you need to explain to a person who has not used a car before how it works?*

▶ *Could you tell how an animal functions just by looking at its cells?*

🔺 Hooke saw cells like this using a microscope. He called them cells because of their shape.

# Unicellular organisms

Some organisms consist of a single, very complex and often quite large cell. Scientists call this group the **unicells**. Like all other living organisms, unicells such as *Euglena* and *Amoeba* feed, reproduce, grow and **respire** (take in oxygen and give out carbon dioxide) and **excrete** (give out waste substances). They can detect chemicals in their surroundings in the minutest of concentrations and move towards or away from them.

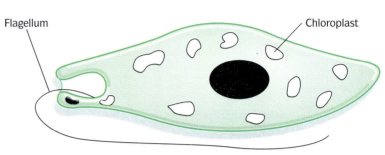

*Euglena* (0.1 mm)
Up to 100 μm long. Cigar-shaped. Bright green because it possesses chloroplasts for feeding by photosynthesis. It is included in the plant kingdom as a member of the Algae. It has a whip-like flagellum for swimming through water.

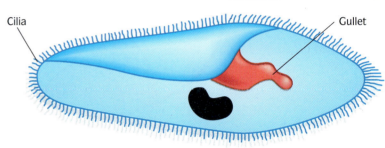

*Paramecium* (0.2 mm)
About 200 μm long. Slipper-shaped. Covered with beating cilia which 'row' the animal through the water. Feed on tiny organisms which are swept into the gullet by cilia.

🔺 Two unicells.

▶ *Look back to the diagrams of animal and plants cells on the review page. Say how unicells differ from animal and plant cells.*

> 1 μm = 1 micrometre
> 1000 μm = 1 millimetre

## Cell observation

You may be given a worksheet to help you learn to use a microscope. You will be able to study plant cells and possibly animal cells too. From your observations make your own drawings of an animal cell and a plant cell. Include some idea of scale in all your drawings.

▶ *For the cells you have seen and read about so far, produce two lists.*
  **a** *List the features common to both plant and animal cells.*
  **b** *List the important differences between plant and animal cells.*

## Cell contents

The contents of a cell are called the **protoplasm**, and this is divided into the **nucleus** and the **cytoplasm**. If the nucleus is the centre of control in the cell, the cytoplasm is the factory carrying out the nucleus' instructions. Where we have organ systems for carrying out the functions of living things, unicells have systems made of chemicals and structures held together by membranes. It is these membrane-bound structures that make up the cell's organelles (small organs).

| Organelle | Function |
|---|---|
| Cell membrane | Controls movement of materials into and out of the cell |
| Nucleus | Controls cellular activity Contains the chromosomes |
| Mitochondrion | Site of respiration |
| Chloroplast | Site of photosynthesis |
| Endoplasmic reticulum | Site of protein synthesis |

🔺 Organelles and their functions.

▶ *Look at this table. Which organelle is only found in plants?*

# Bacteria

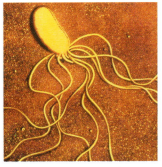
Rod-shaped bacterium with flagellae.

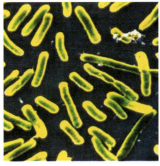
Rod-shaped bacteria.

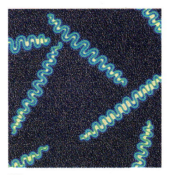
Spiral bacteria.

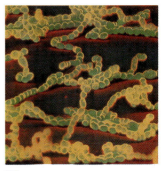
Spherical bacteria (*Cocci*).

**Bacteria** are the smallest and most numerous of all living organisms. The largest bacterium is about $\frac{1}{20}$th of the size of a typical human cell. There are no bacteria bigger than 0.001 millimetres. Bacteria exist as independent cells, although some cluster together in pairs or chains. Like the unicells, they show all the characteristics of living things.

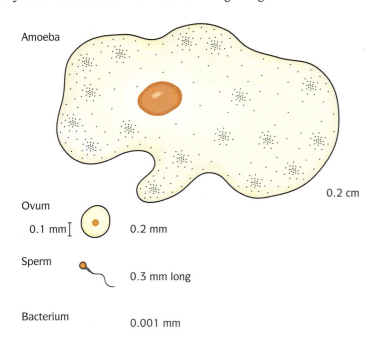

Amoeba

0.2 cm

Ovum

0.1 mm    0.2 mm

Sperm

0.3 mm long

Bacterium    0.001 mm

The size of some cells.

The biggest difference between bacterial cells and the cells you have studied so far, is the lack of structure inside the bacterial cell wall – no nucleus, no mitochondria, no chloroplasts, no endoplasmic reticulum (site of protein manufacture). Instead, the tasks performed by these organelles are carried out by chemicals either attached to the inside of the cell wall, or moving freely inside the cytoplasm.

▶ *Draw a table to show how bacteria are similar to our own cells, and how they are different.*

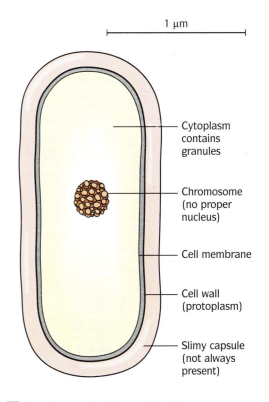

1 μm

Cytoplasm contains granules

Chromosome (no proper nucleus)

Cell membrane

Cell wall (protoplasm)

Slimy capsule (not always present)

*E. coli* – a typical bacterial cell.

## Classifying bacteria

As bacteria have cell walls, scientists used to group them with plants. Scientists now group them separately for many reasons. For example, the structure of their cell wall is completely different from the wall of plant cells.

## Studying microscopic cells

Scientists can use powerful microscopes called electron microscopes to produce images of the cell. These microscopes enlarge things by hundreds or thousands of times more than light microscopes and have revealed much of the internal structure of cells. However, we know that the cell is **dynamic**, that is, its contents are continually moving. Most electron microscopes cannot show this as cells die during sample preparation. Also, a picture on a page, or from a microscope, is in two dimensions and does not show the three-dimensional structure of a cell.

▶ *Look back at the picture of* E. coli. *Can you imagine and describe what a live* E. coli *looks like?*

## Problems with viewing cells

A typical human cell is about 0.02 millimetres in diameter. The best light microscopes enlarge or magnify things by a little over one thousand times.

▶ *Does Hooke's microscope share any features with a microscope you have used at school?*

Imagine a cell in three dimensions. Microscopes show only a thin section through a sample, or perhaps just part of the surface view. Because of this, you must always be careful in drawing conclusions from what you see through a microscope.

🔺 Hooke's light microscope.

🔺 A modern electron microscope.

# Interpreting microscope pictures

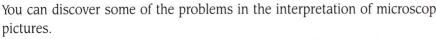

You can discover some of the problems in the interpretation of microscope pictures.

See how different a fruit can look when it is cut in different ways.

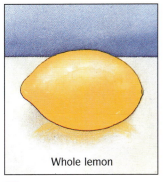

Whole lemon

Half lemon

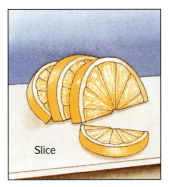

Slice

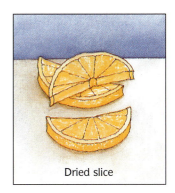

Dried slice

🔺 Four views of a lemon.

▶ *Sketch a thin slice (section) of orange or lemon.*

▶ *What other information might you need before you could draw a picture of the whole fruit?*

▶ *What does this tell you about the problems of looking at thin sections of cells under a microscope?*

Until recently electron microscopes could only view dehydrated specimens. You may have realised that it is nearly impossible to draw a whole lemon when you only know what a slice looks like. Imagine you had to work from a dried lemon slice rather than a fresh one. This gives you an idea of the problems faced by scientists when they interpret pictures from electron microscopes.

## Stains

Cells are mostly water, so they can be difficult to see using a light microscope. To help you see them and their contents you can use special dyes called stains. Stains might react with one particular part of the cell, such as the cell wall or starch grains. They can also increase the contrast between the cell and its surroundings, making it easier to see. For example, a solution of iodine will do both with plant cells, staining areas containing starch and cellulose and increasing the contrast between the cell and its background.

# A matter of scale

Look at this full stop. It is bigger than most of the cells found in the human body.

▶ *How small would you have to be if you wanted to be the same size as, say, a white blood cell?*

▶ *How many white blood cells could you fit into 1 mm$^2$?*

Microscopes produce an enlarged image of objects. A different way to look at very small things might be to make a person very small. 'The Incredible Shrinking Man' is just science fiction, but imagine being the same size as a

🔺 Advertising 'The Incredible Shrinking Man'.

cell and being able to stand next to one. The first thing you would see would be the cell membrane. You might be amazed to see that it is quite soft and constantly moving. Scientists describe this as *fluid*.

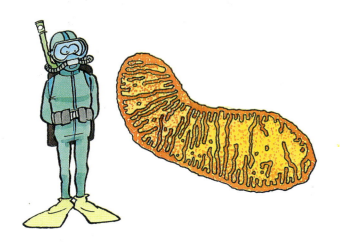

▲ Shrinking down ...

Objects rise from the membrane surface, some floating high, others seeming to sink. Look closely and you see that some of these objects allow you to pass into the cell.

If you jumped through the cell membrane, and became even smaller, you would see just how busy a cell is. You are now in the cytoplasm. Materials are continually passing in and out of the cell across the membrane. You are surrounded by structures that look very like the cell membrane, through which you have just passed. It is like a three-dimensional industrial estate.

Suspended in water are all kinds of different chemicals. Some of the largest are **enzymes**. Enzymes are the chemicals which control reactions in living things. You may read about these in Chapter Four (Human nutrition). Most of the enzymes in the cell are contained inside the membranes you can see. Each separate structure performs a specialised task. You might recognise mitochondria, which provide most of the energy needed by the cell.

As you move through the cell you see another membrane in front of you. Behind this is the nucleus – the control and regulatory centre of the cell. Like the cell membrane it has pores allowing the entry and exit of materials. Off to one side you notice how the membrane seems to reach out into the cytoplasm to form a region of enclosed maze-like tunnels.

Shrink a bit more . . .

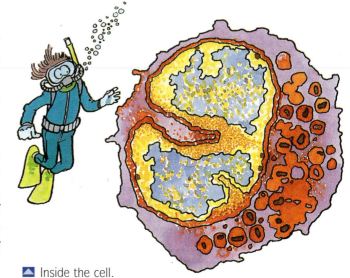

▲ Inside the cell.

Entering the nucleus you see many large chemicals moving to and from a ribbon-like structure in front of you. The ribbon seems to be wrapped around small spheres to give it support. At the most active sites it resembles a knitting basket after an attack by some kittens! Chemicals cluster around the central ribbon. You are watching the genetic material of the cell, the **DNA** (**deoxyribose nucleic acid**), in action. Each thread is just a tiny part of a chromosome. There are 46 such chromosomes in a human cell.

Shrink a bit more . . .

You follow one of the largest chemicals leaving the scene and you enter the maze-like tunnels. The activity inside here is intense. Hundreds of different enzymes are working to produce proteins. You are inside a structure called the endoplasmic reticulum.

Following one of the larger proteins, you find yourself inside a bubble of membrane floating in the cytoplasm. The bubble touches the cell membrane and seems to explode. You are back outside the cell.

▶ *Make a route map of your journey. Label each of the major structures you saw and add notes about them.*

## Diffusion

Somebody walks into the room. You know who it is before you see him because you can smell his aftershave.

The aftershave molecules have energy. This energy causes them to vibrate and move through the air in all directions. This random movement of the molecules causes them to bump into one another and, eventually, to spread evenly throughout the room. This process is helped by the other molecules in air. These are also in motion and will push the individual perfume molecules away from one another. Some molecules will be pushed back towards where they came from. But if you could see what was happening, you would see more molecules moving away from your friend than towards him. This process is called **diffusion** and is defined as the tendency for molecules to move away from an area of high concentration of that molecule to an area of relatively low concentration. Diffusion occurs if there is a concentration gradient.

▲ Diffusion of potassium manganate (VII) through water.

Scientists often speak of the net movement of molecules from one area to another, as the actual molecules are always moving but more move away than return.

## Features of diffusion

There are three main features of diffusion:
■ There has to be a difference in concentration between two points.
■ The lowest concentration must be in the area where the diffusing chemical is needed.
■ It is very slow.

▶ *Imagine you had to get food to your cells and oxygen to your brain by diffusion. What problems might there be?*

▶ *Write down some advantages of having organ systems to transport materials around the body.*

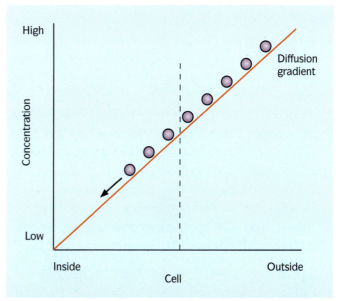

▲ Diffusion – molecules move down the gradient from an area of high concentration to an area of relatively low concentration.

| Problem with Concentration | Problem with Speed | Problem with Membrane |
|---|---|---|
| 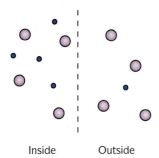 | 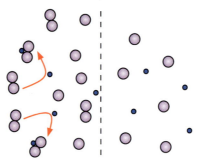 | 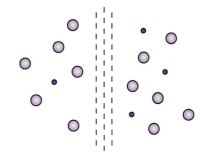 |
| Inside          Outside | | |
| The molecules needed are in a lower concentration outside the cell than inside | Molecules are used up faster than they can enter the cell | Membrane is too thick or distance too great |

🔺 Features of diffusion.

Sometimes we have to take in very rare nutrients from our gut as part of digestion. Usually these are in much higher concentrations inside the body than inside the gut, so they would not diffuse across the gut wall and into the body. There is a mechanism which overcomes this problem. You can read about it later in this chapter.

Diffusion works too slowly to move important materials a large distance. It is fine for moving oxygen across a membrane and into a single cell, but not for getting oxygen to your brain from outside your body. This would take far too long.

## Biological membranes

Another problem with diffusion is that some surfaces are easier to cross than others. A surface which diffusing molecules can cross is said to be **permeable**. As a rule, the thinner a surface the faster diffusion can occur. You would have seen on your journey into the cell that cell membranes have holes (pores) in them to speed up the process of diffusion.

On your journey through the cell you would have seen that membranes are not solid, but are soft and runny. Scientists use a model for membranes called a **fluid mosaic**. It is thought that membranes consist of an oily layer in which a large number of proteins is suspended. Some of these proteins act as pores, allowing chemicals to pass through them. Only molecules small enough to fit into these pores can pass into the cell. So, although biological membranes are permeable, not everything can pass through. For this reason, biological membranes are described as being **differentially permeable membranes (DPMs)**.

▶ *In the past, DPMs have also been described as semi-permeable and selectively permeable. Write a brief report suggesting which term should be used and why.*

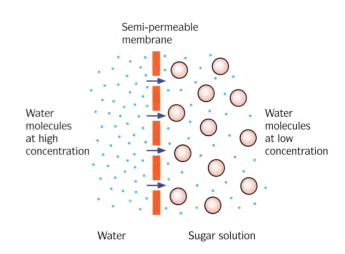

Semi-permeable membrane

Water molecules at high concentration

Water molecules at low concentration

Water          Sugar solution

🔺 Explaining osmosis.

# Osmosis

**Osmosis** is a special form of diffusion. It is the diffusion of water across a DPM.

You may be given a worksheet to help you investigate diffusion and osmosis.

▶ *What characteristic of the water molecule (hint H$_2$O) allows it to pass across DPMs?*

▶ *Aubergines and cucumbers are often salted before use. This makes them 'crisp up' and brings out the flavour. Write a note for a cookery book explaining how this works.*

# Active transport

The cells of the gut can take in some rare chemicals from our food even though diffusion cannot happen. The chemicals may be in tiny concentrations – much lower, in fact, than the concentration of the chemical inside the cells taking them in. Some cells have the ability to collect important chemicals from their surroundings and transport them across their cell membrane against a concentration gradient.

Moving chemicals down a concentration gradient by diffusion does not need energy from the cell. To move chemicals the other way, however, does require energy. Special structures in the cell membrane appear to be able to recognise important chemicals and carry them across into the cytoplasm. This process requires the cell to use its energy store and so is called **active transport**. We collect vitamins from our gut by active transport and plants take in minerals from the soil against concentration gradients.

# Carrier molecules

Special types of protein exist in the cell membrane called **carrier molecules**. Carrier molecules recognise a chemical by its shape and can transport it inside the cell. Vitamin C and iron enter our cells in this way. Many viruses have evolved to make use of these carrier molecules mimicking the shape of the chemicals which are transported. Some scientists believe that high doses of vitamin C may prevent colds because the vitamin blocks the carrier molecules used by the cold viruses.

Other scientists are exploring the possibility of using carrier molecules to deliver highly toxic drugs to specific cells. This is one of Dr Allen's key tasks. Debbie tries to make antibodies that will attach themselves to the carrier molecules on cancer cells. Anything joined to the other end of the antibody will then be taken into the cell by the carrier molecule. If you attached a drug to an antibody in this way, you would have a very effective way of treating a sick cell.

◣ Dr Allen at work.

# Biosynthesis

Cells are the main site of chemical production within our bodies. The production of chemicals by living things is called **biosynthesis** and the study of this process, **biochemistry**.

Cells are often highly specialised. You may have studied nerve cells and sperm cells in humans, or mesophyll cells and root hair cells in plants. These are examples of cells which have evolved for a special task. Other cells have developed which produce specific chemicals such as hormones or proteins. So that complex chemicals can be made, there is a division of labour within the cell. Each major task is carried out by a particular organelle.

### Endoplasmic reticulum (protein synthesis)

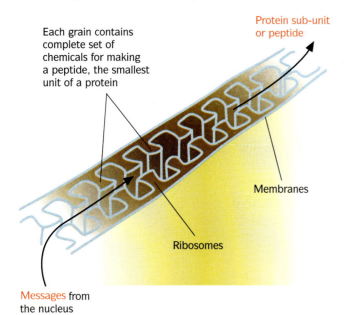

Each grain contains complete set of chemicals for making a peptide, the smallest unit of a protein

Protein sub-unit or peptide

Membranes

Ribosomes

Messages from the nucleus

### Chloroplast (photosynthesis)

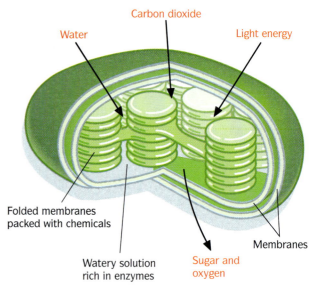

Water

Carbon dioxide

Light energy

Folded membranes packed with chemicals

Membranes

Watery solution rich in enzymes

Sugar and oxygen

### Mitochondrion (respiration)

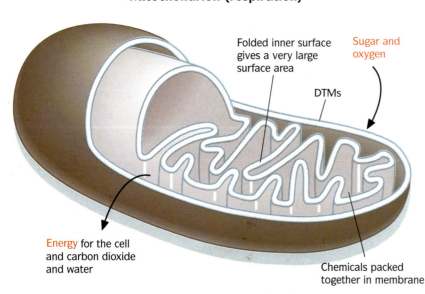

Folded inner surface gives a very large surface area

Sugar and oxygen

DTMs

Energy for the cell and carbon dioxide and water

Chemicals packed together in membrane

▸ *Complex chemicals may be made by a number of different reactions. In small groups discuss why scientists believe that organising different chemical reactions into separate organelles is more efficient than having the chemicals free to move throughout the cell. Make notes of your discussion.*

🔺 Factories in the cell.

# Making new cells

Near the middle of the cell is the nucleus. The nucleus contains most of the genetic material of the cell. Genetic material, arranged into **genes**, controls the characteristics that pass from generation to generation. We often describe these features as inherited characteristics. You may read about this in Chapter Nine (Genetics).

The genetic material, or genes, is organised into long chains called **chromosomes**. These control all processes in the cells, including the production of new cells.

## Bacteria

Bacteria can reproduce very quickly. They make new cells by splitting in two, a process called **binary fission**.

Before they divide, they must produce a duplicate set of all the chemicals inside their cell. Although bacteria do not have nuclei, they still have genes. The bacterium's genetic material organises this complex process of cell division as well as being duplicated itself.

## Plant and animal cells

Like bacteria, other cells produce a second set of chemicals, but they also need a second set of organelles.

▶ *Look back through this chapter. List all the organelles that have to be duplicated before the cell can divide.*

## Mitosis

Some types of cells can divide to form two new daughter cells. In order to do this they must first make copies of all their internal organelles, including their chromosomes. These have to be shared between the two daughters. This process allows growth and is called **mitosis**.

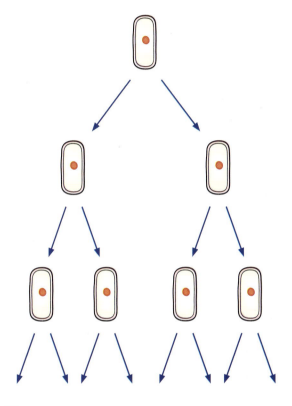

▲ Binary fission – one cell splitting to give two.

## Meiosis

Reproductive cells are highly specialised. They have to carry an accurate copy of genes, but they carry only half a set of chromosomes. Reproductive cells are produced by mitosis. You may read about this in Chapter Nine (Genetics).

The human sperm cell has a very difficult task. It must swim a distance of many centimetres inside a woman's body. At the end of its journey it must join with an ovum (egg cell) to begin the process which results in the birth of a new human being.

The sex cells are formed in a different way from the other cells in our body. Sex cells **(gametes)** are formed by reduction division **(meiosis)**. In meiosis, four daughter cells are formed, each carrying a half set of chromosomes.

▶ *Where is the other half set of chromosomes going to come from?*

▶ *Why do you think that the sex cells are formed in this special way?*

▶ *List all the differences you can think of between mitosis and meiosis.*

BIOLOGY

## Mitosis

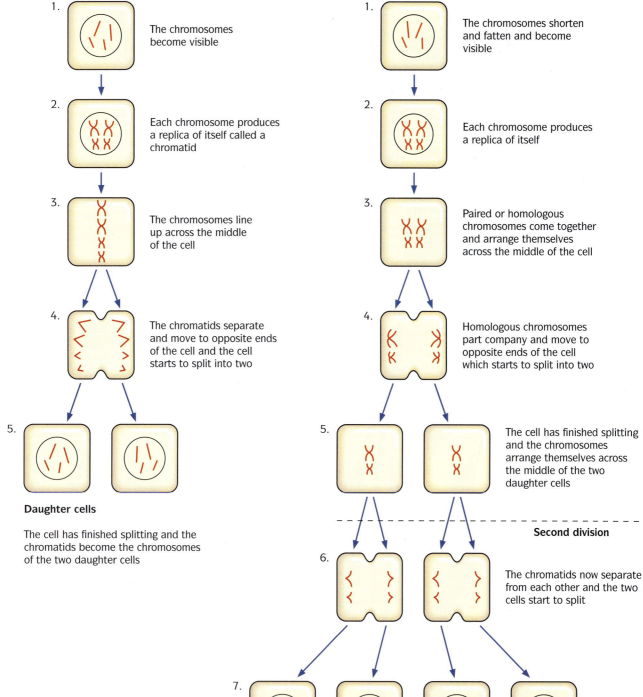

1. The chromosomes become visible

2. Each chromosome produces a replica of itself called a chromatid

3. The chromosomes line up across the middle of the cell

4. The chromatids separate and move to opposite ends of the cell and the cell starts to split into two

5. **Daughter cells**

The cell has finished splitting and the chromatids become the chromosomes of the two daughter cells

## Meiosis

**First division**

1. The chromosomes shorten and fatten and become visible

2. Each chromosome produces a replica of itself

3. Paired or homologous chromosomes come together and arrange themselves across the middle of the cell

4. Homologous chromosomes part company and move to opposite ends of the cell which starts to split into two

5. The cell has finished splitting and the chromosomes arrange themselves across the middle of the two daughter cells

**Second division**

6. The chromatids now separate from each other and the two cells start to split

7. **Daughter cells**

The cells have finished splitting so we finish up with a total of four cells each of which contains half the original number of chromosomes

▲ Cell division by mitosis and meiosis.

BIOLOGY

# Cell specialisation

The production of cells is rather complicated. Even very different cells might start from the same type of cell.

Most of the cells found in blood are made from the same type of cell. Some develop into white blood cells, others into red blood cells. This process is called **differentiation**. Often, once a cell becomes specialised as a result of differentiation, it cannot divide to produce new cells.

Cells specialise after they have divided. For example, the red blood cell loses its nucleus giving it more room for carrying oxygen. After three or four months it is worn out and replaced by a new cell.

# Summary

- Organisms are made up from cells.
- Cells work together to form tissues.
- Tissues work together to form organs.
- Two or more organs make an organ system.
- Cells contain specialised units called organelles.
- Bacteria are single-celled organisms lacking internal membranes.
- Microscopes help us see inside cells but we must be very careful when drawing conclusions from what we see.
- Stains help us to see structures through a microscope.
- Light microscopes magnify up to about one thousand times and electron microscopes to about one million times.
- Materials enter and leave cells in a number of ways.
- These include diffusion, osmosis (a special form of diffusion) and active transport.
- Biochemists study the reactions of chemicals found in living things.
- Bacteria grow and divide in a process called binary fission.
- Cells of plants and animals divide by mitosis or meiosis.
- In mitosis, a parent cell produces two daughter cells.
- Meiosis is used to make the sex cells (gametes). One parent cell produces four daughter cells, each with half the number of chromosomes of the parent.

# Revision Questions

1 List the characteristics of a living organism. Use a cell that you have studied to explain each characteristic.

2 Design a simple poster for a primary school classroom. The aim of the poster is to show why a named animal is considered to be living but a motor car is not.

3 Match the pairs:

| | |
|---|---|
| chloroplast | respiration |
| nucleus | photosynthesis |
| endoplasmic reticulum | chromosomes |
| mitochondrion | protein synthesis |

4 How do cells divide?

5 How can materials get into a cell? How do very large molecules get in?

6 Draw three cells you have studied. For each one explain how it is adapted to its particular task.

7 Imagine that you are Robert Hooke. Write your diary entry for the day you first saw cells in cork. You might like to say what his microscope looked like and include a sketch of it, along with any drawings made.

8 As an organism increases in size, the ratio of its surface area to its volume changes. This affects how quickly materials can diffuse into the organism. The bigger the organism, the longer it will take for chemicals to diffuse into its centre.

For example, for a cubic organism with a side of size 1 cm, its surface area will be 6 $cm^2$ and its volume 1 $cm^3$.

For a 2 cm cube, its surface area will be 24 $cm^2$, its volume $2 \times 2 \times 2 = 8\ cm^3$.

Copy and complete this table:

| Side cm | Surface area (SA) $cm^2$ | Volume (V) $cm^3$ | Ratio (SA/V) |
|---|---|---|---|
| 1 | 6 × 1 = 6 | 1 × 1 × 1 = 1 | 6/1 = 6 |
| 2 | | | |
| 3 | | | |
| 5 | | | |
| 10 | | | |
| 20 | | | |

Copy and complete this statement by crossing out the words which do not apply.

As an organism increases in size, its surface area to volume ratio decreases/increases. This makes it harder/easier for it to rely on diffusion to supply its cells with food and oxygen.

Explain why large plants and animals have systems for transporting food, oxygen and waste.

9 Draw a simple diagram of a cell showing two pairs of chromosomes in its nucleus. Show how that cell would divide by:
a mitosis
b meiosis.

10 Why is meiosis used to produce gametes rather than mitosis?

11 a Why do bacteria divide by binary fission and not mitosis?
b If you started with one bacterium which could divide every twenty minutes, how many bacteria would you have after:
i one hour
ii four hours
iii five hours
iv six hours?
Plot your results on a graph.
Describe the shape of your curve.

12 What is the difference between a cell, a tissue and an organ? Use diagrams to illustrate your answer.

# Health & blood

Perhaps you are wondering:

■ Why *should* or *shouldn't* we do those things?
■ Who says so and what evidence is there?
■ Surely our own bodies have ways of keeping us healthy and protecting us against disease?

This chapter will answer some of these questions and help you to make informed choices about your own health.

**People are much more aware of their health nowadays than ever before. Advertisements on the television and radio, and in the newspapers, tell us that we should not smoke, we should not drink too much, we should take lots of exercise and we should eat only *healthy* food.**

# CHAPTER THREE

# Review

See what you know already about health. Before going any further, do the word search and attempt the tasks. Write the answers in your notes.

There are some key words about health hidden in the word search. The key words will help you answer the Check Three questions. Copy the word search into your notebook and find the words. There are ten words in all; four are written down and six across – and one of them is written backwards.

## WORD SEARCH

| D | S | E | S | I | C | R | E | X | E | A | A | I |
|---|---|---|---|---|---|---|---|---|---|---|---|---|
| R | M | H | E | R | V | I | R | U | S | B | L | M |
| U | O | D | P | L | A | W | T | K | M | N | C | M |
| G | K | Z | B | A | C | T | E | R | I | A | O | U |
| S | I | D | E | J | C | L | S | X | V | V | H | N |
| A | N | T | I | B | I | O | T | I | C | Y | O | E |
| F | G | H | K | E | N | U | G | N | W | R | L | D |
| B | S | O | L | V | E | N | T | S | A | K | I | C |
| V | A | C | V | A | C | C | I | N | E | Z | R | A |

## CHECK THREE

**1** Which of the key words is good for your health? List as many other things as you can think of.

**2** List the key words that are supposed to be bad for you.

**3** Which key words can cause disease?

**4** What things can doctors use to treat you if you are unwell?

**5** Which key word means that you are protected from a disease?

**6** What key word can doctors give you to prevent you from getting infectious diseases in the first place?

# Health

The World Health Organization (WHO) – part of the United Nations – defines health as 'not merely the absence of disease, but a state of complete physical, mental and social well-being'. This definition seems a bit idealistic but certainly, good health means being *free from disease*. Disease is an illness or malfunction of part of the body. Our bodies are being invaded all the time by micro organisms. Some of them cause diseases and are called **pathogens**.

# External defences against disease

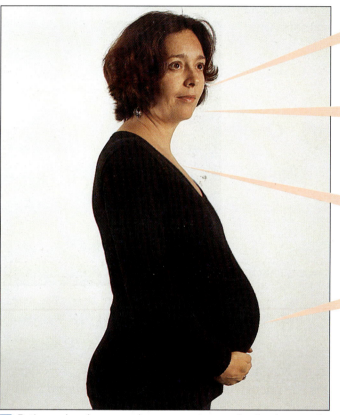

Pathogenic micro organisms can enter our bodies in any of these ways.

Some pathogens are taken into our lungs when we breathe. Examples are the viruses that cause the common cold and influenza (flu).

Some pathogens enter our gut in the food we eat. An example is the bacterium, *Salmonella*, that causes food poisoning.

Our skin is a protective barrier that keeps pathogens outside our bodies.

Some pathogens enter our blood through cuts in the skin. An example is the bacterium that causes tetanus.

Some pathogens can pass from a mother to her fetus through the placenta. An example is the virus called *rubella*. It causes German measles.

Some pathogens are transmitted from one person to another during sexual contact.

Examples are the virus that causes AIDS and the bacteria that cause syphilis and gonorrhoea.

Pathogens can enter the body in a number of different ways. These are shown in the diagram. The body has a number of defensive barriers which help stop pathogens entering and causing disease. These include:

- Sticky **mucus** which lines the air passages traps many of the pathogens entering the body in the air we breathe. Mucus is pushed into the mouth by small hairs called **cilia**. The mucus is then usually swallowed. Any pathogens in it are killed in the stomach's acidic **gastric juice**.
- **Hydrochloric acid** in gastric juice kills pathogens which enter the body in the food that we eat. You may read about this in Chapter Four (Human nutrition).
- The skin is an effective barrier which keeps pathogens outside our bodies. You may read about this in Chapter Eight (Homeostasis).
- Tears flood the surfaces of the eyes each time we blink. Any pathogens on the eyes are washed away.

▶ *How do our bodies protect us against pathogens entering by the lungs and the digestive system?*

▶ *How can pathogens enter the body through the skin?*

▶ *Name two other ways by which pathogens can enter human bodies.*

# Internal defences against disease

Our bodies also have a number of internal defences which help to kill any pathogens that get through the external defences. The internal defences involve the blood and include phagocytosis, immune responses and blood clotting.

## Phagocytosis

**Neutrophils** and **monocytes** are white blood cells which can leave the blood and enter the tissues anywhere in the body. You may read about this in Chapter Five (Breathing and circulation). They swarm around any bacteria they find, then they engulf (surround) the bacteria by **phagocytosis**. Once inside the blood cells, the bacteria are killed.

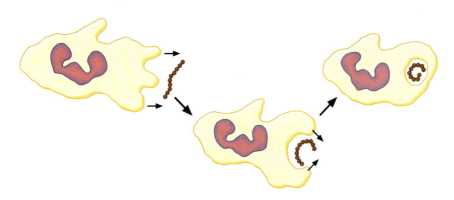

▲ Phagocytosis – this neutrophil has detected the bacteria nearby. It moves towards them and finally engulfs the bacterial cells.

## Immune responses

**Lymphocytes** are another group of white blood cells. They are made in glands called **lymph nodes**. When pathogens enter the body, some lymphocytes produce proteins called **antibodies**. The antibodies kill the pathogens. Other types of lymphocytes attack cells which are infected with viruses.

These actions are called immune responses. The protection they give is called **immunity**. You can sometimes feel the lymph nodes in your neck or under your arms. They can swell up when they are active during an immune response.

All three types of white blood cell recognise the foreign proteins on the outside of the pathogens.

New-born babies can obtain antibodies from their mother in breast milk. Antibodies also pass through the placenta from the mother to the fetus before it is born.

## Counting white blood cells

Some diseases cause the number of white blood cells to increase and some cause a decrease. Doctors can diagnose some diseases by looking at the numbers of white blood cells. You may be given a worksheet to show you how this is done.

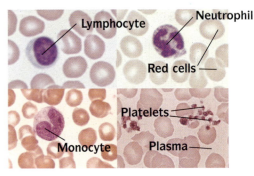

▲ Photomicrographs of a smear of human blood magnified 800 times.

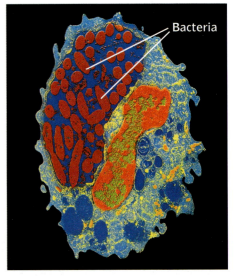

▲ Photomicrograph of blood phagocyte (magnified 6500 times) filled with bacteria it has engulfed.

▶ *Why is it important for phagocytes to be able to leave the blood and enter the tissues?*

**BLOOD CLOTTING**

Blood clots and scabs form at the site of wounds. They prevent pathogens from entering the body. You can read more about clots later in this chapter.

## Transplant rejection

Lymphocytes can also attack the cells of transplanted organs. They respond to the organ because it is foreign. In this way, some patients who have had a transplant reject the organ. Transfused blood can also be rejected if it is not carefully matched to the recipient's blood group. Transplant rejection can be treated by giving the patient drugs which suppress or slow down the immune response. Unfortunately, this leaves the patient unprotected against pathogens.

## Vaccines

**Vaccines** are substances which protect us from certain diseases. They give us immunity. Vaccines are usually injected, but some are taken by mouth. This is called **immunisation**.

Vaccines are made from pathogens and contain the substances which trigger our immune responses. These substances are called **antigens**. After vaccination, our bodies make antibodies. This reaction gives us immunity against the pathogen.

Sometimes the pathogens in vaccines have been killed; sometimes they are alive but deactivated so they cannot cause disease.

Each antibody is only effective against one antigen. For example, a vaccine against whooping cough does not protect us against measles. That is why we have different vaccines to protect us against different diseases.

Some pathogens, like the flu virus, are changing all the time. This makes it very difficult to produce an effective vaccine.

In Britain, parents are offered a vaccination programme for their children which gives protection against childhood diseases. These diseases were once widespread killers, but are now relatively rare in Britain.

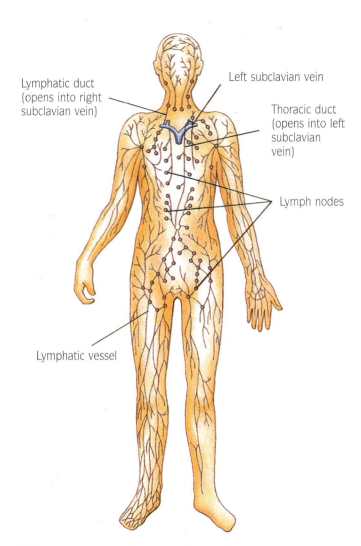

▲ The main parts of the human lymphatic system. All parts of the body contain lymphatic vessels.

# SMALLPOX
## – death of a disease?

SMALLPOX WAS ONE OF the main causes of death in the world. Because of the use of vaccines, smallpox no longer exists. In the 1960s, the World Health Organization started an international programme of mass vaccination. In 1977, the WHO reported the last case of smallpox in Somalia.

*Ali Maow Maalin, the last case of smallpox in 1977.*

| Age of child | Immunisation |
|---|---|
| 2–4 months | Hib (Bacterial meningitis) <br> Diphtheria <br> Whooping cough <br> Tetanus <br> Polio |
| 18–24 months | Measles <br> Mumps <br> Rubella |
| 3–5 years | Diphtheria <br> Tetanus <br> Polio |
| Girls 10–14 years | Rubella |
| Girls/Boys 13 years | Tuberculosis (BCG) |
| School leavers | Tetanus <br> Polio (booster) |

▲ The United Kingdom childhood vaccination programme, 1995. Some vaccines have to be given several times for a child to become completely immune.

BIOLOGY

# Rubella

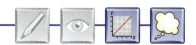

German measles is caused by a virus called rubella. Here are some extracts from a leaflet, *Is Your Daughter Between 10 and 14?* It was produced by the Health Education Authority.

Use the information to research some of the principles of immune responses and the use of vaccines to prevent disease.

---

*You may think German measles is a disease that is almost harmless and not worth bothering about. You may think your daughter has had it and so can't get it again. For either reason, you may think you need not bother about immunisation.*

*But in fact it is very important to have your daughter immunised, not only for her sake, but for the sake of your grandchildren as well.*

### NOT SO HARMLESS AS YOU THINK

German measles is caused by a virus and is highly infectious. The main symptoms are a mild pink rash on the face and chest – perhaps accompanied by a slight fever, some swollen glands and a general feeling of being off-colour. The rash may only last for a few hours and only rarely does it last beyond a few days.

So, for the patient, the disease usually causes little trouble. It may even pass unnoticed.

### DANGER TO THE UNBORN CHILD

However, it is not always as harmless as it appears. If caught by a pregnant woman, it can very seriously affect her baby. Depending on what stage of her pregnancy the mother is at when she catches it, her baby may suffer varying degrees of harm, the most serious being damage to its brain, sight, hearing or heart. Some babies affected in this way die in the first year of their life. Those who live could face a lifetime of handicap.

---

▶ *Rubella is not serious for adults and children. Why is this?*

▶ *What can happen to her unborn baby if a pregnant woman catches rubella?*

---

### A SIMPLE SOLUTION

This need not happen. Immunisation provides highly effective protection against the disease and means that you can ensure your daughter does not run this risk.

You should have your daughter immunised – whether or not you think she has had German measles already.

### HOW IT'S DONE

Protection is given, usually between the ages of 10 and 14, by one simple injection.

In the United States of America, boys as well as girls are immunised. They are trying to wipe out the disease completely. Boys are not immunised in Britain. This gives girls who are not immune to the disease a chance to catch it before they reach reproductive age. Also, it allows the antibodies to be *topped up* in those girls who are immune. Immunisation does not give protection for the whole of a girl's reproductive lifetime.

---

▶ *How does immunisation protect against rubella?*

▶ *If rubella is not serious in children and adults, why immunise them at all?*

▶ *Why immunise girls between 10 and 14? Why not wait until they are older?*

▶ *Give one advantage of immunising girls and not boys against rubella.*

▶ *What benefit is there in immunising both girls and boys against rubella?*

▶ *Why doesn't immunisation against measles also give protection against German measles?*

Here is a bar chart showing the number of cases of rubella reported to the Royal College of General Practitioners between 1977 and 1982. Also shown are the number of abortions associated with rubella in the same period.

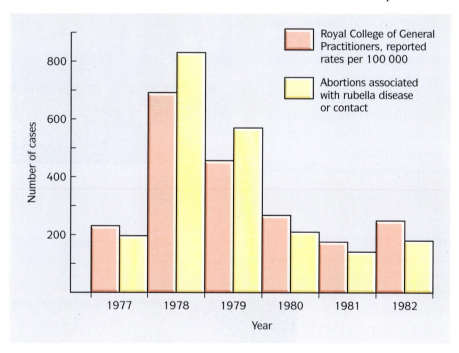

▶ *In which year were the most cases of rubella?*

▶ *When were the most abortions associated with rubella?*

▶ *Why do you think some women decide to have an abortion if they catch German measles at an early stage of pregnancy?*

In 1975, 68 per cent of females were immunised against rubella by the age of 14. In 1982, the figure had risen to 84 per cent – it was 91 per cent in 1992–3.

▶ *Is there any evidence in the bar chart that immunisation against rubella has had a beneficial effect?*

▶ *Do you think you have enough data to say that you have identified a trend?*

# Antibiotics

As well as vaccines, **antibiotics** are used to help prevent and cure certain diseases. Antibiotics are substances which are produced by fungi – usually moulds like *Penicillium*.

Antibiotics are either **bactericidal** – they kill bacteria, or they are **bacteriostatic** – they stop the bacteria growing. Viruses are not affected by antibiotics. Diseases which are caused by a virus cannot be treated with antibiotics.

Sir Alexander Fleming was the first scientist to notice this effect in 1929, but he did not realise the significance of antibiotics at the time. Howard Florey developed penicillin into a useful medicine in the 1940s. Since then, many other antibiotics have been discovered.

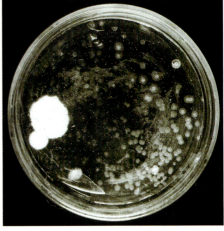

▲ The clear area near to the *Penicillium* mould is where the mould's antibiotic has prevented the bacteria from growing.

# Penicillin resistance

In recent years, doctors have noticed that antibiotics which have been very good at curing bacterial diseases are getting less and less effective. They believe it is because antibiotics have been prescribed too much in the past. People have been given antibiotics more often than they needed and in doses too low to be effective. The result is that bacteria have now evolved resistant strains. Doctors are now being much more careful to give only the minimum doses needed to cure their patients. At the same time, the pharmaceutical companies are spending a lot of time and money trying to find and develop new antibiotics.

▲ Sir Alexander Fleming in his laboratory.

# Investigating drug resistance

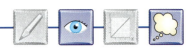

Look at these results of an experiment in which bacteria have been grown on a nutrient jelly. Each of the paper discs contains a different antibiotic, identified by the code written on the discs. Some of the antibiotics prevent bacterial growth, whilst the bacteria are not affected by others. The bacteria are resistant to them.

Look at the photograph and complete the tasks below.

▶ *Which antibiotics prevent bacterial growth?*

▶ *Which antibiotics are the bacteria resistant to?*

▶ *Is it possible to tell whether some of the antibiotics are more effective than the others? How?*

▶ *List the antibiotics in order of their effectiveness against the bacteria.*

▶ *How can a test like this help in finding the best treatment for a patient with a bacterial disease?*

▶ *Why shouldn't the doctor just prescribe a lot of penicillin until the patient is better?*

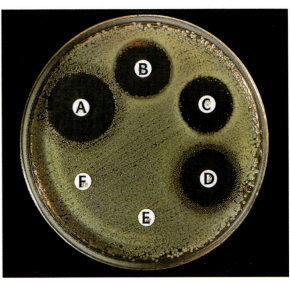

▲ Antibiotics from these paper discs may stop the bacteria growing in the Petri dish.

# Allergy

About a third of the people in Britain are **allergic**. An allergy is an immune response to a type of antigen called an **allergen**. People can be allergic to grass pollen (this gives them hay fever), the fur of cats or dogs, house dust mites or certain foods. Many allergens are breathed into the lungs. Sometimes the allergic response can make it difficult to breathe – this is called **asthma**. You may read about this in Chapter Five (Breathing and circulation).

When the allergic response takes place, a substance called **histamine** is produced in the affected tissues. Histamine causes the unpleasant symptoms of allergy. For example, in hay fever, there can be sneezing, itchiness and sore eyes. Medicines called **antihistamines** are taken to relieve the effects of histamine.

## Testing for allergies

Mites feed on shed human skin scales that make up house dust. There are probably about 10 000 of these small animals in your mattress, even if it is clean. Some people are allergic to them. For such people, the mites cause asthma when they are breathed in. Some people are allergic to pollen and get hay fever.

The skin prick test is used to find out what causes someone's allergy. Different kinds of allergens are scratched into the skin on the arm. The names of the allergens are written on to the arm!

On the right, you can see the swollen reactions to some of the allergens.

▶ *Why is a control used in the skin prick test?*

▶ *What is this person allergic to?*

▶ *Which medicine relieves the symptoms of allergy?*

▶ *Make a list of some of the ways this patient could be helped.*

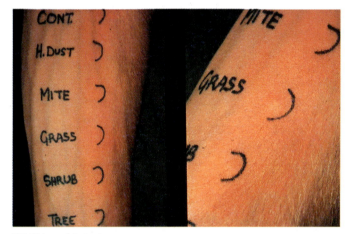

🔺 Skin prick test.

🔺 A house dust mite, magnified 135 times by an electron microscope.

# Blood clotting

Another internal defence mechanism in our bodies is blood clotting, or **coagulation**. When we cut ourselves, the bleeding usually stops after a few minutes – the blood clots. This prevents pathogens from entering the body at the site of the wound.

Blood clots result from the action of small particles in the blood called **platelets**. Platelets are sometimes called **thrombocytes**. Platelets clump together at the site of an injury. They then trigger off a chemical reaction which results in the formation of a protein called **fibrin**. Fibrin is insoluble – it does not dissolve in blood – it deposits inside the blood vessels, traps blood cells and forms a clot or scab.

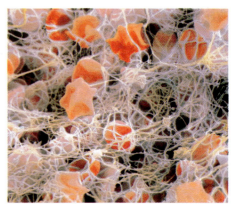

▲ Scanning electronmicrograph of a blood clot, magnified 1525 times. The fibrin strands hold the blood cells together.

## Clots in the wrong place

Sometimes, a clot forms in the blood even when there is no wound. This is called a **thrombus**. If a thrombus forms in an artery leading to an organ, the clot reduces the blood supply and can cause sudden death. For example, a thrombus in the coronary arteries in the heart wall can stop blood reaching all parts of the heart's muscle. This is called **coronary thrombosis**.

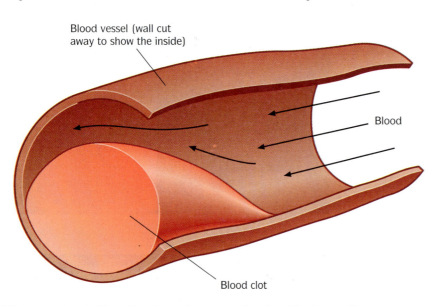

Blood vessel (wall cut away to show the inside)

Blood

Blood clot

▲ A thrombus inside a blood vessel prevents the blood flowing easily.

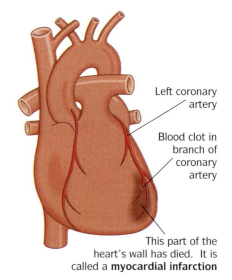

Left coronary artery

Blood clot in branch of coronary artery

This part of the heart's wall has died. It is called a **myocardial infarction**

▲ The coronary arteries in this heart were blocked by a thrombus. The part of the heart which now cannot receive blood has died.

Part of the heart's wall can die or the heart can even stop beating all together – a heart attack. Coronary thrombosis is a major cause of death in Britain. Many factors increase the risk of having a coronary. They include smoking, a high-fat diet and a lack of exercise.

# Lifestyle and health

The health of our bodies can be affected by the way we choose to live. Scientists and doctors have done a lot of research into the effects of things like diet, stress, hygiene, exercise, smoking, alcohol, solvents and other drugs. You may read about the importance of diet to health in Chapter Four (Human nutrition). In this section, you will study a few of the other factors.

## Smoking

We are constantly told that smoking is bad for us and can cause disease – but everyone seems to know someone who smoked a lot and still lived to an old age. Doctors do *not* say you will get smoking-related diseases if you smoke. They *do* say the chances of getting smoking-related diseases are greater if you smoke. It is like running out into a busy road without looking – you might not get run over, but you *probably* will.

One of the main problems with cigarettes, as with other drugs, is that they are addictive. It is the chemical nicotine that makes cigarettes addictive. People who start smoking find they cannot easily give it up. When they try, they can become miserable and bad-tempered. Some try to compensate by overeating and put on too much weight. It is a vicious circle. Eventually they smoke just to avoid the symptoms of not smoking, not because they like it or they have chosen to smoke.

We do not even have to smoke ourselves, as breathing someone else's smoke can be just as harmful. This is called secondary smoking or passive smoking. A mother who smokes can seriously harm her fetus before it is born.

These can affect your health.

## Smoking and health

Here are some general facts about smoking taken from pamphlets published by the Health Education Authority:

You can use the facts and the bar chart to research the effects of smoking on our health and to answer the questions.

▸ *A man smokes 15 cigarettes a day for 10 years. By how many days is the smoking likely to shorten his life? (Hint: You need to know 365 days is one year, 60 minutes is one hour and 24 hours is one day.)*

▸ *If he gives up smoking at the age of 30, how old will he be when the extra risk of death due to cigarettes disappears?*

▸ *Which diseases are smokers more likely to die from than non-smokers? Write them down in order, starting with the highest risk disease.*

▸ *A lot of people say smoking should be banned from all public places, some say smokers have a right to smoke where they like. Some people refuse to believe the evidence that you have read no matter what doctors say. What do you think about smoking? Using as much of the information given above as you need, make out a reasoned case to support what you believe.*

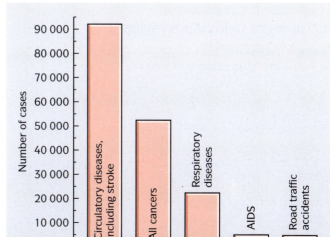

Some major causes of death in 1992.

BIOLOGY

◆ Smoking kills about 115 thousand people each year – that is, one every five minutes.

◆ Out of every thousand people who start smoking when they are teenagers and continue to smoke 20 cigarettes or more a day, one will be murdered, six will die in road accidents and about 250 will be killed before their time by smoking.

◆ On average, for each cigarette smoked, a smoker shortens his or her life by about five and a half minutes.

◆ Over four times as many premature deaths are caused by smoking as by road traffic accidents, alcohol abuse, drugs, suicide and all other known, avoidable risks put together.

◆ Tobacco smoke contains thousands of chemicals. Some of them have marked irritant properties and some 60 are known or suspected **carcinogens** (cancer-causing substances).

◆ About 81 per cent of lung cancer deaths, 18 per cent of coronary heart disease deaths and 76 per cent of chronic bronchitis and emphysema deaths (diseases of the air passages and lungs) are attributable to smoking.

◆ Smoking can also cause asthma, stroke, atherosclerosis and cancers of the mouth, larynx and oesophagus.

◆ Ex-smokers have fewer days of illness and fewer health complaints than smokers.

◆ Only one year after of giving up smoking, the extra risk of heart disease is reduced by half.

◆ After 15 years off cigarettes, ex-smokers have almost the same risk of death as people who have never smoked.

◆ Stopping smoking is beneficial even for those who are already ill. For example, the risk of repeat heart attacks is reduced by 50 per cent or more.

◆ In a household where both parents smoke, their children could be experiencing damage equivalent to smoking 80 cigarettes a year.

## Alcohol

Most people agree that drinking alcohol *in moderation* is not at all harmful. It can even be good for the body. But severe problems can result from excess alcohol. These include:

- Liver damage.
- Increased risk of oesophageal and pancreatic cancer.
- Inflammation of the stomach.
- Loss of interest in food followed by malnutrition. You may read about malnutrition in Chapter Four (Human nutrition).
- Damage to the immune system followed by increased susceptibility to infections.
- Weight gain which affects the heart.
- High blood pressure.
- Damage to the brain and nerves.

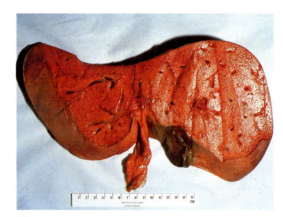

▲ A healthy liver.

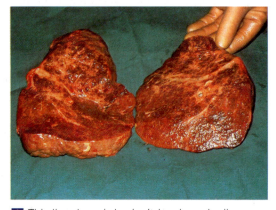

▲ This liver has cirrhosis. It has been badly damaged by excess alcohol.

## Safe levels of alcohol

It is recommended that people over the age of 18 years restrict their alcohol intake to 14 units in women or 21 units in men each week. Pregnant women and people under 18 are advised not to drink at all. 'Measuring alcohol' shows you how much of each drink is one unit.

Overdrinking can be a major cause of ill-health. Here are some startling facts:

■ About a third of all deaths in road traffic accidents are associated with blood alcohol levels over the legal limit.

■ Twice as many people died from liver disease caused by alcohol in 1986 compared with 1956.

■ It is thought that between eight thousand and 25 thousand men die each year because of alcohol abuse.

■ Alcohol abuse leads to between eight million and 15 million lost working days each year in Britain.

■ Drink-driving offences in Britain rose by 33 per cent in women and 40 per cent in men between 1974 and 1989.

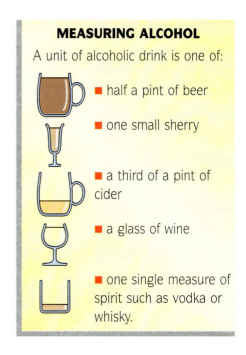

**MEASURING ALCOHOL**

A unit of alcoholic drink is one of:

■ half a pint of beer

■ one small sherry

■ a third of a pint of cider

■ a glass of wine

■ one single measure of spirit such as vodka or whisky.

Just like smoking, drinking alcohol can become an addiction for some people. It is very difficult for an alcoholic to 'kick the habit' and lead a normal life. Many alcoholics do not even recognise the fact that they are addicted to alcohol and do not admit to themselves that they have a problem.

## Solvents and drugs

Solvents, such as glue, and other substances, such as ecstasy, cocaine and heroin, can cause very serious reactions in the body. Their use can be fatal. It is illegal to buy or sell ecstasy, cocaine and heroin.

The worst feature of these non-medicinal drugs is that they can be addictive. People who use them can easily become obsessed with them. The body develops a demand or craving for the drug. It is not a habit which can be broken with a bit of will power. Some drugs, like crack cocaine, are so powerfully addictive that no one has been known to use them and stop afterwards. The addicts cannot survive without their drugs and their whole lives become devoted to getting drugs.

Drug addicts often cannot work or function properly in society and have to steal to get the money to pay for their addiction. The downward spiral into a life of drug use and crime destroys family and other relationships.

## Exercise

Doctors believe taking regular exercise is good for our health. They particularly recommend **aerobic** exercise which increases the volume of oxygen sent in the blood to the body's muscles, including the muscular wall of the heart. This exercise should be vigorous enough to make you feel warm and slightly out of breath and done for at least 20 minutes, three to five times a week. Easy ways to do aerobic exercise include brisk walking, running, riding a bicycle and swimming. Here are some of the benefits of aerobic exercise:

■ Increased fitness of the heart. It pumps blood more efficiently and with less effort. A trained athlete's heart can pump up to six times as much blood as the heart of an unfit person. You may read about this in Chapter Five (Breathing and circulation).

- Blood pressure gets less.
- The blood concentration of a chemical which counteracts the effects of cholesterol rises. Scientists think that cholesterol, which is a fat, may cause heart disease.
- Improved lung function. You may read about lung function in Chapter Five (Breathing and circulation).
- Helps to reduce anxiety and depression.
- Helps to control body weight by *burning off* excess fats in respiration.
- Helps the body's ability to dissolve blood clots.
- Increases the blood concentrations of **endorphins**. These substances are painkillers and might cause the feeling of elation experienced by athletes after hard exercise.
- Helps to make bones stronger.

Use the information above to answer the following questions.

▶ *It is common for people who work indoors to go outside now and then, just for a quick walk in the fresh air. When they come back in, they usually feel much better for the exercise. Explain why this is so.*

▶ *Explain how a trained athlete's resting heart rate might be 40 beats per minute, whereas the average rate is normally about 70 beats per minute.*

▶ *People who suffer from high blood pressure or heart disease are usually advised by their doctor to take regular, but not too strenuous (hard) exercise. Explain the benefit of this advice, bearing in mind their medical condition.*

▶ *Some people have a tendency to make blood clots inside their blood vessels. These clots are called thrombi. How can regular exercise help to prevent thrombosis?*

## Hygiene

You should always wash your hands after blowing your nose or going to the toilet and before you prepare food. You should always wash and brush your teeth before going to bed at night and also after breakfast in the morning. Washing is a simple way of stopping micro organisms passing from person to person. It helps to prevent the spread of disease. Many diseases, such as typhoid and dysentery, which used to be major causes of death in Britain, are now very rare. This is mainly because people are now more aware of the importance of good hygiene.

Hygiene does not just refer to our personal habits. It also refers to the habits of a community. The water supply to our houses and the treatment of sewage in our towns and cities is done hygienically. Before early Victorian times, when proper sewers were built in all major towns, drinking water was often contaminated with sewage.

Study the drawing of a child eating and then answer the questions.

▸ *List all the things you can see in the drawing which are unhygienic and likely to cause disease to spread.*

▸ *What steps could you take to make eating more hygienic than shown here?*

## Summary

- Pathogens are micro organisms which cause disease.
- Pathogens can enter our bodies through lungs, digestive system, skin, by sexual contact or into a fetus through the placenta.
- Neutrophils and monocytes engulf pathogens by phagocytosis.
- Lymphocytes protect our bodies from disease by immune responses. These include the production of special proteins called antibodies. Protection is called immunity.
- Antibodies can cause rejection of transplanted organs or transfused blood.
- Vaccines are preparations of antigens which do not cause disease but bring about an immune response.
- An allergy is a reaction to antigens to which most people do not react at all. Irritation is caused in the tissues by histamine which is produced by the allergic reaction.
- Antihistamine drugs help relieve the symptoms of an allergy. Asthma is an example of an allergic reaction.
- Blood coagulation is brought about by the actions of platelets when blood vessels are damaged. The protein fibrin is formed. It traps blood cells and produces a clot.
- A blood clot formed inside an intact blood vessel is called a thrombus. Thrombi can block blood vessels.
- Certain aspects of lifestyle can affect health, for example, diet, stress, smoking, alcohol, solvents and illegal drugs, exercise and hygiene.
- Smoking, drinking excess alcohol and using solvents and illegal substances are all very unhealthy. They are habits which easily become addictive and often lead to deterioration of body function and possibly death.
- Exercise is positively good for the body, especially the heart and muscles. Lack of regular exercise can be harmful.

# Revision Questions

**1 a** List *three* things that are bad for our health.
  **b** List *three* things that are good for our health.
  **c** Take *one* item from each of your lists and explain its effect on our health.
  **d** Medical science is much more advanced than when your parents were young, but some say that people are less healthy nowadays. Explain how this might be so.

**2** Dave is 28 years old and is 12 kilograms overweight for his body build. He smokes 40 cigarettes a day and drinks a few pints with his mates each night. His job as a company salesman means he does not get much exercise at work. Dave does not take much regular exercise in his own time either. He receives a small basic wage and depends on sales commission to make enough to live on. Some months he does not earn enough from sales to pay his mortgage. Dave's blood pressure is currently very high.
  **a** What health dangers are there in Dave's life style?
  **b** What advice could you give to Dave to help him lead a healthier life?

**3 a** What is a *pathogen*?
  **b** In what ways do the following things protect our body from pathogens:
    *i* skin
    *ii* gastric acid
    *iii* mucus
    *iv* tears?
    Write a few lines on each.
  **c** Explain *one* other way in which the body can protect itself from pathogens.

**4** Write brief notes about each of the following in the protection of our bodies against disease:
  **a** phagocytosis
  **b** antibodies
  **c** blood clots
  **d** antibiotics.

**5 a** What is an *immune response*?
  **b** How do immune responses protect us against disease-causing micro organisms?
  **c** Allergies are immune responses with no obvious protective effects – quite the opposite – they can often be painful and even threaten life. Describe how an allergic response can be caused.

**6** Vaccines and antibiotics are substances which can protect us against disease. Explain the following facts about vaccines and antiobiotics:
  **a** Vaccines can consist of live organisms but they do not cause disease.
  **b** A vaccine only gives immunity against a particular disease.
  **c** Influenza vaccine is not always effective.
  **d** Antibiotics give no protection against viral diseases.
  **e** Antibiotics are generally less effective today than they were ten years ago.

**7 a** Draw a diagram which shows the main stages of blood coagulation, starting with the clumping of platelets and ending with the formation of a clot.
  **b** Explain how blood clots can sometimes form inside blood vessels.
  **c** What might happen if a clot forms in a coronary artery?

**8** You have been asked to appear on a television programme about young people's awareness of a number of health issues in modern Britain. You have been told you might have to participate in studio discussions on any of the following issues:
  **a** the abuse of illegal substances
  **b** excess alcohol
  **c** smoking and health
  **d** exercise.

Prepare some briefing notes to remind you of the main points just before you go to the studio.

# Human nutrition

A report for the Department of Health, called *Diets of British School Children (1989)*, said that the main sources of dietary energy were bread, chips, milk, biscuits, meat products, cake and puddings.

The photographs show a breakfast, a school dinner and an evening meal that might be eaten by a typical student in Britain. You can also see some of the things that might be eaten between meals.

**You might have been told junk food is bad for you or that you should eat more vegetables or to cut down on fatty foods. These are bits of advice we do not want to hear because we often like the foods that are supposed to be bad for us.**

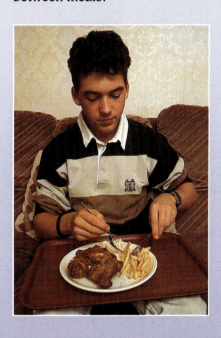

▶ *How does the food shown in the photographs compare with your diet (what you eat)?*

▶ *Do you think these meals represent a healthy diet? Are there any foods that might be bad for your health? Is there enough of the foods that are good for you?*

In this chapter, you will study diet and digestion and see how our diet can affect our health.

# Review

Many people think of a diet as a way of trying to slim or lose weight. In fact, our diet is everything we eat. A *balanced diet* contains foods that give our bodies all the substances they need for healthy growth throughout our lives. Before going any further read this page and attempt the tasks. Write the answers in your notes.

| Substance | Foods | Importance |
|---|---|---|
| **Carbohydrates** Sugars and starches | Potatoes, bread, cereals, sugar, rice, pasta | Provide energy in respiration |
| **Fats** There are saturated and unsaturated fats | Butter, cheese, margarine, oils | Provide energy in respiration; heat insulation (skin); growth of cell membranes |
| **Proteins** | Meat, cheese, fish, eggs, pulses (such as peas, lentils, beans) | Enzymes; growth of cells and tissues |
| **Vitamins** A, D, E, K, B, C | Liver, fruit, vegetables | Needed for a variety of body functions, for example, red blood cell production, respiration, nerve action, blood clotting, vision |
| **Minerals** For example, iron, calcium, sodium, potassium, iodine | Bread, dairy products, vegetables | Needed for a variety of body functions, for example, nerve and muscle action, haemoglobin production, hormone action, absorption of minerals in the intestine |
| **Fibre** | Brown bread, cereals, bran, vegetables | Helps the actions of the digestive system, reduces fat absorption |
| **Water** | | About 67 per cent of our body mass is water. Water forms the main part of cytoplasm and other body fluids; substances are transported in water; biochemical reactions take place in water |

⬛ This table lists the main nutrients (dietary substances) and why we need them.

## CHECK FOUR

**1** Here are some of the main types of chemical substances we need in our diet:
  **a** carbohydrates
  **b** proteins
  **c** water
  **d** fats.

Match them up with the following list of some of the things they do in our bodies:
  **e** Makes up most of the mass of our bodies.
  **f** Heat insulation in the skin.
  **g** Main source of energy in respiration.
  **h** Needed to make and for growth of cells and tissues.

**2** Choose two vitamins and two minerals and say why they are essential in a healthy diet.

**3** What foods are a good source of fibre?

**4** How does dietary fibre affect our health?

**5** What foods are naturally rich in vitamins?

**6** Would you say that you eat a balanced diet? List everything you ate yesterday and then check that you ate some of each of the main nutrients in the table above.

**7** What must happen to the food we eat before it can be absorbed into our blood?

**8** List some things that you can eat that you think are good and some that are bad for your health.

**9** Explain how regular brushing and flossing can help prevent tooth decay.

# A healthy diet

The National Advisory Committee on Nutritional Education (NACNE) and the Committee on Medical Aspects of Food Policy (COMA) have recommended the following changes in the British diet:

- eat *less fat*
- eat *more fibre*
- eat *less sugar*
- eat *less salt*

People should also avoid becoming overweight.

# Eat less fat

Fats contain **fatty acids**. Some of these are essential in our diet. You can read about the different kinds of fats in Chemistry, Chapter Two.

Some fats are **saturated**; they do not have any double bonds between their carbon atoms. Saturated fats include animal fat (lard) and they are also found in dairy products, such as milk, cheese and butter.

Other fats are **unsaturated**; they have one **(monounsaturates)** or more **(polyunsaturates)** double bonds. Unsaturated fats are found in sunflower oil, olive oil and some other vegetable oils. They are also found in margarine made from these oils.

Scientists think that saturated fats may increase the level of **cholesterol** in your blood. Cholesterol can harden your arteries and lead to heart disease. Blood vessels damaged in this way can also cause blood clots to form, leading to thrombosis. You may have read about this in Chapter Three (Health and blood). Polyunsaturated fats might be good for your heart because they provide fatty acids without increasing cholesterol to unhealthy levels.

Fats also contain a lot of energy which is released in your cells by respiration. A diet rich in fats can lead to a person gaining too much weight. This can strain the **cardiovascular system** (heart and blood vessels) and lead to heart disease and high blood pressure. This chart can be used to check a person's weight.

People whose weight is in the chart's white *underweight* zone could eat more

| Nutrient | Effect of deficiency |
|---|---|
| Vitamin A | Poor skin; poor vision in dim light |
| *Vitamin B$_1$ | Beri-beri; nerve and muscle disorders; heart failure |
| *Vitamin B$_2$ | Poor skin |
| *Vitamin B$_6$ | Anaemia |
| *Niacin | Pellagra; dark, scaly skin |
| *Vitamin B$_{12}$ | Pernicious anaemia |
| *Folic acid | Anaemia |
| Vitamin C | Scurvy; bleeding gums and under skin, poor wound healing |
| Vitamin D | Poor bone development; rickets in children |
| Vitamin K | Slow blood clotting |
| Iron | Anaemia |
| Calcium, phosphate or magnesium | Poor bone development |
| Sodium chloride | Low blood pressure |
| Potassium | Weak muscles |
| Iodine | Low thyroid hormone output, leading to slow metabolism and retarded growth |
| Protein | Poor growth and development; poor wound healing |

*There are a number of types of vitamin B.

🔺 A lack of any of the **nutrients** (dietary substances) from our diet leads to **nutritional deficiency diseases**. Some examples of vitamins and minerals are summarised in this table.

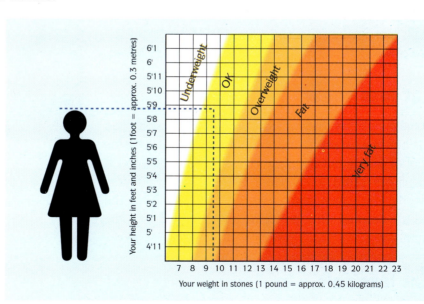

🔺 Chart relating height to weight. An example is shown for a woman who is 5 feet 8¾ inches tall and who weighs 9 stones 8 pounds. The lines joining these values cross in the yellow 'weight OK' zone. She is normal weight for her height.

than they do, provided they eat a well-balanced diet and do not just fill up with fats and sugar. Very underweight people should see their doctor.

*Overweight* and *fat* people (green and orange zones) should try to lose weight. People whose weight is in the red zone should see their doctor and must lose a lot of weight. Some people think they are fat when they are not. In extreme cases this is called **anorexia**. People with anorexia can become dangerously ill because they do not eat properly. Their diet must be carefully controlled, so that, if they need to, they lose weight safely.

### Cholesterol – good or bad?

Because scientists think that high blood cholesterol can contribute to heart disease, many people think of cholesterol as a harmful substance. However, cholesterol is very important as it is found in all cell membranes. It is also needed for the production of steroid hormones, such as the sex hormones. Most of the cholesterol in the blood is formed in the liver from saturated fats which we eat in our diet.

It is the *amount* of cholesterol in the blood that is important to our health. The risk of heart disease increases when the blood cholesterol level rises above 150 mg (milligram) per 100 cm$^3$. The risk of heart disease doubles with every 50 mg increase above 200 mg per 100 cm$^3$.

▶ *What is the best way to avoid too much cholesterol in the blood? Eat less cholesterol or cut down on saturated fats? Explain your answer.*

## Eat more fibre

Fibre can help food travel through the digestive system. The muscles in the gut need exercise to stay healthy. Fibre gives them something to squeeze against! Fibre can prevent constipation. The special type of fibre in oat bran can lower the amount of cholesterol in our blood and so help prevent heart disease. There is also evidence that high fibre intake can reduce the risk of cancer of the bowel, which is one of the commonest cancers in Britain.

## Eat less sugar

Some people say that refined sugar (the white sugar you can buy in a packet) is *empty calories* because it contains a lot of energy, but no useful nutrients. Eating too much sugar can cause tooth decay. It feeds bacteria in the mouth which then make acid. This acid dissolves the teeth's **enamel** (the protective coating) and rots the teeth.

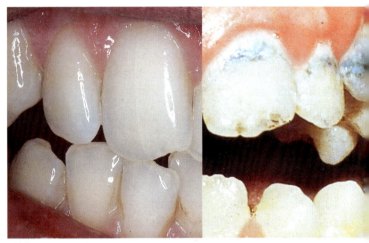

🔺 Compare the normal and the decayed teeth. Tooth decay is caused by too much sugar in the diet and poor dental hygiene. Regular brushing and flossing removes trapped food and many of the bacteria.

## Eat less salt

Too much salt in your diet can cause an increase in blood pressure. This might damage the heart.

# Daily allowances

People above the age of 12 are recommended to eat 70–75 grams of fats each day. In general, we should all eat less fat and try to eat mostly unsaturated fats. People above the age of 12 are recommended to eat 25–30 grams of fibre each day.

It is recommended that we cut the average sugar intake to half its present level. The energy required by people depends on the amount of exercise they do. On average, most adults must take in between 1900 and 2550 Calories each day.

The recommended daily salt intake is just 6 grams. The average salt intake in the United Kingdom in 1989 was about 8–12 grams a day.

Most food manufacturers print nutritional information lists on their food packages. These lists tell you the energy value of the food, what the food contains and also how much there is of each of the ingredients. You can use the lists to help you decide what you will eat and so help you to keep to a healthy diet. However, this information is not printed on fresh food. This table lists approximate values for a variety of fresh foods.

▶ Prepare some notes for a leaflet entitled 'Fat Facts', aimed at reducing the reader's saturated fat intake.

▶ Why is refined sugar sometimes called empty calories?

▶ Why should we avoid being overweight?

| Item of diet | Energy (kJ) | Protein (g) | Fat (g) | Carbohy- drate(g) | Minerals (mg) | *Vitamins | | | | | |
|---|---|---|---|---|---|---|---|---|---|---|---|
| | | | | | | A (µg) | D (µg) | B$_1$ (mg) | B$_2$ (mg) | Nicotinic acid (mg) | C (mg) |
| Apples | 197 | 0.3 | 0 | 12.0 | 4.3 | 5 | 0 | 0.04 | 0.02 | 0.1 | 5 |
| Bananas | 326 | 1.1 | 0 | 19.2 | 7.4 | 33 | 0 | 0.04 | 0.07 | 0.8 | 10 |
| Beef | 940 | 18.1 | 17.1 | 0 | 8.9 | 0 | 0 | 0.06 | 0.19 | 8.1 | 0 |
| Bread, white | 1068 | 8.0 | 1.7 | 54.3 | 101.7 | 0 | 0 | 0.18 | 0.03 | 2.6 | 0 |
| Bread, wholemeal | 1025 | 9.6 | 3.1 | 46.7 | 31.0 | 0 | 0 | 0.24 | 0.09 | 1.9 | 0 |
| Butter | 3006 | 0.5 | 81.0 | 0 | 15.2 | 995 | 1.25 | 0 | 0 | 0.1 | 0 |
| Cabbage | 66 | 1.7 | 0 | 2.3 | 38.4 | 50 | 0 | 0.03 | 0.03 | 0.5 | 23 |
| Carrots | 98 | 0.7 | 0 | 5.4 | 48.6 | 2000 | 0 | 0.06 | 0.05 | 0.7 | 6 |
| Cheese, cheddar | 1708 | 25.4 | 34.5 | 0 | 810.6 | 420 | 0.35 | 0.04 | 0.50 | 5.2 | 0 |
| Cod | 321 | 17.4 | 0.7 | 0 | 16.3 | 0 | 0 | 0.08 | 0.07 | 4.8 | 0 |
| Cream, double | 1848 | 1.8 | 48.0 | 2.6 | 65.0 | 420 | 0.28 | 0.02 | 0.08 | 0.4 | 0 |
| Eggs | 612 | 12.3 | 10.9 | 0 | 56.1 | 140 | 1.50 | 0.09 | 0.47 | 3.7 | 0 |
| Liver | 1020 | 24.9 | 13.7 | 5.6 | 22.8 | 6000 | 0.75 | 0.27 | 4.30 | 20.7 | 20 |
| Margarine | 3019 | 0.2 | 81.5 | 0 | 4.3 | 900 | 8.00 | 0 | 0 | 0.1 | 0 |
| Milk | 274 | 3.3 | 3.8 | 4.8 | 120.1 | 40 | 0.03 | 0.04 | 0.15 | 0.9 | 1 |
| Oranges | 150 | 0.8 | 0 | 8.5 | 41.3 | 8 | 0 | 0.10 | 0.03 | 0.3 | 50 |
| Parsnips | 210 | 1.7 | 0 | 11.3 | 55.6 | 0 | 0 | 0.10 | 0.09 | 1.3 | 15 |
| Peas | 208 | 5.0 | 0 | 7.7 | 14.2 | 50 | 0 | 0.25 | 0.11 | 2.3 | 15 |
| Potatoes, boiled | 339 | 1.4 | 0 | 19.7 | 4.5 | 0 | 0 | 0.08 | 0.03 | 1.2 | 10 |
| Rice | 1531 | 6.2 | 1.0 | 86.8 | 4.4 | 0 | 0 | 0.08 | 0.03 | 1.5 | 0 |
| Sugar, white | 1680 | 0 | 0 | 100.0 | 1.0 | 0 | 0 | 0 | 0 | 0 | 0 |
| Tomatoes | 52 | 0.8 | 0 | 2.4 | 13.4 | 117 | 0 | 0.06 | 0.04 | 0.7 | 21 |

▲ Average nutritional content per 100 grams of a variety of fresh foods. Minerals are mostly calcium and iron.

*1 mg = 1/1000th g
1 µg = 1/1000th mg

# Food additives

Food additives are substances that are added to food for three main reasons.
These are to:
- keep food *fresh* and stable
- alter and improve the *taste*
- improve the *texture* and *appearance* of the food.

Many people are worried that some food additives might damage our health.
The use of food additives is controlled in the United Kingdom by the Ministry
of Agriculture, Fisheries and Food (MAFF) and a law called the Food Act. The
MAFF is advised on the safety and possible **toxicity** (poisonous effects) of
food additives by the Food Advisory Committee.

▶ *What does the MAFF do?*

## E numbers

The law requires all food manufacturers to list the additives in their products
on the food packages. Most of the additives are given a code number, called
an **E number**. E is for European Union.

This table gives an example of each of the commonly used additives, what
it is called and what it is used for.

| E numbers | Substance | Reason for the additive |
|-----------|-----------|-------------------------|
| E102 | Tartrazine | Colour |
| E220 – E227 | Sulphur dioxide | Preservative (helps prevent food decay by micro organisms such as bacteria and fungi) |
| E321 | Butylated hydroxytoluene | Anti-oxidant (prevents discolouration of food by the air) |
| E412 | Guar gum | Improves texture |

▶ *Examine some food packaging to find some more examples of E numbers.*

Some additives are used to add flavour to the food. Others, like monosodium
glutamate, do not have any flavour on their own, but enhance the flavour of
the food. Monosodium glutamate is often used in Chinese food. Some additives give a sweet taste to food without the calories in sugar, for example,
aspartame and saccharin. These sweeteners can be important in food
designed for people with **diabetes** who need to restrict their sugar intake.
You can read about diabetes in Chapter Seven (Hormones).

▶ *Produce a poster for consumers to tell them about the advantages of using
food additives. Alternatively, produce a poster for a doctor's surgery
showing that food additives may be bad for our health and that fresh food
is better for us.*

# Food facts – marketing foods

You can tell a lot about food from its packaging. You can examine the constituents (ingredients) of some common foods and relate them to a healthy diet.

The photographs show the packages of three foods that are considered to be healthy. Look at the information on the food labels and answer the questions below.

▶ *How have the manufacturers emphasised the healthy aspects of these foods?*

▶ *Use the package labels and the nutritional information boxes to answer the following questions:*
  **a** *What is the energy content of 100 cm³ of the high juice orange drink (undiluted)?*
  **b** *What vitamins are present in the sunflower margarine? Why are they important in our diet?*
  **c** *How much of the daily recommended intake of fibre is provided by one serving of the Oat and Bran Flakes?*

▶ *Compare each of the brands shown in the photographs with two other brands of similar foods. Draw up a table of brand names in order of nutritional merit (best first). You will have to say how you have decided on the order. For instance, 'provides the most energy' or 'contains the most vitamins'. If there are any cases where two brands score the same, use their price to place them in your table.*

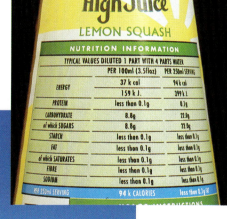

**High Juice — LEMON SQUASH**

## NUTRITION INFORMATION
TYPICAL VALUES DILUTED 1 PART WITH 4 PARTS WATER

|  | PER 100ml (3.5floz) | PER 250ml SERVING |
|---|---|---|
| ENERGY | 37 k cal | 94 k cal |
|  | 159 k J. | 399 k J. |
| PROTEIN | less than 0.1g | 0.1g |
| CARBOHYDRATE | 8.8g | 22.0g |
| of which sugars | 8.8g | 22.0g |
| STARCH | less than 0.1g | less than 0.1g |
| FAT | less than 0.1g | less than 0.1g |
| of which SATURATES | less than 0.1g | less than 0.1g |
| FIBRE | less than 0.1g | less than 0.1g |
| SODIUM | less than 0.1g | less than 0.1g |
| PER 250ml SERVING | 94 k CALORIES | less than 0.1g of |

**SAINSBURY'S OAT & BRAN FLAKES**
*Fortified with vitamins & iron*
HIGH IN FIBRE
NATURALLY LOW IN FAT
500 grams

## NUTRITION INFORMATION
TYPICAL VALUES

|  | PER 100g (3.5oz) | PER 30g SERVING |
|---|---|---|
| ENERGY | 343 k cal | 103 k cal |
|  | 1453 k J. | 436 k J. |
| PROTEIN | 11.6g | 3.5g |
| CARBOHYDRATE | 64.3g | 19.3g |
| of which SUGARS | 14.5g | 4.3g |
| STARCH | 49.8g | 14.9g |
| FAT | 4.4g | 1.3g |
| of which SATURATES | 1.0g | 0.3g |
| FIBRE | 12.5g | 3.8g |
| SODIUM | 1.1g | 0.3g |
| VITAMIN D | 2.8µg (56% RDA) | 0.9µg (17% RDA) |
| VITAMIN C | 34mg (56% RDA) | 10.2mg (17% RDA) |
| THIAMIN (B1) | 1.4mg (100% RDA) | 0.4mg (30% RDA) |
| RIBOFLAVIN (B2) | 1.6mg (100% RDA) | 0.5mg (30% RDA) |
| NIACIN | 18mg (100% RDA) | 5.4mg (30% RDA) |
| VITAMIN B6 | 2mg (100% RDA) | 0.6mg (30% RDA) |
| FOLIC ACID | 200µg (100% RDA) | 60µg (30% RDA) |
| VITAMIN B12 | 1µg (100% RDA) | 0.3µg (30% RDA) |
| IRON | 7.8mg (56% RDA) | 2.4mg (17% RDA) |
| RDA means Recommended Daily Allowance | | |
| PER 30g SERVING | 103 CALORIES | 1.3g FAT |

**SAINSBURY'S High Juice LEMON SQUASH** — 1 litre

**KRAFT Vitalite sunflower spread**
HIGH IN ESSENTIAL POLYUNSATURATES
LOW IN SATURATES
VIRTUALLY CHOLESTEROL FREE
500 g

A AND D.
FOR FRYING
comments, or
s about
's Not Butter!
all us free on
onday to Friday
5pm.
FOODS LTD.
WEST SUSSEX

## NUTRITION INFORMATION
100g PROVIDES

| ENERGY | 1544kJ/375kcal |
|---|---|
| PROTEIN | 3 g |
| CARBOHYDRATE | 0.8g |
| (of which sugars | 0.8g) |
| FAT | 40 g |
| (of which saturates | 8 g) |
| (and polyunsaturates | 19 g) |
| (cholesterol | Trace) |
| FIBRE | 0 g |
| SODIUM | 0.6g |

# Eating food

Carry out a survey of the diets eaten by students in your school year or in your class. To do this, you can design a short questionnaire to find out what foods the people in your survey have eaten on a particular day. Make sure the questions are short and simple and will tell you the kind of information you are trying to find out. Select a reasonable number of people for your questionnaire. Make sure your sample is not too large but is representative of the students in your year or class. You might choose to pool all the data collected by your class.

Write a report of your findings. In your report, describe how you carried out the survey and say how reliable you think your data are. (Hint: you will need to think about the number of people you included in your survey.) Work out a way to summarise your results so that conclusions can be drawn from them.

# Food tests

You might be given a worksheet to help you carry out some food tests. The purpose of the exercise is to become familiar with some of the chemical properties of common foods and to find out how they can be detected.

# Digestion

Most of the food we eat is not in a form that can be absorbed directly into the blood. First, it has to be digested. Digestion is the process by which food is broken down into molecules small enough to pass through the gut wall and enter the blood. Digestion takes place in the **digestive system** – sometimes just called the gut. It is brought about by the action of **digestive enzymes** that are secreted by **digestive glands**. The diagram opposite shows the main parts of the human digestive system.

▶ *What is digestion and why must it take place?*

▶ *List the main parts of the digestive system that food passes through after it has been swallowed. What are the main digestive glands?*

Food is pushed through the digestive system by the action of muscles in the gut wall. The action is called **peristalsis**.

## Chewing – mechanical digestion

A lot of the food we eat is taken into the mouth in big pieces which can't be broken down by enzymes. They have to be broken down mechanically into smaller pieces. This is done by the teeth during chewing. The main result of chewing is to increase the surface area of the food, so more of it can be digested at a time by digestive enzymes. Chewing also moistens food.

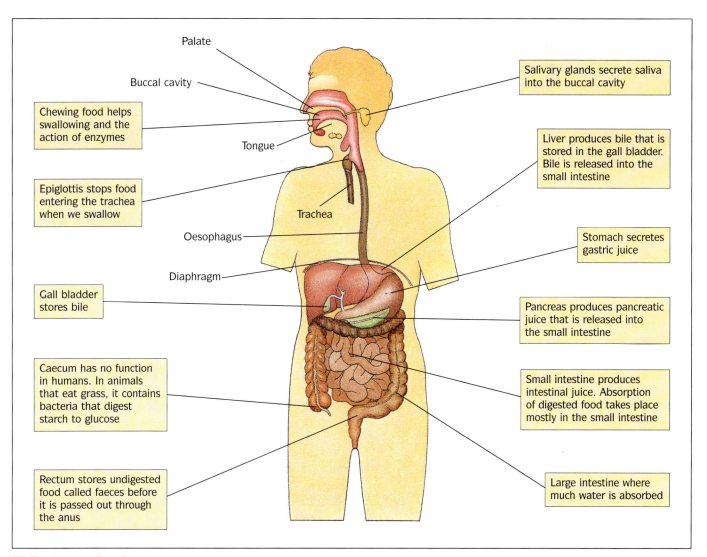

Palate

Buccal cavity

Chewing food helps swallowing and the action of enzymes

Tongue

Epiglottis stops food entering the trachea when we swallow

Trachea

Oesophagus

Diaphragm

Gall bladder stores bile

Caecum has no function in humans. In animals that eat grass, it contains bacteria that digest starch to glucose

Rectum stores undigested food called faeces before it is passed out through the anus

Salivary glands secrete saliva into the buccal cavity

Liver produces bile that is stored in the gall bladder. Bile is released into the small intestine

Stomach secretes gastric juice

Pancreas produces pancreatic juice that is released into the small intestine

Small intestine produces intestinal juice. Absorption of digested food takes place mostly in the small intestine

Large intestine where much water is absorbed

🔺 The human digestive system.

▶ *Explain carefully how chewing food before it is swallowed helps digestion.*

▶ *Suggest why meat-eating animals do not have to chew their food as much as vegetation-eaters.*

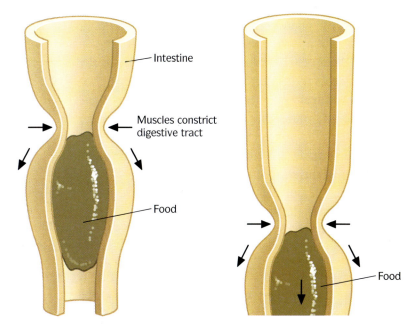

Intestine

Muscles constrict digestive tract

Food

Food

🔺 Peristalsis. Waves of muscle contraction pass down the wall of the digestive system, pushing food and digestive juices through the system.

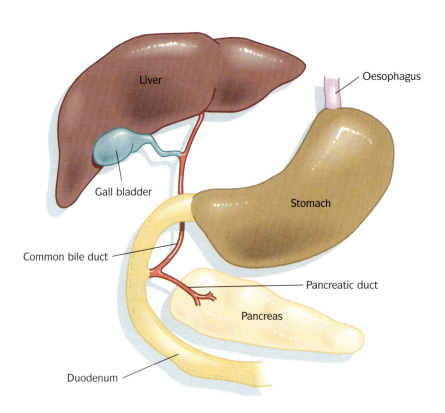

△ Animals which eat a lot of vegetation, like this cow, spend time chewing as vegetation is difficult to break down.

△ Most chemical digestion and absorption of food takes place in the stomach and small intestine.

## Stomach

The lining of the stomach secretes **gastric juice** which contains two main materials:

- **Hydrochloric acid**. This acid gives gastric juice a pH below 2. The main function of the acid is to kill any bacteria that might be in the food. It is one of the body's defences against infection. Hydrochloric acid also changes the molecular structure of proteins, that is, it **denatures** them. You may have read about the structure of proteins in Chemistry, Chapter Fourteen.
- **Pepsin** is a digestive enzyme which breaks down proteins to smaller chemicals called **polypeptides**. This is only the start of the process of protein digestion. The polypeptides will be further digested to amino acids in the small intestine. Pepsin is unique among the body's enzymes in being able to work well in an acid solution.

△ Meat-eating animals, like this lion, rip and tear at their food.

After leaving the stomach, a little at a time, the partially digested food is still very acid and is called **chyme**. On entering the small intestine, chyme is mixed with three main juices: bile, pancreatic juice and intestinal juice.

## Coping with acidity

The hydrochloric acid in gastric juice acts as a disinfectant, killing most bacteria that might be in food. The stomach wall secretes a layer of sticky mucus which forms a lining on the wall's inner surface. Mucus protects the stomach wall against the acid in the gastric juice. In some people, the stomach produces too much acid for the mucus to cope with. The acid corrodes the stomach wall, and causes gastric ulcers. These can be very painful.

A gastric ulcer can be seen inside the stomach with the aid of an **endoscope**. This is a flexible tube which can be pushed down the oesophagus and into the stomach. The endoscope contains a lot of narrow glass fibres along which a doctor can see into the stomach.

Recent research suggests that most ulcers are caused by a bacterium called *Helicobacter pylori* which is resistant to gastric acid. In the past, many gastric ulcer sufferers had to take medicines throughout their lives or even have parts of their stomachs taken out. Nowadays, many sufferers have been completely cured by a course of antibiotics.

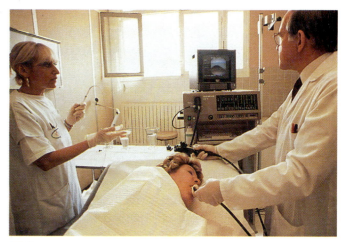

▲ The doctor is looking into the patient's stomach through an endoscope.

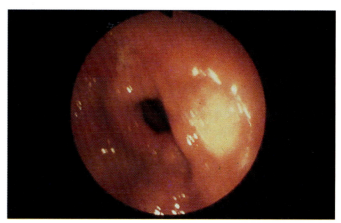

▲ This is what a gastric ulcer looks like, seen through the endoscope.

## Bile

**Bile** is made in the liver. It contains no digestive enzymes but does contain the following substances which are important to digestion:

■ **Sodium hydrogencarbonate** ($NaHCO_3$). This chemical neutralises the hydrochloric acid still in the food that enters the small intestine from the stomach. The chyme must be neutralised to a slightly alkaline pH of about 8 so the digestive enzymes in the small intestine can work properly.

■ **Bile salts**. These are chemicals which break fats down to small droplets. We say the fats are **emulsified**. In this form the fats are more easily digested by enzymes in the small intestine.

■ **Bile pigments**. These are substances produced from the breakdown of old red blood cells. They are excreted via the digestive system and give faeces their characteristic colour.

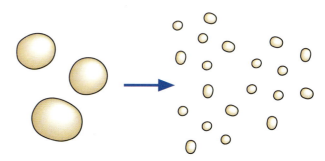

▲ Emulsification of fats by bile salts. The small fat droplets are more easily digested by lipase.

BIOLOGY

# Antacids

Sodium hydrogencarbonate neutralises hydrochloric acid by the following reaction:

$$NaHCO_3 + HCl \rightarrow NaCl + H_2CO_3$$

The word equation is:

sodium hydrogencarbonate + hydrochloric acid → sodium chloride + carbonic acid

Carbonic acid is a weak acid which does not damage the lining of the intestine.

**Antacids** are substances which can be given to people with too much acid in their stomach. They act in the same way as the sodium hydrogencarbonate in bile and pancreatic juice. An example of an antacid is calcium carbonate ($CaCO_3$).

▶ *Write out in words and then the chemical equation showing how calcium carbonate neutralises gastric acid. Use the equation for sodium hydrogencarbonate to help you.*

## Pancreatic and intestinal juices

**Pancreatic juice** and **intestinal juice** contain enzymes which complete the digestion of the food. Pancreatic juice is secreted by the pancreas and intestinal juice is secreted by glands in the wall of the small intestine.

The actions of the digestive enzymes secreted by the main glands of the digestive system are summarised in this table. Substances which are easily absorbed are written in bold.

| Secretions | Glands | Enzymes and other digestive agents | Function |
|---|---|---|---|
| Saliva | Salivary glands | | Saliva lubricates swallowing |
| | | Amylase | Digests starch to maltose |
| Gastric juice | Stomach | Pepsin | Digests proteins to polypeptides |
| | | Hydrochloric acid | Kills micro organisms |
| | | Intrinsic factor | Helps to absorb vitamin $B_{12}$ |
| Pancreatic juice | Pancreas | Amylase | Digests starch to maltose |
| | | Lipase | Digests fats to **fatty acids** and **glycerol** |
| | | Trypsin and chymotrypsin | Digest proteins to polypeptides |
| | | Sodium hydrogencarbonate | Neutralises gastric acid |
| Bile | Liver | Sodium hydrogencarbonate | Neutralises gastric acid |
| | | Bile salts | Emulsify fats |
| | | Bile pigments | Excretion products of haemoglobin from old red blood cells |
| Intestinal juice | Wall of the small intestine | Peptidase | Digests polypeptides to **amino acids** |
| | | Lipase | Digests fats to **fatty acids** and **glycerol** |
| | | Amylase | Digests starch to maltose |
| | | Maltase | Digests maltose to **glucose** |
| | | Sucrase (invertase) | Digests sucrose to **glucose** and **fructose** |
| | | Lactase | Digests lactose to **glucose** and **galactose** |

- *Why must the acid in chyme be neutralised when it enters the small intestine? How is this achieved?*

- *List some substances which are absorbed easily into the blood.*

- *Explain why most carbohydrates are absorbed as monosaccharides (single sugar units like glucose, galactose and fructose).*

- *What happens to the protein in our food before it can be absorbed into the blood?*

## The effects of acidity on enzymes

The purpose of this exercise is to investigate the effects of acidity, that is, pH, on the actions of digestive enzymes.

In an experiment, six test tubes were set up in a rack. A small volume of **buffer solution** was added to each tube. A buffer solution is a mixture of salts which can keep a fixed pH. The pH in each tube was marked as shown in this photograph.

Then, a small volume of amylase solution was added to each tube together with a small volume of starch solution. The tubes were carefully shaken to mix the contents together and a stop clock was started.

Every half minute, a drop of the mixture was taken out of each tube and added to a drop of iodine in potassium iodide solution on a white tile. In the presence of starch, the iodine solution turns blue-black. If the starch has been digested to maltose by the amylase, the iodine stays brown.

The colour reactions were noted for each tube over a period of 5 minutes. The results are shown in this table.

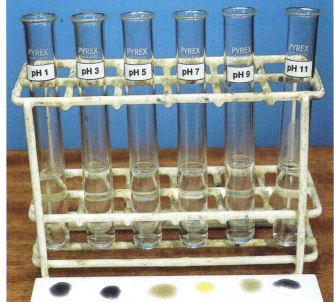

▲ Setting up the experiment.

- *Plot a graph of the time the amylase takes to digest the starch against the pH.*

- *Use your graph to explain the following statements:*
  **a** *Amylase in saliva has little effect on starch digestion because food is usually swallowed quickly into the stomach.*
  **b** *Sodium hydrogencarbonate (NaHCO₃) in pancreatic juice and bile is needed for pancreatic amylase to work properly.*

- *Some people do not have any amylase in their saliva, but this does not affect their digestion at all. Why is this so?*

| Time | pH | | | | | |
|------|----|----|----|----|----|----|
| (minutes) | 1 | 3 | 5 | 7 | 9 | 11 |
| 0.5 | | | | | | |
| 1.0 | | | | ▓ | | |
| 1.5 | | | | ▓ | | |
| 2.0 | | | | ▓ | | |
| 2.5 | | | | ▓ | ▓ | |
| 3.0 | | | ▓ | ▓ | ▓ | |
| 3.5 | | | ▓ | ▓ | ▓ | |
| 4.0 | | | ▓ | ▓ | ▓ | |
| 4.5 | | | ▓ | ▓ | ▓ | |
| 5.0 | | ▓ | ▓ | ▓ | ▓ | ▓ |

▲ The results of the experiment to investigate amylase. Orange squares show when amylase action was recorded.

> In another experiment like the one above, pepsin was used instead of amylase and small squares of exposed photographic film were added instead of starch. Pepsin digests the protein gelatin on the film's surface which then turns from black to clear. This table shows the results.

> Plot a graph of the time it takes pepsin to digest the gelatin against pH.

> Use both your graphs to predict in what pH the enzymes in intestinal juice would work best. This is their **optimum pH**. Explain your answer.

You may be able to develop your answer to the last question into an investigation.

| Time (minutes) | pH | | | | |
|:---:|:---:|:---:|:---:|:---:|:---:|
| | 1 | 3 | 5 | 7 | 9 |
| 1 | ■ | ■ | ■ | ■ | ■ |
| 2 | ■ | | ■ | ■ | ■ |
| 3 | ■ | | ■ | ■ | ■ |
| 4 | | | ■ | ■ | ■ |
| 5 | | | | ■ | ■ |

🔺 The results of an experiment to investigate pepsin action. When active, pepsin dissolves the black photographic emulsion – shown as white squares.

# Absorption of digested food

Food that is digested in the gut is absorbed into the blood. Absorption takes place mostly from the wall of the small intestine. The lining of the small intestine has a very large surface area. This is because millions of **villi** (one is a **villus**) project into the cavity of the intestine. The villi increase the area for absorption of food by about 12 times.

Much water is absorbed across the wall of the **large intestine**. A lot of this water was secreted as part of the digestive juices, some of it was already in the food or drinks you swallowed.

During absorption, nutrients enter the blood and lymph vessels inside the villi. They are then transported to the liver where some substances, such as glucose, are stored. You may read about this in Chapter Seven (Hormones). The nutrients are then carried in the blood to the rest of the body where they are assimilated (absorbed) into the cells and tissues. You can now understand the phrase 'you are what you eat'!

Any undigested or unabsorbed food left in the large intestine leaves the body through the anus as **faeces**. Bacteria from the digestive system make up about half the mass of faeces. Faeces are not excreted, because they never became a part of our cells or tissues, but simply passed straight through the body **(defaecation)**.

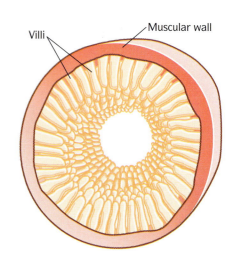

🔺 Villi in the small intestine (adult life-size).

> Write brief notes explaining:
> **a** How villi help the absorption of digested food.
> **b** Where the blood containing absorbed food goes to.
> **c** The difference between absorption and assimilation.
> **d** The difference between defaecation and excretion.

# Disorders of the digestive tract

You can consider the functions of the digestive system and what can go wrong.

Here are some facts about the digestive actions of the gut:
- The inside of the stomach is lined with a layer of mucus. This layer stops gastric juice and pepsin corroding the stomach wall.

- The enzymes made by the digestive glands mostly go into the cavity of the gut. A small amount of the enzymes goes into the blood.
- People with gall stones usually cannot digest fat properly.
- Some people cannot swallow properly. They have to take plenty of liquids with their food.
- **Pancreatitis** is a sudden overactivity of the pancreas, often caused by alcohol abuse. Large amounts of amylase appear in the urine after an attack of pancreatitis.
- Gastric ulcers can occur if the stomach makes too much acid.
- Solid deposits in the bile can block the bile ducts.
- The salivary glands of some people do not make saliva properly.

▶ *Write out these facts into four pairs. Explain how the facts in each pair are linked.*

▶ *List the different ways in which the digestive system can malfunction (not work properly).*

## A model gut

You may be given a worksheet to help you consider food absorption in more detail. You can make a model gut using visking tubing, which has similar properties to the wall of the small intestine.

## Summary

- Our diet must contain a balanced mixture of nutrients.
- The main constituents of a balanced diet are carbohydrates, fats, proteins, vitamins, minerals, fibre and water. These constituents help our bodies to grow and function properly.
- Some diets are unhealthy. They might contain too much or too little of the substances required.
- Many of the substances in food must be broken down into small molecules before they can be absorbed into the blood. They must be digested by enzymes.
- After swallowing, food enters the stomach where it meets gastric juice. This contains hydrochloric acid (which kills micro organisms) and pepsin (which starts to digest proteins).
- Partially digested food (chyme) passes into the small intestine where it meets bile, pancreatic juice and intestinal juice.
- Bile contains sodium hydrogencarbonate (which neutralises gastric acid), bile salts (which emulsify fats) and bile pigments (the excreted remains of haemoglobin from old red blood cells).
- Pancreatic juice contains sodium hydrogencarbonate, amylase (which digests starch to maltose), lipase (which digests fats to fatty acids and glycerol) and enzymes which digest proteins to polypeptides.
- Intestinal juice contains many enzymes which complete the digestion of all foods.
- The products of digestion are absorbed into the blood and lymph in millions of villi in the wall of the small intestine. Much water is absorbed across the wall of the large intestine. Any substances remaining in the large intestine are passed out of the body through the anus as faeces.

## Revision Questions

1 **a** *i* List *four* examples of *junk food*. (Do not confuse this term with *instant* or *fast food* which are not necessarily junk.)

   *ii* List *two* reasons why junk food is supposed to be bad for you.

  **b** What do nutritionists recommend for a healthy diet? In your answer say what is recommended for fat, salt, fibre and refined sugar. In each case, state why.

2 **a** What is meant by a *balanced diet*?

  **b** *i* Suggest meals which would provide a healthy diet for a day.

   *ii* Explain your choice.

3 **a** Make a labelled drawing showing the main parts of the human digestive system. Include the oesophagus, stomach, pancreas, liver, gall bladder and the small and large intestines.

  **b** Indicate on your drawing where the following things take place:

   *i* digestion and absorption of food

   *ii* production of digestive juices.

4 Construct a table to show the following:

  **a** The main foods which provide carbohydrates, fats, proteins, vitamins C and D, calcium and iron.

  **b** The reason why these nutrients are needed in a healthy diet.

5 A recent report for the Department of Health, *The Diets of British Schoolchildren,* stated: 'The main sources of dietary energy in the diets of British schoolchildren were bread, chips, milk, biscuits, meat products, cake and pudding'. Do you think the diets of British schoolchildren are healthy or can they be improved in any way? Explain your answer.

6 Imagine you swallow a small piece of bread.

  **a** Describe what happens to the bread inside your digestive system up to the point of it being absorbed into your blood.

  **b** What might happen to the digested bread after absorption?

7 The following information is taken from a 25 gram packet of potato crisps.

| Nutrition | | |
|---|---|---|
| | **per 25 gram packet** | **per 100 gram** |
| Energy | 560 kJ | 2240 kJ |
| Protein | 1.5 g | 6 g |
| Carbohydrate | 12 g | 48 g |
| Fat | 9 g | 36 g |
| Fibre | 1 g | 4 g |
| Salt | 0.5 g | 2 g |

  **a** How much energy is provided by 25 grams of crisps?

  **b** The recommended daily amount of fibre is 28 grams. How many 25 gram packets of crisps would provide this much fibre? Show your working.

  **c** Crisps contain large amounts of fat and salt. What are the dangers to health of eating:

   *i* too much fat

   *ii* too much salt?

  **d** Which important group of nutrients is missing from the list given on the crisp packet?

8 Explain the advantages of the following things in the processes of digestion and absorption:

  **a** Acid in gastric juice.

  **b** The mucus which lines the stomach.

  **c** Emulsification of fats by bile salts.

  **d** Villi in the walls of the small intestine.

  **e** The length of the intestine.

# Breathing & circulation

The person on the operating table in the photograph is having open heart surgery. One of his heart valves is not working properly, so he is having an artificial one inserted.

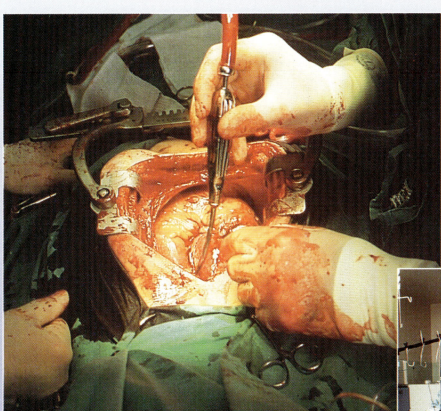

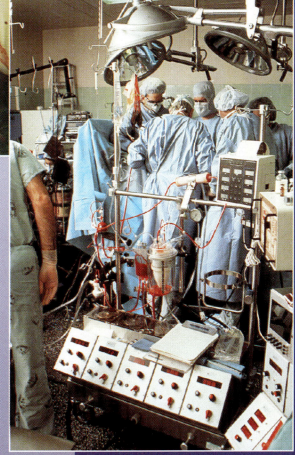

The operation will take about five hours. During this time, the patient's heart is stopped, so the surgeons can cut it open and insert the new valve. The patient's blood is circulated artificially by the machine shown on the right. The machine also adds oxygen to the patient's blood. It is called a heart-lung machine.

This kind of operation is only possible because scientists have designed a machine which can replace two important body functions while the surgeons work on the patient. One function is getting oxygen into the blood vessels of the lungs – breathing. The other function is the pumping action of the heart – circulation of the blood.

Oxygen is needed to allow our cells to obtain energy from food. This chapter explains how oxygen reaches our cells and what happens to it when it gets there.

# Review

You may have made a poster like this earlier in your science course. Before going any further, read this page and attempt the tasks. Write the answers in your notes.

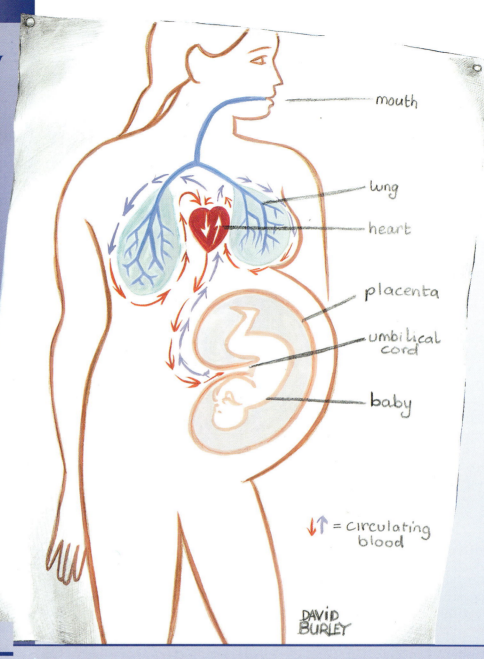

mouth

lung

heart

placenta

umbilical cord

baby

↓↑ = circulating blood

DAVID BURLEY

## CHECK FIVE

1 Copy out the passage below and fill in the missing words from the list underneath:

Blood is pumped around the body by the _____. The blood flows to the organs through large vessels called _____. It flows back to the heart through vessels called _____. Inside the organs, the blood flows through very small vessels called _____. These can only be seen with the aid of a microscope. Substances from the blood pass across the walls of these vessels and into the _____. A fetus gets vital substances from its mother's blood in an organ called the _____.

    veins       placenta     tissues
    arteries   heart        capillaries

2 Draw a diagram of the lungs and the main air passages which take air to them when you breathe. Label as many parts as you can.

3 In what way is smoking supposed to be bad for our lungs and heart?

4 Summarise respiration using a simple word equation.

5 What is a fetus? How does the placenta help it to survive?

# Breathing in

Tony has asthma. Sometimes, he cannot breathe easily because the air passages leading to his lungs become narrow and so he gasps for air. Asthma sufferers can breathe in or inhale a substance which makes their air passages wider. Breathing then becomes easier again.

▲ Tony is asthmatic. His medication helps him control his symptoms.

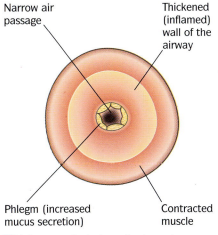

Narrow air passage

Thickened (inflamed) wall of the airway

Phlegm (increased mucus secretion)

Contracted muscle

▲ Microscopical view of a bronchus before an asthma attack.

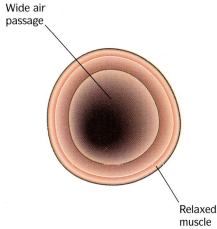

Wide air passage

Relaxed muscle

▲ The same bronchus after treatment with a broncho-dilator.

Sometimes, people can stop breathing altogether. This can happen if someone is electrocuted or has been under water for a few minutes. It might be possible to start their breathing again by giving them assisted breathing, sometimes called **artificial respiration** or **resuscitation**.

The helper blows air into the person's lungs. After this is done a few times, and if the heart is still beating, the person should start breathing on their own.

▲ The woman shown here is being given assisted breathing.

# Breathing

Air is pulled into the lungs and then pushed out before being drawn in again. This *in and out* movement of air is called breathing. It is brought about by movements of the ribs and diaphragm as shown in these diagrams.

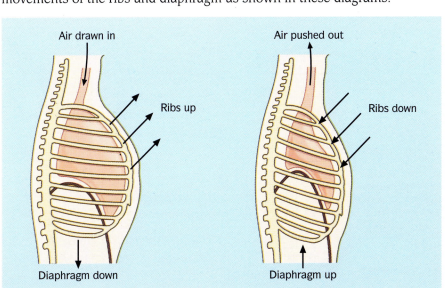

Air drawn in

Ribs up

Diaphragm down

Air pushed out

Ribs down

Diaphragm up

▲ Breathing.

## Asthma

During an asthma attack, the patient coughs and wheezes and has great difficulty breathing. Many asthma sufferers are allergic to particles in the air, such as dust or pollen. However, in some people asthma attacks can also be brought on by exercise. Attacks are caused by contraction of the muscles in the walls of the air passages which become narrower, and if the airways are constricted, not enough oxygen reaches the blood. During an attack the skin under the finger nails can turn white or blue. This is because **haemoglobin**, the chemical which carries oxygen in the red blood cells, goes bluish when it is not carrying much oxygen. It goes bright red when it combines with a lot of oxygen.

## Using a peak flow meter

You may be given a worksheet to help you study breathing. You can use a peak flow meter to measure the fastest rate that you can blow air out of your lungs.

## Gas exchange

The lungs take oxygen from the air we breathe. They also excrete into the air carbon dioxide produced in respiration. These processes are called gas exchange.

When we breathe, air is drawn into our lungs through a system of tubes called the **air passages**. They end in hundreds of millions of tiny air sacs called **alveoli** (single, alveolus). The surface area of all the alveoli together is enormous. In an adult human it is about the playing area of a tennis court. Gas exchange takes place in the alveoli.

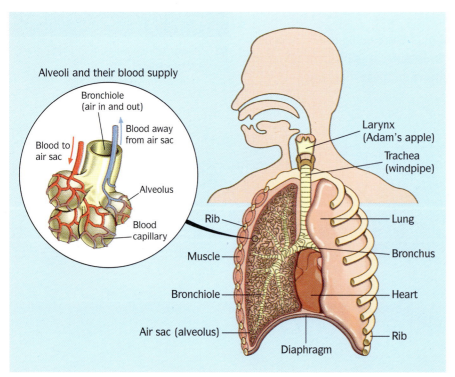

Alveoli and their blood supply

Bronchiole (air in and out)

Blood away from air sac

Blood to air sac

Alveolus

Blood capillary

Rib

Muscle

Bronchiole

Air sac (alveolus)

Larynx (Adam's apple)

Trachea (windpipe)

Lung

Bronchus

Heart

Rib

Diaphragm

⬛ Microscopical view of the air passages ending in alveoli in the lungs.

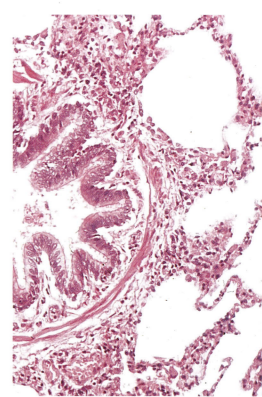

⬛ Microscopical view of a bronchiole (left) and alveoli (magnified 200 times).

▶ *What two features of alveoli enable the exchange of large volumes of respiratory gases?*

▶ *During exercise, breathing gets faster and deeper. Why is this so?*

## Clear airways

A sticky substance called **mucus** is found on the inner surface of the walls of the **trachea, bronchi** and **bronchioles**. Mucus traps any dust, bacteria and pollen which we breathe in. The mucus is pushed up into the **pharynx** at the back of the mouth by small hairs. The mucus is swallowed. The small hairs are called **cilia**. They line the air passages and beat in a rhythm. This stops the alveoli getting blocked up by particles in the air. It also takes away micro organisms which might cause disease in the lungs.

▶ *The air we breathe contains dust, bacteria and pollen. Explain why these do not normally block up the lungs.*

▶ *How is the physio helping to move the mucus?*

▶ *What would happen if the mucus stayed in the lungs?*

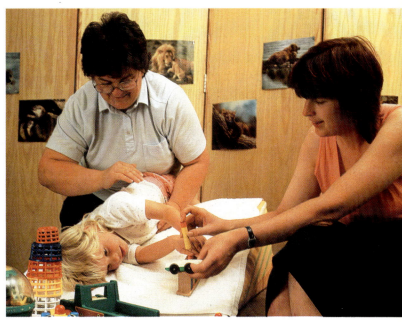

This child has cystic fibrosis. The mucus in her air passages is very thick and sticky. She needs help to bring it up out of her lungs and into her mouth.

## Transport of respiratory gases

Oxygen is carried in the blood from our lungs to all parts of our bodies. The blood is red because it contains a red substance called haemoglobin. Haemoglobin carries oxygen and is found in the red blood cells. Blood rich in oxygen is said to be **oxygenated**.

▶ *List the different types of cells shown in the photograph, putting the commonest found in blood at the top and the rarest at the bottom.*

### Red blood cells

In a healthy person, red cells only last about four months in the blood. After this time, they have to be replaced by new ones. These are made in the marrow of some of our bones. **Bone marrow** makes new red cells at a rate of about nine thousand million cells per hour.

The red cells make up nearly half of the volume of our blood. Each one is a disc shape with a dent in the middle and has no nucleus. The shape gives the red cells a big surface area for a small volume. The bigger the surface area the red cells have, the more oxygen they can take in when the blood enters the lungs.

▶ *What advantage is there in the red cells having no nucleus?*

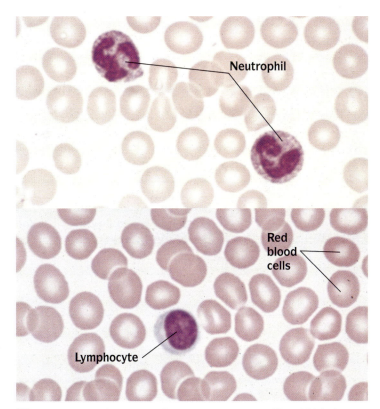

Photograph of a smear of human blood, magnified 1200 times.

BIOLOGY

## Anaemia

If the blood cannot carry oxygen to the body's organs properly, anaemia occurs. Sometimes, the red cells are shaped like spheres and have a smaller surface area, even though their volume is normal. This type of anaemia is called **spherocytosis**. Another type of anaemia happens when the bone marrow doesn't produce enough red blood cells.

A common cause of anaemia in Britain is carbon monoxide. This gas is found in the exhaust fumes of car engines and in cigarette smoke. Carbon monoxide reacts irreversibly with haemoglobin to make **carboxyhaemoglobin** – and stops it from taking up oxygen. About 15 per cent of the haemoglobin in the blood of people who smoke cannot carry oxygen because of carbon monoxide. Pregnant women who smoke stop a lot of oxygen getting to their fetuses.

▸ *People with anaemia are usually pale, short of breath and short of energy. Why should these effects be caused by anaemia?*

◣ Normal biconcave disc-shaped red blood cell.

## Surface area:volume problem

The two cells shown in the diagrams are each $80\,\mu m^3$ in volume (a micrometre is a millionth of a metre). The normal disc-shaped cell has a surface area of about $120\,\mu m^2$. The sphere-shaped cell has a surface area of about $90\,\mu m^2$.

▸ *Calculate the surface area:volume ratio for each cell.*

▸ *Explain why the disc-shaped cell can carry more oxygen than the spherical one, even though they each contain the same amount of haemoglobin.*

◣ Spherical red blood cell.

## The blood of taxi drivers

|  |  | Average concentration of carbon monoxide in the blood (percentage) | Range of concentration (percentage) |
|---|---|---|---|
| Day drivers | Non-smokers | 2.3 | 1.4–3.0 |
|  | Smokers | 5.8 | 2.0–9.7 |
| Night drivers | Non-smokers | 1.0 | 0.4–1.8 |
|  | Smokers | 4.4 | 1.0–8.7 |

◣ The percentage of carbon monoxide in the blood of city taxi drivers.

▸ *Name two sources of carbon monoxide in the air breathed by the taxi drivers.*

▸ *Which source is likely to contribute most to the high value (5.8 per cent) of carbon monoxide in their blood?*

▸ *Why is there a difference in the blood concentration of carbon monoxide in day and night drivers?*

▸ *How does carbon monoxide affect the normal functioning of the blood?*

# Other blood functions

Blood is mainly concerned with the transport of substances around the body, not just respiratory gases.

- Blood transports nutrients from food needed for cell metabolism: inorganic substances such as sodium, potassium, calcium and iron and organic substances such as sugars, fatty acids and amino acids. These substances are called **metabolites** because they are needed for **metabolism**, the chemical reactions which take place in cells.
- Blood transports waste materials produced by metabolism to the kidneys for excretion. An example of a waste product is urea.
- The blood also transports **hormones** from ductless glands, where they are produced, to the organs where they have their effect.
- The blood is also important in the transport of heat. In this way, heat which is mostly produced in organs, such as the liver, can be evenly distributed to nearly all parts of the body.
- Blood is also part of the body's defences against disease. It does this by phagocytosis, immune responses and blood clotting.

## Circulation

All the organs in the body must have a good supply of blood. The blood brings oxygen and food to them and takes away their waste materials. Blood circulates the body in the **cardiovascular system**, that is, the heart and blood vessels.

## The heart

The heart's job is to pump blood to all the body's organs.

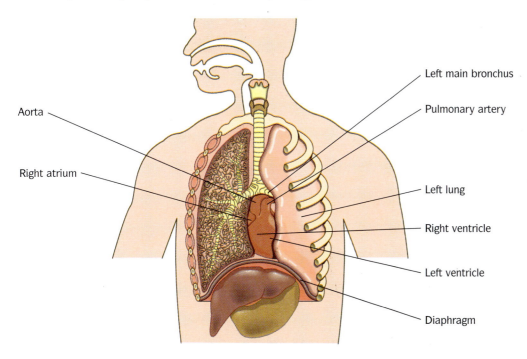

⬆ The heart is in the middle of the chest, but you do not need to cut open the chest to see it. Doctors can look at a person's heart by using X-rays and ultrasound.

## X-rays

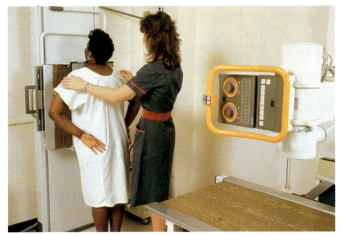

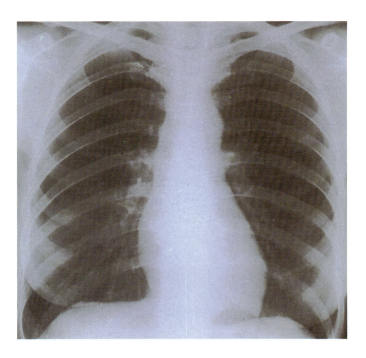

⬛ When X-rays are passed through the chest, some of them are absorbed by the heart. The X-rays which are not absorbed pass straight through the chest and on to an X-ray sensitive film. When the film is developed, a picture of the chest is produced showing the outline of the heart.

## Ultrasound scans

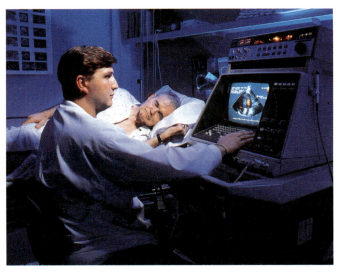

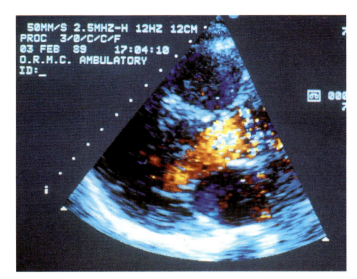

⬛ This man is having an ultrasound scan of his heart. The picture appears instantly on a screen and can be recorded on video or as a photograph. Ultrasound is sound of very high pitch – so high, we cannot hear it. If a beam of ultrasound is passed through the chest, some of it bounces off the heart. These **ultrasound echoes** are detected by a probe and used to make a picture of the heart.

## The heart's structure

You may be given a worksheet to help you with a dissection of the heart.

If you cut open the heart and look inside, you would find there are four chambers. Two are called **atria** (single, atrium) and two are called **ventricles**.

**Arteries** carry blood away from the heart. **Veins** bring blood back to the heart. The heart in the diagram on the next page has been cut open to show the main features inside.

# How the heart works

The heart is two pumps. The right side of the heart collects blood from the body and pumps it to the lungs. The left side of the heart collects blood from the lungs and pumps it to the body.

Every time the blood goes round the circulation, it passes through the heart twice: first one side, then the other. For this reason, it is called a **double circulation**.

## How the heart pumps blood

The muscle in the walls of the atria contracts. At the same time, the ventricles relax. Because of this, the blood pushes the **mitral** and **tricuspid valves** open and is forced into the ventricles from the atria.

Next, the muscle in the walls of the ventricles contracts. At the same time, the atria relax. Because of this, the blood pushes open the **semi-lunar valves** and rushes into the arteries.

▸ *Write out the route taken by a blood cell starting from the lungs going round the body and then back to the lungs.*

▸ *What would happen if there was a hole in the wall between the left and right ventricles?*

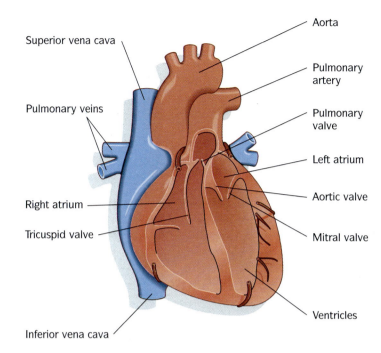

Superior vena cava
Pulmonary veins
Right atrium
Tricuspid valve
Inferior vena cava

Aorta
Pulmonary artery
Pulmonary valve
Left atrium
Aortic valve
Mitral valve
Ventricles

🔺 Inside the heart. The muscle wall of the ventricles is thicker than the atria. This is because the ventricles have to pump blood further than the atria do.

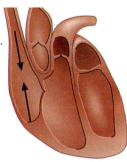

1 Blood enters the atria from the main veins.

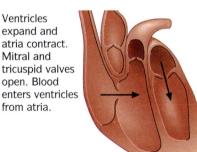

2 Ventricles expand and atria contract. Mitral and tricuspid valves open. Blood enters ventricles from atria.

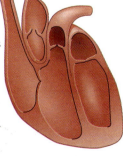

3 Atria stop contracting. Mitral and tricuspid valves close.

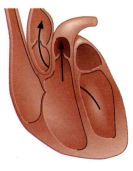

4 Ventricles contract. Aortic and pulmonary valves open. Blood enters main arteries from ventricles.

🔺 The cardiac cycle. Blood enters the left atrium of the heart from the lungs. After circulating the body, it returns to the right atrium.

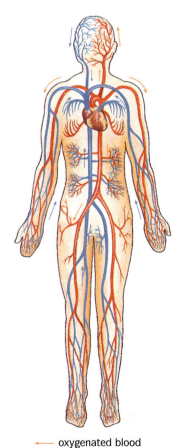

→ oxygenated blood
→ de-oxygenated blood

🔺 Double circulation.

## Valve replacement

Sometimes one of the heart's valves might fail to work properly. It is possible to replace the faulty valve with an artificial one. In the past, valves from pigs' hearts were used.

▲ A ball-in-cage type of artificial heart valve.

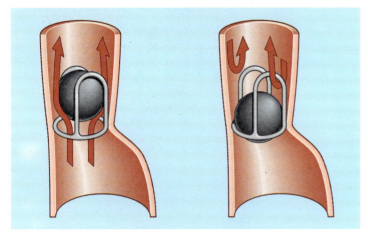

▲ The artificial valve working inside the heart.

▶ *State two differences and two similarities between the artificial valve and a normal heart valve.*

▶ *How is the blood stopped from going back into the ventricles from the arteries when the ventricles relax? How is the blood stopped from going back into the atria when the ventricles contract?*

## The heart's own blood supply

The muscle in the walls of the heart, just like any other organ, must have a good blood supply. The blood which passes through the four chambers cannot give any oxygen to the heart. This is because the heart muscle is too thick. Blood is taken to the heart muscle by **coronary arteries**. They are joined to the aorta, just where it leaves the left ventricle. The blood returns from the heart muscle to the right atrium by **cardiac veins**.

### Heart disease

Sometimes the coronary arteries become narrow. This can be caused by thickening of the artery walls, perhaps because of smoking or a poor diet. You may read about this in Chapter Four (Human nutrition). Narrowing of the coronary arteries is very dangerous. It can cause a heart attack. Poor blood supply to the heart can cause pain in the chest after mild exercise. This is called **angina**. A blood clot in the coronary arteries can block them completely. This is called **coronary thrombosis**. Sudden blockage of the arteries can make the heart stop altogether – this can be fatal.

Doctors can look at the coronary arteries in a person's heart by using X-rays. A narrow plastic tube called a **catheter** is pushed into one of the coronary arteries.

Once in place, a substance which absorbs X-rays is injected into the arteries through the catheter. An X-ray picture is then taken of the coronary artery just as the substance enters it. The procedure is then repeated for the other coronary artery. Any narrowing in the coronary arteries can usually be seen on the X-ray pictures.

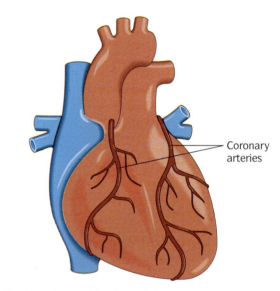

Coronary arteries

▲ The heart's own blood supply.

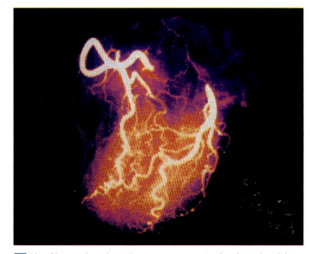

▲ An X-ray showing the coronary arteries in a healthy heart.

BIOLOGY

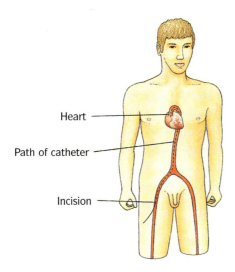

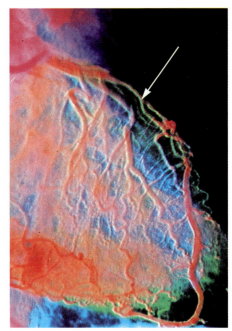

▶ *Which part of the heart shown in the X-ray photograph is poorly supplied with blood?*

🔺 A catheter in place inside the heart. It is threaded into the heart through the aorta from an artery in the abdomen. The patient is usually awake while this is done, only a local anaesthetic is needed.

If the narrowing is severe, the patient may be given a **bypass** operation. Small parts of veins are taken from the patient's own leg. They are then transplanted to the coronary arteries so that the blood can flow easily to the heart muscle. The narrow sections of the arteries are bypassed as shown in this diagram.

▶ *Explain why the wall of the heart needs its own blood supply when blood flows through the chambers all the time.*

▶ *How can a blood clot in a coronary artery lead to a heart attack?*

🔺 X-ray taken during catheterisation. The arrow points to narrowing of the coronary arteries.

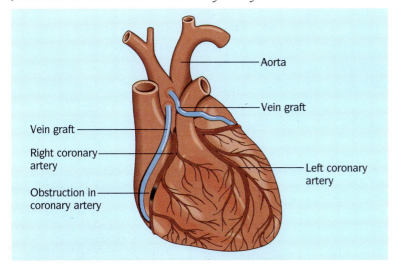

🔺 The result of a coronary artery bypass operation.

# Control of the heart

The heart beats about 70 times a minute. This is called the **heart rate**. Heart muscle is **myogenic**, which means that it beats on its own without nerve stimulation. The rate of beating and the volume of blood pumped can be modified by nerves from the cardiac centre in the brain.

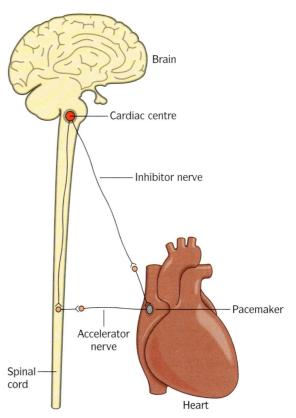

🔺 The nerves controlling the heart bring impulses from the cardiac centre in the brain.

# Respiration

Staying alive needs energy. The body takes its energy from food. Fats and carbohydrates, such as glucose, are especially rich in energy and the body releases this energy through a carefully controlled process called **respiration**.

## Aerobic respiration

Look at the equation for respiration:

glucose + oxygen → water + carbon dioxide + energy

This reaction releases large amounts of energy. The amount released can be shown as part of the equation. Instead of *energy* we would write $\Delta E$ is –2880 kilojoules/mole. This means that for every standard quantity of glucose used in respiration (that is, one mole), 2880 kilojoules of energy are released. You can read about moles in Chemistry, Chapter Fifteen.

▶ *Write down the chemical formulae of the chemicals involved in the process. Write a balanced equation for respiration.*

### Blood pH

The brain detects the rate of energy use in the body indirectly. Carbon dioxide is very soluble and dissolves in our blood to form a weak acid. As carbon dioxide is produced during respiration, it dissolves in blood making it increasingly acidic. During exercise, for example, the amount of carbon dioxide in the blood increases. The brain is very sensitive to the pH of the blood. As the pH falls, the brain sends out impulses from the **cardiac centre**, speeding up the heart rate. At the same time, impulses are sent to muscles which increase the breathing or **ventilation rate**.

The result of these changes is that more blood is pumped around the body and that more oxygen can be taken in from the lungs. It also means that more carbon dioxide can be lost from the blood when it reaches the lungs. As the level of dissolved carbon dioxide falls, the acidity of the blood also decreases. The brain can detect this as an increase in pH.

The brain now sends out impulses to the heart and muscles controlling breathing, causing the heart rate and the breathing rate to slow down. You may read about mechanisms which act to keep body conditions constant in Chapter Eight (Homeostasis).

The cardiac centre is also sensitive to changes in blood pressure and can respond by altering breathing and heart rates.

This process is entirely automatic which is just as well. You are not able to think about breathing and your heart rate 24 hours a day!

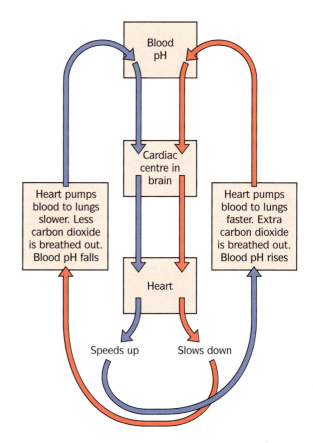

▲ A summary of the homeostatic control of the heart.

## PACEMAKERS

Sometimes the heartbeat is not controlled properly. An artificial pacemaker can be put into the body. The pacemaker sends small electrical pulses along a wire to the heart. In this way, the heart's normal rate can be restored.

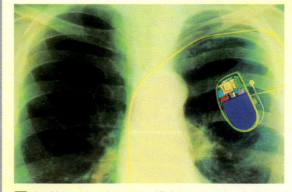

▲ An X-ray showing an artificial pacemaker inside a person's chest. You can see the wire electrode connecting the pacemaker to the heart's wall.

▶ *Write a summary of the changes to the heart rate and the ventilation rate which take place during exercise.*

# Cellular respiration

Cells contain small reserves of glucose for use in respiration. Glucose is stored as **glycogen**, which can be converted to glucose when needed. You may read about glucose and glycogen in Chapter Seven (Hormones). An inability to manage glucose levels in the body results in the condition known as **diabetes**.

You may have read about **mitochondria** in Chapter Two (Cells). Mitochondria contain many enzymes which allows them to take energy from glucose and to use it to make a chemical called **ATP**. When our cells use energy it is ATP which provides it.

# The body plc

Imagine the cell as a factory. It needs a supply of *raw materials*, a *good workforce* and a *distribution network* to get its products to its customers.

Unfortunately, we do not always have enough raw materials for our cells to work efficiently. For instance, if you do not eat the right types of foods you might be short of essential raw materials. Exercise ensures that we are fit, that is, we have a good workforce. To a scientist, *fit* means an efficient circulatory system, healthy heart and lungs and healthy or toned muscles. However, even in the fittest people, the rate at which raw materials reach the cell might be too slow in times of great need.

When top class sprinters run 100 metres, it is impossible for their cells to receive oxygen fast enough to supply all the energy needed by the muscle tissue. Our cells have evolved a system which allows them to survive without oxygen for a short while. This type of respiration is called **anaerobic respiration** – anaerobic means without air or oxygen.

# Anaerobic respiration

Our cells can break down glucose without oxygen, but the process is very inefficient:

glucose → lactic acid + energy

In this reaction $\Delta E$ is $-150\,kJ/mol$, less than a tenth of the energy made available to the cell than through aerobic respiration.

As well as not using oxygen in the breakdown, no carbon dioxide is formed. The cell stores the lactic acid until oxygen becomes available to break it down further:

lactic acid + oxygen → carbon dioxide and water

## Oxygen debt

The amount of oxygen needed to break down the lactic acid formed during exercise is called the **oxygen debt**. Top class athletes have muscle tissue which is very tolerant to lactic acid.

## CRAMP

This reaction occurs in muscle tissue during strenuous exercise and results from a build-up of lactic acid. Lactic acid is poisonous. Too much lactic acid and it stops muscles from functioning (**cramp**). You may have seen an athlete receiving treatment for cramp in the legs. Normally, the legs are lifted up and the toes moved back and forth, pumping blood into the leg muscles. This makes more oxygen available to the muscles, allowing the accumulated lactic acid to break down.

## Heart transplants

Doctors can **transplant** a new heart into the body of a patient whose heart has failed and cannot be cured. The **donor** of the new heart is usually an accident victim. The main problem about transplants is **immune rejection**. You may read about this in Chapter Three (Health and blood). The person receiving the transplant makes antibodies and lymphocytes which attack and destroy the new heart. Rejection can be controlled and there are many people today in the world who have had successful heart transplants.

▲ This woman has had a heart transplant and now wins medals at the transplant games.

## Exercise and heart rate

You may be given a worksheet to help you find out about the effects of exercise on heart rate.

## Movement of metabolites between blood and the tissues

**Arteries** take blood to the organs. Deep inside the organs, the arteries divide into many small vessels called **capillaries**. The capillaries form a network of vessels throughout the tissues. They have very thin walls through which metabolites pass easily between the blood and **tissue fluid**. Tissue fluid is a liquid quite like blood plasma, which bathes the cells. Once inside the tissues, metabolites **diffuse** to the cells through the tissue fluid. Diffusion is very slow and so all cells must be very close to a capillary. You may have read about diffusion in Chapter Two (Cells).

Some of the blood cells can squeeze between the cells making up the capillary walls. In this way, blood **phagocytes** can enter the tissues and destroy any bacteria that might be there. You may have read about this in Chapter Three (Health and blood).

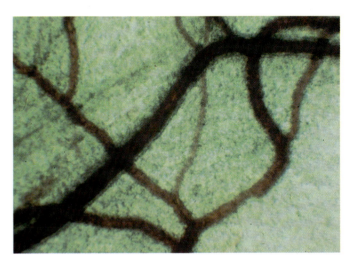

▲ Photograph showing a network of blood capillaries, magnified.

## Blood supply to a fetus

An embryo developing inside its mother's uterus is called a **fetus**. A fetus gets food, oxygen and hormones from its mother's blood. The fetus's carbon dioxide and other waste materials pass into its mother's blood for excretion.

In order for metabolites to pass between the mother and her fetus in this way, their blood vessels must come close to each other. This happens in the **placenta**. The placenta brings the two sets of vessels together, but the two circulations do not mix.

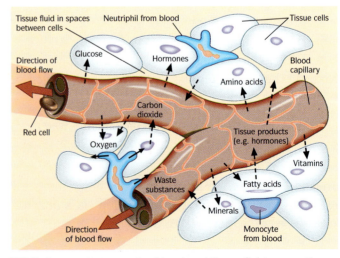

▲ Exchanges between the blood and tissue fluid across the capillary walls.

# Summary

- Respiratory gas exchange takes place in the alveoli in the lungs. Oxygen is absorbed by the blood from the atmosphere, carbon dioxide is removed from the blood to the atmosphere.
- Breathing is brought about by contraction and relaxation of the diaphragm and intercostal muscles between the ribs.
- Air enters the trachea, and then the bronchi. In the lungs the bronchi divide into bronchioles, then into alveoli.
- The air passages are kept clear by cells which secrete mucus and have cilia. Dust and bacteria are trapped in the mucus and wafted by the cilia up into the mouth.
- Oxygen is absorbed by the red blood cells oxygenation. They contain haemoglobin which transports the oxygen to the tissues. Red blood cells are biconcave disc–shaped.
- A lowering of the blood's ability to carry oxygen is called anaemia.
- Blood transports respiratory gases, metabolites, waste substances, hormones and heat around the body. Blood also helps defend the body against infection and disease.
- The heart pumps blood through arteries to the organs. Blood returns to the heart through veins. The left side of the heart pumps oxygenated blood from the lungs. The right side pumps deoxygenated blood to the lungs to pick up more oxygen. Blood flows through the heart twice on each complete circuit of the body – double circulation.
- Each side of the heart consists of an atrium (upper chamber) and a ventricle (lower chamber). Ventricles have thicker muscle walls than atria and do most of the pumping.
- The direction blood flows through the heart is regulated by valves. Between the atria and the ventricles are two valves. These stop blood flowing back into the atria when the ventricles contract. The aortic and pulmonary valves stop blood flowing back into the ventricles between beats.
- The heart wall muscle has its own blood supply via the coronary arteries. Blood clots in these arteries can cause a heart attack.
- Respiration is the controlled release of energy from food.
- Aerobic respiration is the most efficient form of respiration. It can only occur if oxygen is present.
- Anaerobic respiration releases about one tenth of the energy of aerobic respiration. It also produces lactic acid which is poisonous.
- The amount of oxygen required to break down lactic acid formed during anaerobic respiration is called the oxygen debt.
- The heart rate and the volume of blood pumped on each beat is controlled by the heart's pacemaker.
- Capillaries have very thin walls which allow metabolites to pass between the tissues and blood in the capillaries.
- The placenta brings the blood of a mother and her fetus close together without the two circulations mixing.

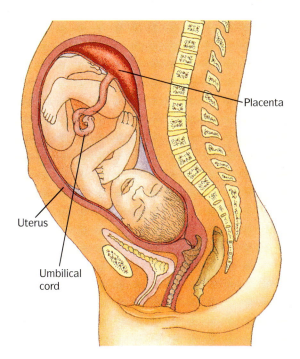

Placenta

Uterus

Umbilical cord

🔺 A fetus inside its mother's uterus. As well as supplying it with blood, the placenta anchors the fetus to the wall of the uterus.

# Revision Questions

1 Movements of the ribs and diaphragm are responsible for breathing. Make a series of drawings to show how these movements are brought about.

2 **a** List *four* main functions of blood.
 **b** Mammals have a *double circulation*. What is meant by this?
 **c** Look back at the ultrasound view of an adult human heart. Which parts of the heart do the following things:
  *i* Pump deoxygenated blood to the lungs to collect oxygen?
  *ii* Receive oxygenated blood from the lungs?
  *iii* Stop oxygenated blood flowing back into the heart from the arteries?
  *iv* Deliver blood to the muscular wall of the heart?
  *v* Stop oxygenated and deoxygenated blood mixing inside the heart?

3 Mammals get oxygen for aerobic respiration through the lungs.
 **a** *i* By what process does oxygen pass from air in the lungs to blood in capillaries?
  *ii* Give *one* feature of the lungs which helps this process to happen quickly.
 **b** Red blood cells transport oxygen to body tissues. Suggest and explain *one* feature of red blood cells which helps them to do this.
 **c** Aerobic respiration provides energy for mammals.
  *i* Write out a word equation to represent *aerobic respiration.*
  *ii* Give *two* ways in which mammals use energy.
 **d** When mammals run for a long time, they also obtain energy by anaerobic respiration.
  *i* Give *one* difference between aerobic and anaerobic respiration.
  *ii* Anaerobic respiration will only continue for a short time before it stops. What causes it to stop?

4 Look back at the double circulation diagram.
 **a** Write out the stages in a heart beat in the form of a list, beginning with blood entering the atria from the veins.
 **b** *i* What happens to the heart rate during physical exercise?
  *ii* What happens to the breathing rate at the same time?
  *iii* Explain why these changes should take place?

5 **a** The trachea produces mucus. What is the job of this mucus?
 **b** Name the type of cell that produces mucus.
 **c** Cigarette smoke contains substances which stimulate mucus secretion **(phlegm)** which cause a persistent cough. Explain how the production of too much mucus reduces the efficiency of the lungs.
 **d** Structures called cilia remove mucus. Where, in the respiratory system, would you find cilia?
 **e** How do the cilia remove mucus?
 **f** What is the effect of cigarette smoke on the cilia?
 **g** Explain why smokers find great difficulty in giving up the habit.
 **h** Carbon monoxide is a major constituent of cigarette smoke. Explain why it reduces oxygen availability to the cells of the body.
 **i** Give *one* other adverse effect of smoking on health.

6 **a** Make up a table to summarise the main functions of the different types of blood vessels.
 **b** Give *two* features of capillaries which help them to deliver oxygen and nutrients to the tissues.

# Nervous system

The athletes shown here are just starting a 100 metre race – the winner will become the world champion. The starter's gun has just fired and the race will be over in less than 10 seconds. Already the athletes' bodies have started to move and will run down the track at about 36 kilometres per hour (22.5 miles per hour).

You might be wondering how they knew when to start and how they started so quickly without bumping into each other or falling over. Or how their muscles are co-ordinated. They might have been startled and jumped when the gun fired. In other circumstances that might have been the right thing to do, but here they were expecting the gun's sound to tell them when to start the race. All this activity, which happened in a fraction of a second, is co-ordinated by their nervous systems.

In this chapter, you will study some of the ways the nervous system controls our bodies.

# Review

The nervous system contains the following things:

■ *Sense organs*, for example the eyes. They contain cells called *receptors* which change stimuli such as light into *nerve impulses*.

■ Nerve cells, called *neurones*, which carry impulses from place to place inside the body.

■ *Brain* and *spinal cord* which send impulses to the right place within the body.

The brain is found inside a part of the skull called the cranium.

The cranium supports and protects the brain.

The brain controls the heart and breathing rates and body movements.

It also allows us to think and behave intelligently, remember things from the past and be aware of our surroundings.

The spinal cord runs the length of the back inside the vertebral column.
The column is made of bones called the vertebrae. The vertebrae protect the spinal cord from injury when we move about.

The spinal cord sends nerve impulses to the correct parts of the body. This makes sure the body's actions are co-ordinated.
The spinal cord also sends impulses from the body to the brain.

The nerves carry impulses from the body's receptors to the spinal cord; the nerves also carry impulses from the spinal cord to the effectors.

▲ The main parts of the human nervous system.

## Before going any further, read this page and attempt the word search. Write the answers in your notes.

When we see danger, such as a car coming straight at us, our brain makes the heart and breathing speed up and it controls our legs so we can run out of the way quickly. The brain makes us aware of what is happening and keeps a memory of the event. These actions give our muscles more oxygen which helps us to run quickly. We can recognise danger the next time and we can predict and avoid danger in future.

### CHECK SIX

Hidden in the word search are seven things connected with the nervous system. Copy out the word search into your notebook.

Find the words and briefly describe what each of them means.

## WORD SEARCH

| D | B | N | A | G | R | O | E | S | N | E | S |
|---|---|---|---|---|---|---|---|---|---|---|---|
| J | R | I | D | S | J | L | O | Z | E | C | X |
| M | A | M | S | H | B | C | V | E | R | S | U |
| K | I | P | R | E | F | L | E | X | V | G | H |
| E | N | U | D | L | A | N | I | T | E | R | L |
| A | F | L | E | N | S | O | K | B | D | F | G |
| C | S | S | P | I | N | A | L | C | O | R | D |
| F | S | E | F | Y | M | D | W | W | G | Y | K |

# Nerve cells

Nerve cells are called **neurones**. A bundle of neurones make up a nerve. Each neurone sends **impulses** (small electrical signals) from one place to another inside the body. Neurones can be very long cells. Some of them reach from the bottom of your back to the tip of your toes, and that can be more than a metre in a tall person. Neurones in the brain are very short.

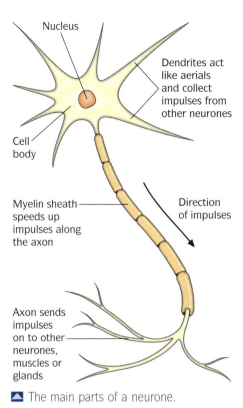

▲ The main parts of a neurone.

Nucleus

Dendrites act like aerials and collect impulses from other neurones

Cell body

Myelin sheath speeds up impulses along the axon

Direction of impulses

Axon sends impulses on to other neurones, muscles or glands

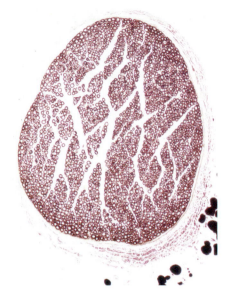

▲ Photograph of a transverse section through a human nerve, magnified 800 times. Some of the neurones are wide and some of them are narrow.

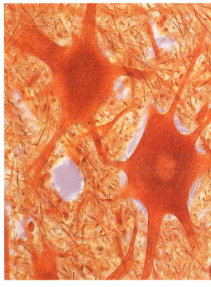

▲ Photograph of a vertical section through the brain, magnified.

You can see that neurones have a long, thread-like extension called an **axon** which carries the impulses from place to place. The axon is often covered by a fatty sheath called **myelin**. Myelin increases the speed of the impulses and insulates neurones from one another, preventing 'short circuiting'. Some travel as fast as one hundred metres a second. That is nearly ten times faster than the world record for sprinting!

▶ *Make a note about the differences between axons and dendrites.*

▶ *Why are the neurones in the brain shorter than the ones in our legs?*

The final destination of nerve impulses is either a muscle or a gland. When stimulated by impulses, muscles contract and glands produce chemicals.

## Brain waves

The boy in the photograph is having an **electroencephalogram** (**EEG**) taken.

Silver electrodes on his scalp detect tiny electrical signals (nerve impulses) coming from his brain. The pattern of these signals can change, for example, during an epileptic fit. The EEG recording can help doctors to diagnose the patient's condition.

▶ *What differences can you see in the two EEG traces shown here?*

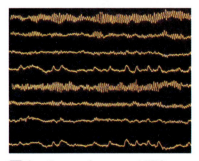

▲ Small part of a normal EEG trace.

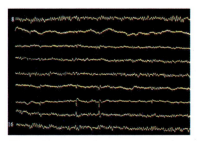

▲ Small part of an EEG trace from someone with epilepsy. Notice the 'spikes' attached to the waves.

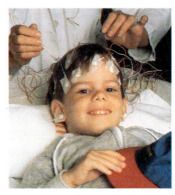

▲ Taking an EEG.

# Transcription speeds

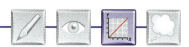

Doctors can measure how fast nerve impulses travel. The **median nerve** contains neurones which send impulses from the spinal cord along our arms to the muscles in our fingers. You can examine the results of an experiment to find out about nerve impulses.

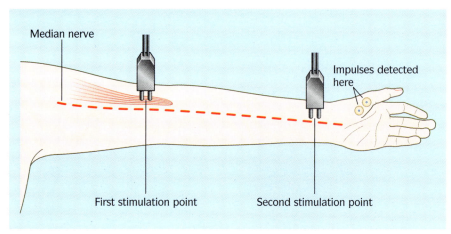

🔺 Electrodes in place, ready to record the speed of impulses along the median nerve in someone's arm.

The median nerve is stimulated by a small electric current applied to the skin about half-way up the arm. This creates impulses which go down the median nerve to the fingers. Small wires placed on the fingers detect the impulses when they arrive. A trace is produced on a monitor screen.

A second electric current is applied to the median nerve through the skin, but much nearer the fingers this time. Another trace records the arrival of the impulses in the fingers. The distance between the two stimulation points is measured. Here are some typical trace results.

Trace A was produced when the nerve was stimulated near the elbow. Trace B was produced when the nerve was stimulated at the wrist. The distance between the elbow and the wrist was 19 centimetres.

> 1 millisecond = 1 ms = $\frac{1}{1000}$ of a second

▶ *How long did it take for the impulses from the elbow to reach the fingers?*

▶ *How long did it take the impulses from the wrist to reach the fingers?*

▶ *How long did it take for the impulses to go from the elbow to the wrist?*

▶ *What was the speed of the impulses in the median nerve? Write your answer in metres per second (m/s). The normal speed for the median nerve is between 50 and 70 metres per second.*

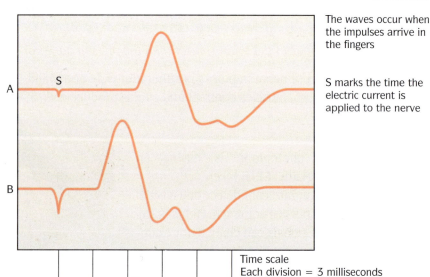

The waves occur when the impulses arrive in the fingers

S marks the time the electric current is applied to the nerve

Time scale
Each division = 3 milliseconds

🔺 Oscilloscope traces recording the arrival of impulses in the muscles of the hand.

# Nerve pathways

Nerve pathways consist of a series of neurones which take impulses from one place to another inside the body. As you read this book, you can see the words printed on the page in front of you. Your eyes are sensitive to the light reflecting off the page. After entering your eyes, the light stimulates a layer of receptor cells at the back of the eye, called the **retina**. These light–sensitive cells send impulses along a pathway to the back of the brain. It is here that you are aware of what your eyes are seeing. Your brain interprets the impulses for you and so you see a picture of this page. Follow the pathway the impulses take in the diagram on the right.

Feel the page with your fingertips. There are thousands of receptor cells in the skin of your hands which are sensitive to touch. When they are activated, they send impulses along another pathway to a different part of your brain where you interpret the impulses as the sensation of touch. Follow this pathway on the above diagram, feeling it with your fingers as you go.

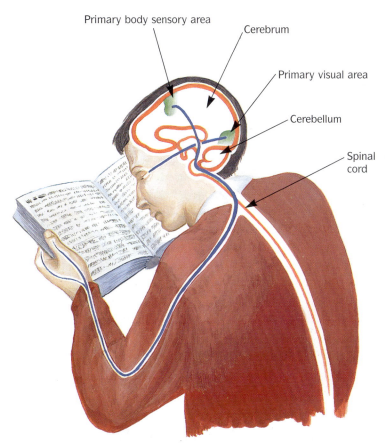

Primary body sensory area

Cerebrum

Primary visual area

Cerebellum

Spinal cord

🔺 The conduction pathways involved in turning the page of a book.

## Reading by touch

Blind people can learn to read by touch. **Braille** is a system of raised bumps imprinted in thick paper. The different patterns of the bumps correspond to particular letters of the alphabet.

▶ *Can you think of ways in which people with hearing loss can learn to communicate, using other senses?*

You hear sounds with your ears. They are also your organs of balance. You smell things with your nose and taste food with your tongue. Receptor cells which are sensitive to these stimuli send impulses to the brain along nerve pathways.

The pathway from the eyes to the primary visual area in the brain is much shorter than the pathway from the fingertips to the body-sensory area in the brain. If you watch your fingers touch an object, you will experience the feel of the object straight away.

▶ *Why is there no delay between seeing and feeling in this case?*

▶ *Explain why someone with an injury to the back of the brain might have problems seeing things properly.*

🔺 A visually-impaired person playing a Braille word game with their fingertips.

# Reflex pathways

Nearly everything we do is automatically controlled by the nervous system. We respond to many stimuli without even knowing about them. These actions are called **reflexes**. Many reflex pathways go through the spinal cord.

▶ *Make a sketch of this pathway. Add some notes to your drawing explaining how the reflex prevents excessive damage to the hand.*

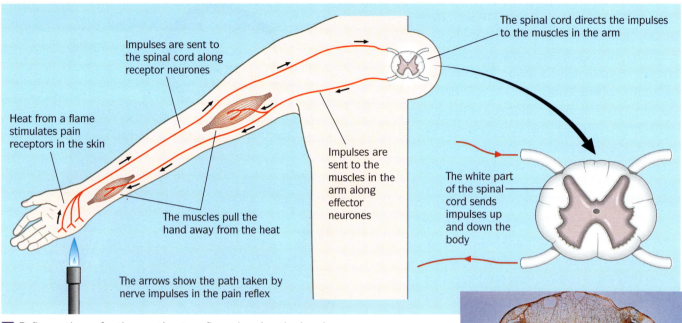

The spinal cord directs the impulses to the muscles in the arm

Impulses are sent to the spinal cord along receptor neurones

Heat from a flame stimulates pain receptors in the skin

Impulses are sent to the muscles in the arm along effector neurones

The white part of the spinal cord sends impulses up and down the body

The muscles pull the hand away from the heat

The arrows show the path taken by nerve impulses in the pain reflex

▲ Reflex pathway for the reaction to a flame burning the hand.

You can see that the reflex pathway in the diagram contains just three neurones. The **sensory neurone**, from the pain receptors in the skin, a **connector neurone** in the spinal cord and a **motor neurone** to the muscles. The connector neurone directs the impulses along the appropriate route. Other connector neurones (not shown in the diagram) send impulses up to the brain. These neurons conduct the impulse which causes the person to feel pain.

▲ Photograph of a transverse section through the spinal cord, magnified 25 times.

## Synapses

The junctions between each of the neurones are called **synapses**.

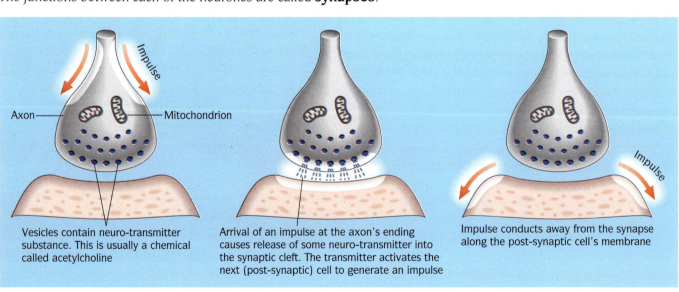

Impulse

Axon — Mitochondrion

Vesicles contain neuro-transmitter substance. This is usually a chemical called acetylcholine

Arrival of an impulse at the axon's ending causes release of some neuro-transmitter into the synaptic cleft. The transmitter activates the next (post-synaptic) cell to generate an impulse

Impulse conducts away from the synapse along the post-synaptic cell's membrane

Impulse

▲ How synapses work.

▶ *Use the magnification of the photograph to work out the distance across the synapse.*

Synapses are a bit like road junctions, they allow impulses to take a number of different routes. Just like road junctions, they slow down the traffic. Impulses travel along single neurones at speeds of up to 100 metres per second. But when a pathway contains a synapse, the average speed of impulses along the pathway might be only about 40 metres per second. This is because of the way synapses work.

▶ *Why do synapses slow down the speed of impulses along a pathway?*

▶ *Why is it important that the neuro–transmitter is broken down just after it has activated a synapse?*

## Myasthenia

In a rare disease called myasthenia, the body's own defence system stops the neuro–transmitter at nerve endings activating the muscles.

▶ *Suggest what the symptoms of myasthenia might be.*

# Inborn and conditioned reflexes

When we are babies, a lot of our behaviour is controlled by **inborn reflexes**. Doctors test these as part of the routine examination of babies. The results are useful in assessing the development of a baby's nervous system. The photographs show some inborn reflexes.

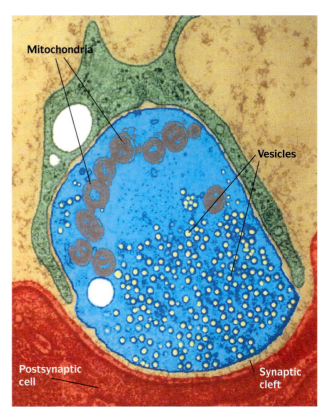

Mitochondria
Vesicles
Postsynaptic cell
Synaptic cleft

🔺 Photograph of a synapse, magnified 24 000 times. The mitochondria provide energy from respiration. The vesicles contain the chemical transmitter.

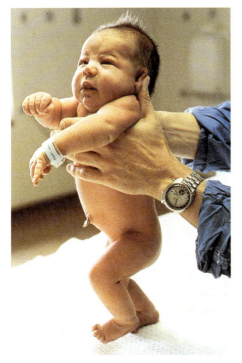

🔺 Walking reflex.

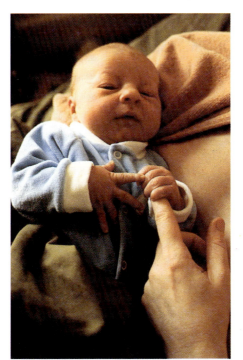

🔺 Grip reflex.

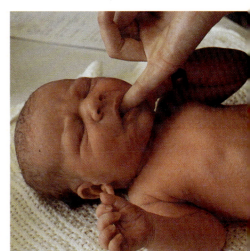

🔺 Sucking reflex.

It is possible to learn reflexes. This is called **conditioning**. The Russian scientist Ivan Pavlov described **conditioned reflexes** in 1910. Pavlov noticed that hungry dogs make saliva by reflex action when they are given food. Saliva helps them swallow the food, so this is a useful response when they are feeding. Dogs do not have to learn to make saliva. The reflex is inborn. The response is completely automatic, even young puppies do it.

Pavlov noticed that his dogs also made saliva when the local church bells rang out at midday. Sometimes the dogs were eating at this time, sometimes they were waiting for their food. The dogs had learned to link the ringing bells with feeding time. Pavlov said his dogs were conditioned to make saliva when the bells rang.

▸ *What two things must happen for a dog to associate ringing bells with feeding?*

▸ *Can you think of any of your own behaviour that is controlled by conditioning?*

▸ *Plan an experiment to test your ideas about conditioned reflexes.*

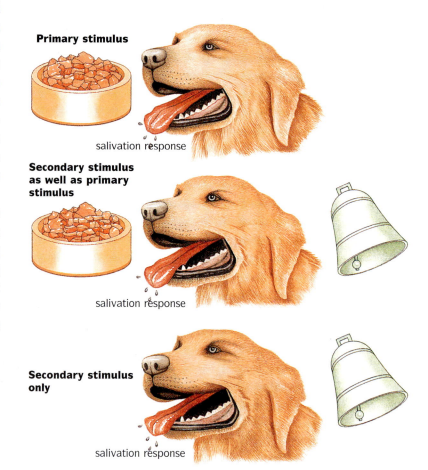

**Primary stimulus**

salivation response

**Secondary stimulus as well as primary stimulus**

salivation response

**Secondary stimulus only**

salivation response

🔺 Summary of Pavlov's experiment.

## The autonomic nervous system

Part of the nervous system is called the **autonomic nervous system**. This automatically controls many of the body's activities by reflex action. This table summarises the actions of the autonomic system. Notice that there are two sets of nerves, sympathetic and parasympathetic, which act in opposite ways on most of the organs.

| Target | Sympathetic effect | Parasympathetic effect |
|---|---|---|
| Iris of eye | Pupil dilation | Pupil constriction |
| Bronchi | — | Constriction of airways |
| Heart | Increased cardiac output | Decreased cardiac output |
| Gut sphincters | Increased tone | Relaxation |
| Urinary bladder | Relaxation of urinary bladder wall | Contraction of urinary bladder wall |
| Sweat glands | Stimulates secretion | — |
| Salivary glands | Decreases secretion | Increases secretion |
| Stomach | Decreases secretion | Increases secretion |
| Pancreas | Decreases secretion | Increases secretion |
| Genitalia | — | Vasodilation in erectile tissue |

🔺 The main actions of the autonomic nervous system.

▸ *Many of the body's vital functions, such as heart rate and breathing are controlled by reflexes which pass through the medulla oblongata in the hind-brain. These reflexes do not need any voluntary control by the brain. Why should this be so?*

# Marketing by reflex

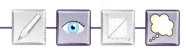

The purpose of this exercise is to see how reflex nervous activity can be used to control our behaviour. The advertising industry uses conditioned reflexes to get us to buy certain brands of goods. The technique is to show us the product – this is the **primary stimulus** – and at the same time, show us something that is very attractive to us – the **secondary stimulus**. Sometimes, the secondary stimulus has nothing to do with the primary one.

When we see the product in the shops, we subconsciously think of the secondary stimulus that is attractive. We then link it with the product, which might not be attractive at all. The chances are that we will want to buy the product, thinking we are buying something else as well. Here are a couple of advertisements.

🔺 Try to identify the secondary stimulus in these adverts.

▶ *In what ways do you think these advertisements use the conditioning technique?*

▶ *Do you think the technique is a good way to promote the sale of goods?*

▶ *Spend an evening watching the advertisements on television. (Have this book with you in case you have to prove it really is for homework.) Make a table to list them as either conditioning or factual. Factual advertisements are ones which tell you the benefits of the product in a factual way and leave you to make up your own mind.*

▶ *What proportion of the advertisements you watched used conditioning?*

▶ *Write an account of what you think about the use of conditioning in advertising. Include the results of your TV survey.*

# The brain

Your brain is the least understood part of your body. Here are some views of the human brain.

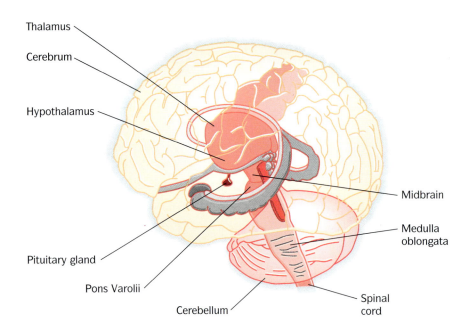

 The main parts of the brain.

| Part of brain | Functions |
|---|---|
| Cerebrum (cerebral hemispheres) | Conscious awareness of senses. Interpretation of sensory information. This is called **perception**. Voluntary control of body's muscles. Memory, personality, intelligent thought, language and speech. |
| Thalamus | Directs impulses from the senses to the appropriate parts of the cerebrum. Directs impulses from the cerebrum to the appropriate parts of the body. |
| Hypothalamus | Contains the thermoregulation centre and centres which cause feelings of hunger and thirst. |
| Pituitary gland | Releases hormones into the blood. |
| Midbrain | Controls wakefulness and sleep. |
| Medulla oblongata | Contains the cardiac and respiratory centres. |
| Cerebellum | Controls posture and balance. Controls delicate movements such as writing or playing a musical instrument. |

 The functions of the main parts of the brain.

▶ *Use your knowledge of the brain to explain how strokes can affect very different parts of the body.*

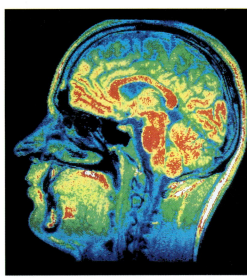

 Picture of a vertical section through a person's brain taken by **magnetic resonance imaging (MRI)**.

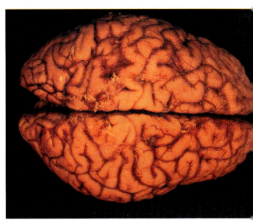

 The surface of the human brain is highly folded.

## STROKES

A **stroke** is damage to the brain caused by blood clots or bleeding. Some stroke patients suffer loss of sensation and voluntary control in certain parts of their bodies and not all over. Other stroke patients suffer loss of sensation and control in different parts of their bodies. The effects of a stroke depend on which parts of the brain are damaged and on how serious the damage is.

## Parkinson's disease

In Parkinson's disease there is abnormal production of a neuro-transmitter called **dopamine**. This is found in a part of the brain controlling body movements. The first signs of Parkinson's disease usually include involuntary shaking of the head and hands, and continuous rubbing together of the thumb and forefinger. If the disease worsens, the person experiences loss of automatic movements such as arm swinging while walking and the ability to write legibly and speak clearly.

Research carried out in the 1980s led to a treatment for Parkinson's disease which involves transplanting dopamine-producing cells into the patient's brain. The cells were taken from the brain tissue of aborted fetuses. This treatment appears to be successful in a lot of cases.

▶ *Many people think human fetuses should not be used for any purpose, even to cure other people of diseases. Prepare a letter to your local newspaper giving your views.*

## The eyes

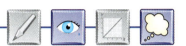

You may be given a worksheet to guide you through a dissection of an eye.

Each of our eyes is a ball filled with a watery liquid. The cells which are sensitive to light are found in a layer called the retina, on the inside and at the back of the eyes.

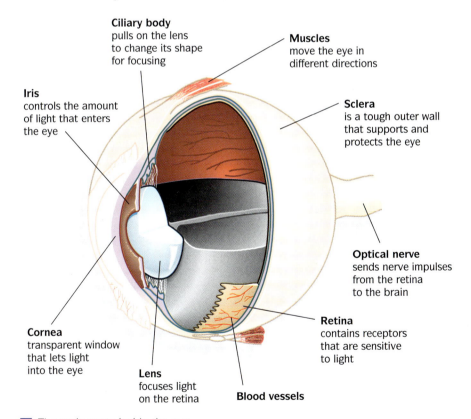

**Ciliary body**
pulls on the lens to change its shape for focusing

**Muscles**
move the eye in different directions

**Iris**
controls the amount of light that enters the eye

**Sclera**
is a tough outer wall that supports and protects the eye

**Optical nerve**
sends nerve impulses from the retina to the brain

**Cornea**
transparent window that lets light into the eye

**Lens**
focuses light on the retina

**Blood vessels**

**Retina**
contains receptors that are sensitive to light

▲ The main parts inside the eye.

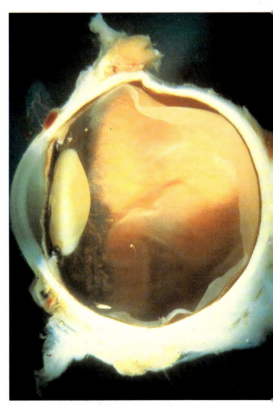

▲ Photograph of a vertical section through the eye, magnified.

The front surfaces of the eyes are protected by a thin layer of cells called the **conjunctiva**. Sometimes, this gets damaged and inflamed and can be very painful – a condition called conjunctivitis. The front of the eye is usually washed by tears and cleaned every time we blink. Blinking wipes away any dust that gets on to the eyes, just like the wash-wipe on a car's windscreen.

# Controlling light entering the eye

You might have found it difficult to see when suddenly going into the dark, for instance going into a cinema from the brightly lit foyer. But after a few seconds, your eyes adjust to the dark and you can see quite well. You might have come out of a dark cinema in the daylight and had to close your eyes for a few seconds until they got used to the bright light. You will agree, the amount of light entering your eyes is important and has to be adjusted in different conditions.

   Cover one of your eyes with your hand and look into a mirror with the other eye. Now, quickly look at your covered eye as you take your hand away.

▶ *What changes can you see in the uncovered eye?*

▶ *Explain why these changes help the eye to see in dark and bright conditions.*

▶ *What kind of nervous reflex pathway could bring about these changes?*

## Focusing light

Light from objects in our surroundings makes **images** on the retina. The lens makes the images sharp and clear on the retina. The light is **focused**.

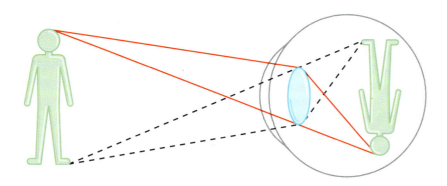

🔺 The light rays from an object travel through the lens and are focused on the retina. The image on the retina is upside down.

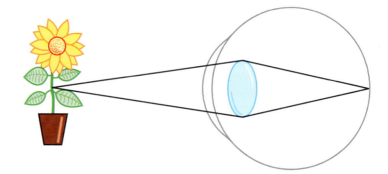

🔺 Focusing an object which is near to the eye.

🔺 Focusing an object which is far away from the eye.

The direction of light is changed by the lens and also a little by the cornea – the light is **refracted**. You may read about refraction in Physics, Chapter 2. Light from near objects must be refracted more than light from far objects. This is done by the lens changing shape. The process is called **accommodation**.

## More on focusing

Hold up one of your fingers a few inches in front of one of your eyes. Focus on it so that it appears sharp and clear. Now quickly focus on something behind your finger and far away. Look at your finger again.

▶ *Can you detect a short period of time when your finger is blurred?*

▶ *Does the same thing happen when you focus on the far object again?*

▶ *Explain all your observations.*

## Colour vision

Most people see things in colour. Some other animals can too.

▶ *Look carefully at the photograph. What number can you see?*

People with normal colour vision can see a number '5'. People with one kind of **colour blindness** see a number '2'.

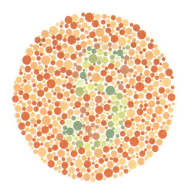

🔺 This picture is part of a test of colour vision called the Ishihara test.

*"The above has been reproduced from Ishihara's Tests for Colour Blindness published by KANEHARA & CO., LTD, Tokyo, Japan, but tests for color blindness cannot be conducted with this material. For accurate testing, the original plates should be used"*

Nearly everyone can see in colour, even people with colour blindness. Colour blindness can be caused by a lack of receptor cells called **cones** in the retina. Some people think that bulls get angry when they see red. In fact we know that bulls are colour blind. Their eyes do not have any cones at all.

Some jobs depend on good colour vision. Two examples are flying an aircraft and driving a train. Pilots and train drivers have to react quickly to colour signals: some warning them of danger, others giving the all-clear.

▶ *Can you think of other jobs that rely on good colour vision?*

▶ *What advantages are there in being able to see in colour?*

▶ *Plan an experiment to discover whether or not a named animal can see colour.*

# Optical illusions

Sometimes, we do not see what our eyes are looking at. Images can be mis-interpreted in some way by our brains to create **illusions**.

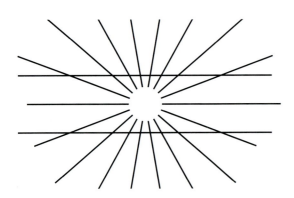

🔺 Are the three horizontal lines parallel? Check it out with a ruler.

🔺 This is a picture of two women, but you can only see one at a time.

🔺 These are not just spots. What else can you see?

# Summary

- Nerve cells, called neurones, send impulses from one place to another inside the body. Impulses are small electrical signals. Myelin increases the speed at which impulses travel along neurones – up to about one hundred metres per second.
- Impulses travel along nerve pathways – sequences of neurones joined at synapses.
- Many nerve pathways control body activities automatically, that is by reflex. Inborn reflexes are present at birth. Conditioned reflexes are learned.
- In a reflex pathway, impulses travel along sensory neurones to the central nervous system (brain or spinal cord) and then along motor neurones to muscles.
- Impulses pass from one neurone to the next at a synapse by secretion of a chemical transmitter from the first neurone's ending on to the membrane of the second neurone.
- The autonomic nervous system controls body organs, such as the heart and breathing, by automatic reflex.
- The brain is the body's main controller. It contains areas which control body movement, receive and interpret sensory information from the sense organs, create memory, provide intelligence and affect personality.
- The eyes contain a layer of light-sensitive cells making up the retina.
- Entry of light into the eye is controlled by the opening and closing of a diaphragm called the iris.
- Light is refracted and focused on to the retina by a lens. Distant and close objects are brought into focus by the action of ciliary muscles which change the shape of the lens.
- Cone cells in the retina are sensitive to light of different wavelengths. The brain recognises this as colour vision.

# Revision Questions

1.  **a** What are the main parts of the nervous system?
    **b** Complete the following: Nerve cells are called _____ . They transmit _____ from one place to another in the body. Each nerve cell has a long _____ which is surrounded by a fatty sheath called _____ . This _____ the speed of transmission which can be as fast as _____ metres per second.

2.  **a** What is a reflex?
    **b** Explain why all vital body functions, like the heartbeat and breathing, are controlled by reflexes.
    **c** List two other activities that are controlled by reflexes and explain what might happen if they were not controlled automatically.

3.  **a** List the things that you can detect with each of your sense organs.
    **b** You are surrounded by radio waves, but you can only detect them by turning on the radio and listening to the programmes. Explain why this is so.

4.  **a** What evidence is there from your everyday life that nerve impulses travel very quickly along nerve pathways?
    **b** Look back at the photograph of a synapse and the diagrams of how synapses work. Explain why synapses slow down the speed of impulses along nerve pathways.

5.  **a** List the complex activities carried out by the brain.
    **b** These activities take place in the surface layer of the brain called the cerebral cortex (grey matter). In what way is the cerebral cortex adapted to allow all these activities to be located there?
    **c** Many of the body's vital functions are controlled by reflexes which pass through the medulla oblongata in the hind-brain. These reflexes do not need any voluntary control by the brain. Why is this so?

6.  If you suddenly look up from this page, distant objects quickly come into focus. How do your eyes change in order to keep objects in sharp focus, whether they are near or far from your eyes?

7.  Look back at the diagrams illustrating how to record the speed of impulses in someone's arm. The drawing below shows a similar experiment to measure the speed of impulse conduction along a nerve in the arm.

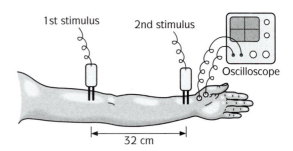

▲ Figure A.

Here are the results:

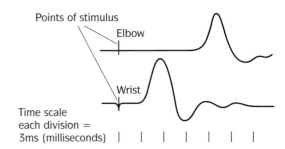

▲ Figure B.

   **a** How quickly did the impulse travel along the arm's nerve? How does this compare with the results for the experiment earlier in this chapter?
   **b** The person whose arm is shown in figure A injured his elbow in a fall. Explain how this might have affected impulse conduction in his arm.
   **c** When his arm was stimulated by the electrodes, the person jumped a little in his chair and was aware of a small shock, although this was harmless. Explain these reactions.

# Hormones

At Christmas time, the wonderful story of Britain's miracle babies

## Six little mouths to feed, six little stockings to fill

Two down . . . four to go—all smiles as Graham and Janet feed Sarah (left) and Lucy. The other four babes have to wait their turn.

**WORLD EXCLUSIVE** by Howard Reynolds and Clive Hatfield

TWO HUNGRY mouths gurgle happily at their bottle. Four more wait their turn.

In this chapter you will study hormones and see how they work. You will also see how hormones can be used in medicine and agriculture for the benefit of people and how they sometimes cause problems.

**The mother of these babies was told by her doctor that she could not have any children. She was *infertile*. However, she was treated with hormones which stimulated her *ovaries* to produce eggs, and, as you can see, six of them were released together.**

# Review

Before going any further, read this page and attempt the tasks. Write the answers in your notes.

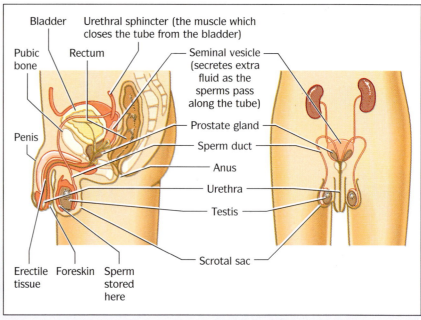

▲ Male reproductive system.

Bladder
Urethral sphincter (the muscle which closes the tube from the bladder)
Pubic bone
Rectum
Seminal vesicle (secretes extra fluid as the sperms pass along the tube)
Penis
Prostate gland
Sperm duct
Anus
Urethra
Testis
Scrotal sac
Erectile tissue
Foreskin
Sperm stored here

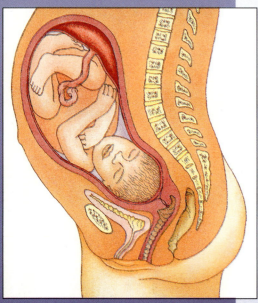

▲ A fetus developing inside its mother.

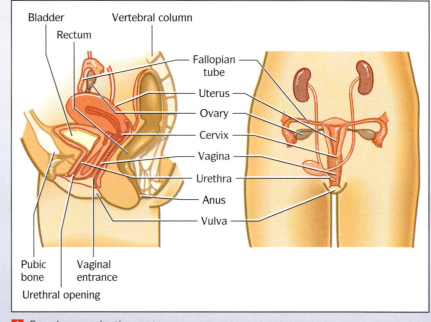

▲ Female reproductive system.

Bladder
Vertebral column
Rectum
Fallopian tube
Uterus
Ovary
Cervix
Vagina
Urethra
Anus
Vulva
Pubic bone
Vaginal entrance
Urethral opening

## CHECK SEVEN

**1** Most carbohydrate digested in the intestine is absorbed into the blood in the form of the sugar, glucose. What is the main use of glucose in the body?

**2** What are the jobs of the parts of the reproductive systems labelled in the diagrams above?

**3** Where, inside its mother, does a fetus develop?

**4** How long does a fetus develop inside its mother before it is born?

**5** What is a placenta and what job does it do?

**6** Why do plants grow so their leaves are turned towards the light?

**7** Why do the roots of a plant grow down into the soil?

# Hormones

Hormones are chemical substances which move around our bodies in the blood. Plants also make hormones. You may read about plant hormones later in this chapter. Animal hormones are made in glands in different parts of the body. They are **ductless glands** – the hormones are released directly into the blood. Another word for ductless is **endocrine**.

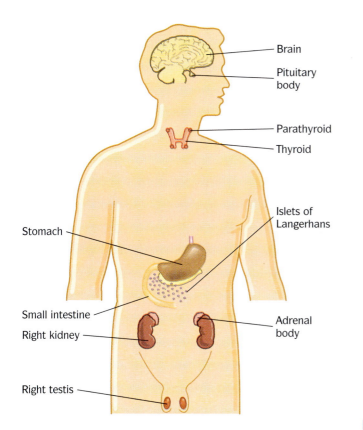

Brain

Pituitary body

Parathyroid

Thyroid

Islets of Langerhans

Stomach

Small intestine

Right kidney

Adrenal body

Right testis

Duct

Exocrine gland

Endocrine gland

Blood

🔺 The main ductless glands in the human body.

🔺 Ductless glands **secrete** (release) hormones directly into the blood.

Hormones affect our bodies in a number of different ways.

| Endocrine gland | Hormones produced | What the hormone does |
|---|---|---|
| Thyroid gland | Thyroxine | Controls growth and metabolic rate |
| Parathyroid gland | Parathyroid hormone | Controls blood calcium |
| Islets of Langerhans | Insulin | Controls blood sugar |
| Islets of Langerhans | Glucagon | Controls blood sugar |
| Adrenal body | Aldosterone | Controls blood sodium chloride |
| Adrenal body | Adrenaline | Prepares the body for stress |
| Testes | Testosterone | Secondary sexual characteristics in male |
| Ovaries | Oestrogen | Secondary sexual characteristics in female |
| Ovaries | Progesterone | Prepares uterus for fetus |
| Pituitary gland | Trophic hormones | Control other ductless glands, eg gonads and thyroid |
| Pituitary gland | Prolactin | Milk production in mammary glands |
| Pituitary gland | Growth hormone | Controls growth |

🔺 Summary of the functions of the main ductless glands.

*Check your understanding of the diagrams on page 95 by writing the answers to the following questions in your notes.*

▶ *Where is the thyroid gland?*

▶ *Which gland produces adrenaline?*

▶ *What do trophic hormones from the pituitary gland do?*

▶ *Which glands and hormones control the production of gametes (sperm and eggs)?*

Let us study the ways hormones work by looking at two hormones in detail – *insulin* and *glucagon*.

## Insulin and blood sugar

Insulin controls the concentration of sugar in the blood.

Blood sugar is important in two main ways:
- It is the main source of *energy in respiration*. You may have read about respiration in Chapter Five (Breathing and circulation).
- Sugar affects the *water content* of cells and tissues.

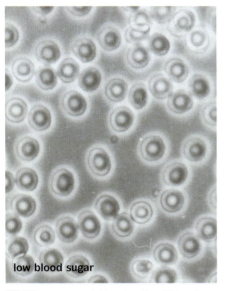 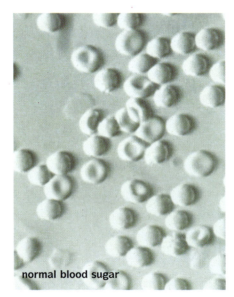 

low blood sugar  normal blood sugar  high blood sugar

🔺 Effects on red blood cells of blood sugar.

▶ *Look at the photographs above. What happens to the red cells if the blood sugar level rises too high or drops too low?*

▶ *What effects might this have in the body?*

The blood sugar concentration must be kept at a level that does not harm the cells.

### Where blood sugar comes from

The main sugar in the blood is **glucose**. All the glucose in our blood comes from the carbohydrate in the food we eat. Carbohydrate is converted to glucose by digestion in our intestines. You may have read about this in Chapter Four (Human nutrition). Glucose is then absorbed into the blood which is taken to the liver.

In the liver cells, large numbers of glucose molecules are joined together to make huge molecules called **glycogen**, sometimes called **animal starch**. Glycogen is insoluble and does not affect the water content of cells. It acts as a store of glucose.

Think of glucose molecules as pound coins. Fifty pound coins would bulge and even rip open your pocket or your purse. But if you change the money into a single fifty pound note, you could easily store it flat. Glycogen is like the fifty pound note. It is easily stored and does not disrupt the cells.

## How blood sugar is controlled

In an organ called the **pancreas**, there are special cells which produce the hormone called insulin. Insulin controls the amount of sugar in the blood. When the concentration of glucose is high more insulin is released and the glucose is converted to glycogen. When the concentration of glucose falls, less insulin is secreted and less glycogen is made.

Not only does insulin affect the level of sugar in the blood, but the sugar also controls the secretion of insulin. When the blood sugar concentration is high, more insulin is made. Glucose is made into glycogen. As the level of glucose falls, less insulin is secreted. For this reason, it is called a **negative feedback control**. The result is a relatively constant concentration of blood sugar. This is an example of **homeostasis**. You may read about this in Chapter Eight (Homeostasis).

If the blood sugar level drops too low, the pancreas produces another hormone called **glucagon**. Glucagon has the opposite effect to insulin. Glucose is released from the glycogen stored in the cells of the liver and so the blood sugar level rises.

▶ *Draw a diagram, similar to the one for insulin, to show how glucagon works by negative feedback.*

▶ *Your blood sugar level drops when you do some strenuous physical activity. Why is this so?*

▶ *How do insulin and glucagon adjust the blood sugar?*

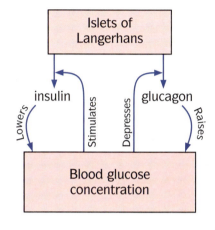

▲ Control of blood sugar by insulin.

## What happens when blood sugar is not controlled

Sometimes, the pancreas does not make enough insulin. This condition is called **diabetes mellitus**. When not enough insulin is present, the following things happen:
- Glucose from the gut is not converted into glycogen.
- Glycogen in the liver is broken down too quickly.
- The blood sugar level rises.
- When the blood sugar level is too high, some of it is removed from the blood in the urine. Urine does not normally contain sugar.
- The body's cells lose water by osmosis.

Mild symptoms of diabetes include tiredness, being very thirsty and having to urinate frequently.

Untreated, diabetes can lead to a loss of consciousness called **coma** and eventually death.

Serious diabetes can be treated very successfully by regular injections of insulin. The insulin used for injection used to be taken from the pancreas of animals such as pigs. Nowadays, it is made by bacteria which have been given human genes. This process is called **genetic engineering**. You may read about genetic engineering in Chapter Nine (Genetics).

Mild diabetes can be controlled by making adjustments to the diet. Very sugary foods must be avoided.

▸ *What would happen in the body if there is too much insulin?*

▸ *People with diabetes must not have too much sugar in their food. Why is this?*

▸ *Sometimes, people with diabetes eat sugary sweets just after taking their insulin injection. Suggest a reason why.*

## Insulin and diabetes

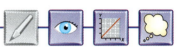

If you drink a sugary drink, like a cola, your blood sugar concentration would increase and, then would decrease again as glucose converts to glycogen. You can look at the results of an experiment in which a man had a sugary drink and then tested his blood glucose concentration. You will be able to follow the action of insulin on his blood sugar level.

It is possible to find out how much glucose there is in someone's blood by a simple test using **Glucostix**. Glucostix are short strips of plastic with pads of paper on the end. The paper contains chemicals which change colour when glucose is added to them. The colour they turn depends on the concentration of glucose.

Blood to be tested is placed on to a Glucostix reagent pad. The blood is removed from the pad after exactly 30 seconds. After a further 90 seconds, the colour produced on the reagent pad is compared to a special colour chart. The concentration of the glucose is then read off the chart's colour scale.

▸ *Suggest why the reaction is allowed to take place for an exact period of time (30 seconds).*

Look at the diagram showing the results of a Glucostix test. You can read off the sugar levels from the colour chart shown to the right.

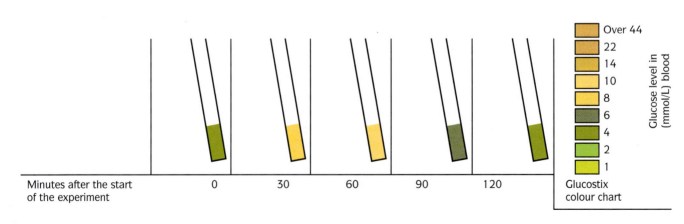

🔺 Results of an experiment in which Glucostix were used to test a man's blood after taking a sugary drink.

- *How much glucose is there in the man's blood at each stage of the experiment?*
- *Plot a graph of blood glucose concentration against time.*
- *How long does it take for the blood glucose to return to the level it was at the start of the experiment?*
- *Why does the blood glucose level rise during the first part of the experiment?*
- *Why does the blood glucose level fall during the second part of the experiment?*
- *In what ways would the results be different for someone with diabetes? Explain your answer.*

## Sex hormones

Sometimes many hormones from different glands can interact with each other to control body processes. Examples of these are the **sex hormones**.

Sex hormones are made in the **gonads**: the **testes** in males and the **ovaries** in females. The male sex hormone is called **testosterone**, the female sex hormone is called **oestrogen**.

Sex hormones control the development of the **secondary sexual characteristics**. These are the features of the body which attract males and females for the purpose of sexual reproduction.

- *Some athletes have taken testosterone to improve their performance. Use the table to suggest how this might work.*

| Male | Facial hair (beard) develops<br>Voice deepens<br>Shoulders become broader<br>Muscles develop<br>Growth of hair in armpits and possibly<br> on chest<br>Growth of pubic hair |
|---|---|
| Female | Breasts grow<br>Uneven distribution of fat under the skin<br> changes body proportions<br>Growth of hair in armpits<br>Hips broaden<br>Growth of pubic hair |

🔺 Summary of the main secondary sexual characteristics in men and women.

The testes and ovaries produce sex hormones when they are stimulated by another hormone called **follicle stimulating hormone (FSH)**. FSH is produced by the **pituitary gland**, which is found just underneath the brain. You may have read about this in Chapter Six (Nervous system). FSH affects the gonads, so it is called a **gonadotrophin**.

### Sex hormones in males

FSH stimulates the testes to make sperm. The pituitary gland produces another hormone called **interstitial cell stimulating hormone (ICSH)**. ICSH stimulates the testes to make testosterone. This complicated interaction of hormones is shown in the diagram.

Testosterone suppresses the production of ICSH by the pituitary gland. This is a negative feedback control mechanism.

- *ICSH output increases in a boy at puberty. What effect does this have on the production of testosterone and the development of the boy's body?*

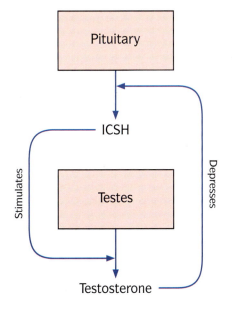

🔺 Testosterone production is controlled by another hormone called ICSH.

## Sex hormones in females

FSH from the pituitary gland in females stimulates the ovaries to make eggs – strictly called **ova** (single, ovum). FSH also stimulates the ovaries to produce oestrogen and starts a very complicated negative feedback mechanism involving two other hormones. Follow the main stages in the diagram.

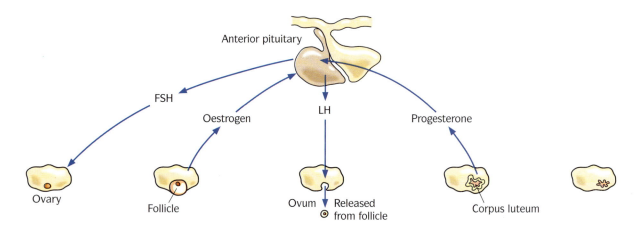

Anterior pituitary

FSH

Oestrogen

LH

Progesterone

Ovary

Follicle

Ovum — Released from follicle

Corpus luteum

▲ The hormonal control of ovulation.

You can see there are two hormones from the pituitary gland, FSH and **luteinising hormone (LH)**. These interact with two hormones from the ovaries, oestrogen and **progesterone**. The process causes a single ovum to be released from one of the ovaries. This is called **ovulation**.

The ovum might be fertilised and develop into a fetus inside the mother's uterus. If it is not, the whole process starts again after a month and another ovum develops. This is called the **menstrual cycle**.

▶ *The contraceptive pill increases the level of oestrogen and progesterone in the woman's blood. How does this stop an ovum being fertilised?*

# Treatment of infertility

Unfortunately, some women are infertile because their ovaries do not produce ova properly. In some cases this can be treated by giving the woman injections of gonadotrophin. This hormone, just like FSH, stimulates ova to develop in the ovaries.

A serious drawback of the treatment is that, very often, a lot of ova develop at once. Normally, only one ovum develops at a time. Consequently, the treatment has resulted in multiple births, six or seven babies at once. The babies are more likely to be born too early – premature – and possibly with serious disabilities.

Doctors can assess how many ova are being stimulated in a woman by scanning her ovaries with **ultrasound**. You may have read about ultrasound in Chapter Five (Breathing and circulation).

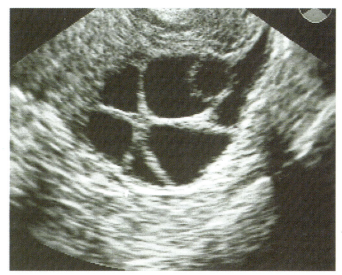

▲ Ultrasound scan showing several follicles in an ovary of a woman who was treated for infertility. Each follicle contains one ovum.

▶ *The ultrasound scan shows several follicles in an ovary. How many can you see?*

# Hormone contraception

Fertility can be increased by giving hormones which stimulate ovulation. The opposite effect (preventing an ova from being released) can be brought about by giving hormones which stop the production of FSH in the pituitary gland. Oestrogen and progesterone work like this. These hormones can be taken daily by mouth in the form of a tablet. **Oral contraception** is usually just called the pill.

▶ *Female sex hormones stop any more ova developing in the ovaries during pregnancy. Why would it be a major problem if a woman became pregnant again while she already had a fetus developing inside her womb (uterus)?*

# Hormones in agriculture

Hormones have also been used in agriculture. Bovine somatotropin, BST, is a growth hormone in cattle.

BST has been produced on a large scale by genetically engineered bacteria. When injected into cows, BST has been shown to increase milk production by possibly as much as 25 per cent. It has also been used to increase growth in beef cattle by as much as 15 per cent. Pig or porcine somatotropin, PST, has been given to pigs to increase their body weight.

Some people see the use of these hormones as a good way to provide for people who do not have enough food. Others think the hormones might be harmful to the consumer.

# Plant hormones

Plants produce hormones which control their growth and development.

An important group of plant hormones is called the **auxins**. Auxins are made in the tips of growing shoots and roots. They are transported back to the growing region just behind the tip where they stimulate growth.

🔺 In the past, cows were injected with growth hormone to increase their milk production. This is no longer allowed in Britain.

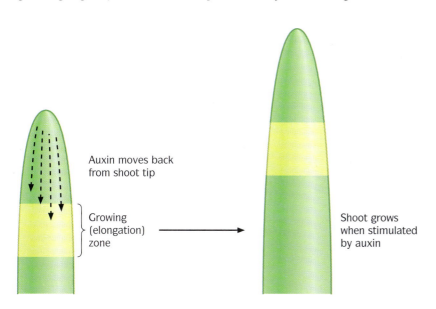

Auxin moves back from shoot tip

Growing (elongation) zone

Shoot grows when stimulated by auxin

🔺 Movement of auxin inside the shoot of a plant. The auxin causes growth in a region just behind the shoot's tip.

## Shoots

Auxins were discovered when scientists were investigating why plant shoots grow towards light. This response is called **positive phototropism**. We say *positive* because they grow *towards* the light. *Photo* means light and *tropism* means growth.

🔺 The result of positive phototropism. The light is coming from the right. Plants need light for photosynthesis.

They found that auxins move away from the light side and into the darker side of the shoots. The auxins then stimulate growth mostly on the dark side, causing the shoot to grow towards the light.

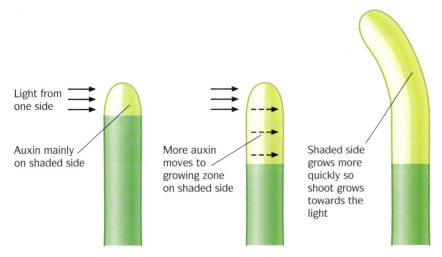

Light from one side

Auxin mainly on shaded side

More auxin moves to growing zone on shaded side

Shaded side grows more quickly so shoot grows towards the light

🔺 Movement of auxin away from the light inside a shoot. Auxin stimulates growth on the dark side of the shoot.

# Auxins and growth

Study these pictures and consider some of the ways in which auxins affect the growth of plant shoots.

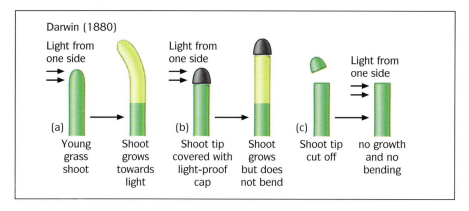

Darwin (1880)

Light from one side → (a) Young grass shoot → Shoot grows towards light

Light from one side → (b) Shoot tip covered with light-proof cap → Shoot grows but does not bend

(c) Shoot tip cut off → Light from one side → no growth and no bending

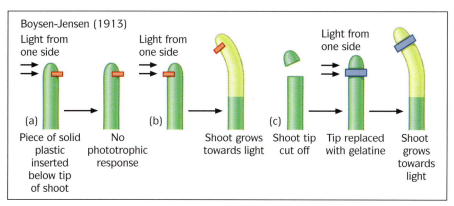

Boysen-Jensen (1913)

Light from one side → (a) Piece of solid plastic inserted below tip of shoot → No phototrophic response

Light from one side → (b) → Shoot grows towards light

(c) Shoot tip cut off → Tip replaced with gelatine → Light from one side → Shoot grows towards light

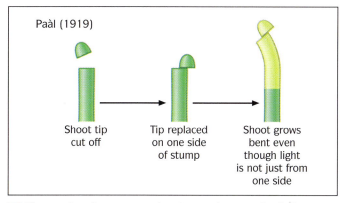

Paàl (1919)

Shoot tip cut off → Tip replaced on one side of stump → Shoot grows bent even though light is not just from one side

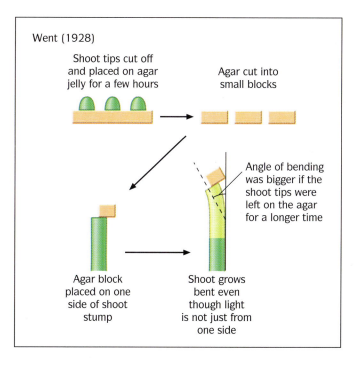

Went (1928)

Shoot tips cut off and placed on agar jelly for a few hours → Agar cut into small blocks

Agar block placed on one side of shoot stump → Shoot grows bent even though light is not just from one side

Angle of bending was bigger if the shoot tips were left on the agar for a longer time

🔺 The results of some experiments on the growth of plants.

Use the diagrams to answer the following questions.

▸ *Briefly describe each experiment and its results.*

▸ *What do the results tell you about how auxins work?*

▸ *What steps were taken in each experiment to make sure the results were reliable?*

▸ *What general results would you expect if the experiments were repeated on the roots of a seedling? Explain your answer.*

## Roots

Auxins are also made in root tips. You have seen that in shoots, growth is stimulated by high concentrations of auxins. In roots the opposite happens and growth is stimulated by smaller concentrations of auxin. This means that roots grow away from light. Auxins concentrate on the dark side and the root grows more on the light side.

Roots are **negatively phototropic**.

▶ *Why are plant shoots positively phototropic and roots negatively phototropic?*

## Geotropism

Shoots and roots also respond to gravity. Shoots grow upwards, away from the pull of the Earth's gravity – **negative geotropism**. Roots grow downwards, towards the Earth – **positive geotropism**.

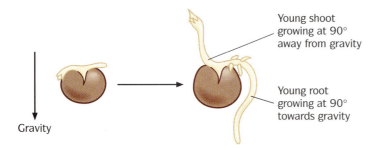

Young shoot growing at 90° away from gravity

Young root growing at 90° towards gravity

Gravity

🔺 Geotropism in a plant's shoot and root.

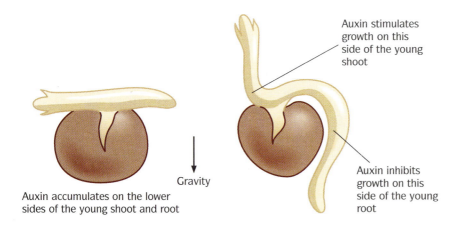

Auxin stimulates growth on this side of the young shoot

Auxin inhibits growth on this side of the young root

Gravity

Auxin accumulates on the lower sides of the young shoot and root

🔺 Movement of auxin inside the shoot and root.

▶ *Explain how gravity can cause the shoot to grow upwards and the root to grow down. (Hint: the shaded area is where most of the auxin is found.)*

▶ *What would happen if you turned the seed upside down? Explain the growth in terms of positive and negative geotropism.*

# Studying plant growth

You may be given worksheets to help you study the effects of light and gravity on the growth of seedlings.

## Commercial uses of plant hormones

Many substances have been made which act on plants just like auxins. **Synthetic auxins** are widely used as follows:

- **Rooting compounds** which stimulate young plants and plant cuttings to form roots.
- Formation of **wound tissue** which helps plant tissue to knit together after grafting.
- Sprayed on to fruit trees to delay fruit falling off. This produces bigger fruit crops.
- **Weedkillers**. Plants like grasses and cereals are less sensitive to synthetic auxins than many weeds, such as dandelions and thistles. The auxin totally disrupts the growth of the weeds, which soon die. Grasses and cereals are unaffected and free to grow without being choked by the weeds.

▶ *Which of the uses of plant hormones listed above are illustrated in the photographs?*

## Safer weedkillers?

A word of caution. Some synthetic auxins are poisonous to insects. Many insects are important **pollinators**. The insects spread pollen from plant to plant, such as fruit trees. Pollination is necessary for the plants to reproduce. Many pollinator insects also use weeds as a source of food. Consequently, the indiscriminate use of auxins as weedkillers can be more harmful than leaving the weeds alone or digging them up by hand.

# Summary

- Animal hormones are chemicals produced by ductless glands and released into the blood.
- Hormones control a range of body functions including growth and reproduction.
- Hormones also regulate the concentration of chemicals in the blood, such as glucose.
- Plant hormones are produced at the growing tips of shoots and roots.
- Plant hormones control plant growth.
- Insulin and glucagon control blood sugar concentration.
- Insulin lowers the blood sugar level, glucagon raises it.
- Excess sugar is deposited as glycogen in the liver. It is also stored in muscle tissue.
- Secretion of insulin and glucagon is controlled by blood sugar by negative feedback. This is an example of homeostasis.
- Lack of insulin leads to diabetes. Blood sugar rises. Treatment can be by insulin injections or dietary regulation.
- Untreated, diabetes can lead to coma and death.
- Sex hormones control secondary sexual characteristics.
- Testosterone is a male sex hormone. It is made when the testes are activated by interstitial cell stimulating hormone (ICSH) from the pituitary gland.
- Female sex hormones are oestrogen and progesterone. They are made when the ovaries are activated by follicle stimulating hormone (FSH) and luteinising hormone (LH) from the pituitary gland.
- FSH also stimulates the testes to make sperm and the ovaries to make eggs (ova).
- Interaction between FSH, oestrogen, LH and progesterone controls the production of eggs, the ovarian cycle (menstrual cycle).
- An egg is produced once a month except during pregnancy or when the contraceptive pill is taken.
- The contraceptive pill prevents egg production. It acts like oestrogen and progesterone during pregnancy.
- Gonadotrophin (like FSH) stimulates egg production. It can be used to treat infertility. Multiple births are a serious risk.
- Growth promoting hormones have been used in agriculture to increase milk yields in cattle and growth in cattle and pigs.
- Main plant hormones are called auxins.
- Auxins are responsible for the growth of shoots towards light (positive phototropism).
- Auxins are responsible for growth of roots down into the soil (positive geotropism).
- Plant hormones are used in horticulture and agriculture to kill weeds, stimulate root formation in cuttings, delay fruiting and make grafts knit together.

# Revision Questions

**1 a** What is a hormone?

**b** Construct a table to show the organ of origin and the function in the human body of *three* hormones.

**2** Copy and complete the following:
An important group of plant hormones are _____ . They are produced in the tips of the _____ and _____ . The hormones move back to the _____ zones. They cause plant shoots to grow towards the light – this is called positive _____ . They also cause the roots to grow down into the soil. This is called positive _____ .

**3** Make a poster illustrating the way hormones control ovulation by the ovaries in women.

**4** Someone you know has no children. They want to have a family of their own and have been trying unsuccessfully for several years. They are afraid to go to the doctor for help. What could you tell them about possible treatments for infertility? (Remember, infertility can result from different possible causes.)

**5 a** Why is it important for the shoots of young plants to grow towards light?

**b** Describe how plant hormones (auxins) make shoots grow towards the light.

**c** Draw a series of sketches showing an experiment which demonstrates how auxins work in phototropism.

**d** Describe a control you would use in the experiment and explain why this is necessary.

**6 a** A scientist used three identical plants for an experiment on auxins.
Plant A was untreated and used as a control.
Plant B had its growing tip removed and the cut surface was wiped with a smear of petroleum jelly (Vaseline).
Plant C had its growing tip removed and the cut surface was wiped with a smear of petroleum jelly containing auxin.

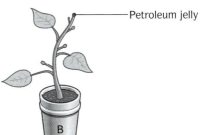
Petroleum jelly

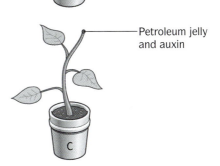
Petroleum jelly and auxin

▲ The result of the experiment.

*i* Describe how the appearance of plant B differs from plant A.

*ii* Suggest *one* effect of auxin which can be deduced from this experiment.

*iii* How does this experiment support the hypothesis that auxins are made in the growing tip of a plant? Explain your answer.

**b** Auxins can be used as selective weedkillers. When sprayed on plants, they encourage the growth of stems and leaves whilst preventing the normal growth of roots.

When sprayed on a lawn in dry weather, broad-leaved weeds such as dandelions and daisies grow rapidly, then wilt and die. Grasses have narrow, vertical leaves and appear to be unaffected by the auxin spray.

*i* Suggest how most of the auxin in the spray enters the plants. Give a reason for your answer.

*ii* Explain why these auxins cause the weeds to shrivel and die.

**7** The graph below shows changes in blood sugar concentration in two people after taking a meal containing a lot of carbohydrate.

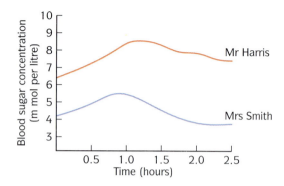

**a** How long does it take for Mrs Smith's blood sugar level to return to what it was before she ate her meal?

**b** Where has the sugar from the meal gone to in Mrs Smith's body?

**c** Explain why it took some time for Mrs Smith's blood sugar concentration to return to the level it was before her meal.

**d** Mr Harris has diabetes. What effect has this had on his blood sugar level, before and after his meal?

**e** Draw graphs showing the blood sugar levels for Mrs Smith and Mr Harris between meals, before and after a short period of strenuous physical work.

# Homeostasis

Space has no air, no water and is very, very cold. It is not an easy place to survive in – we need air, water and heat. Helen Sharman and the other astronauts must have had help to survive in space so that they did not suffocate and their bodies did not dry up or freeze.

Similarly, humans have developed ways to survive on Earth. We have plenty of air and usually enough water, but the temperature is not always comfortable.

In this chapter, you will study some of the ways we and other mammals control our bodies' internal environment. This is called homeostasis.

**Helen Sharman was the first British astronaut. When in space, she lived in a very hostile environment.**

# Review

**Before going any further, read this page and attempt the tasks. Write the answers in your notes.**

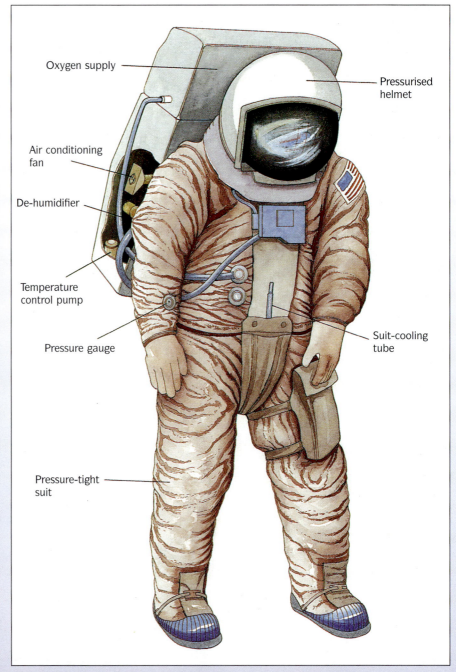

Oxygen supply

Pressurised helmet

Air conditioning fan

De-humidifier

Temperature control pump

Pressure gauge

Suit-cooling tube

Pressure-tight suit

🔺 A North American space suit.

## CHECK EIGHT

**1** Look at the drawing of a space suit. Write out a specification for each of the labelled units. Include the following things:
   **a** What must each unit monitor?
   **b** How must the units respond when changes take place in space?
   **c** What would happen to the astronaut if one of the units failed? Answer this question for each of the units.

**d** What limitations does a space suit put on an astronaut working in space?
**e** Why do astronauts only wear their space suits when they go outside the space capsule?
**f** Do our bodies have any parts which do the same things as the units in the space suits?

# Homeostasis

As long ago as 1857 the French scientist Claude Bernard noticed that animals must maintain a relatively steady set of conditions inside their bodies in order to stay healthy. The internal environment must not change too much or the body will not work properly. Mammals, including people, keep their body temperature fairly constant. They also regulate the chemical content of their blood so that it changes only very little. This control of the internal environment is called **homeostasis**.

# Temperature regulation

Our body temperature is kept at about 37°C. The figure charts the temperature of a woman during a day. Her temperature only changes by about 1.5°C.

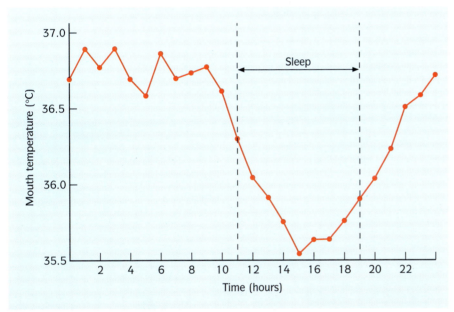

🔺 Daily changes in body temperature of a young woman. Notice the small range on the temperature scale.

The body temperature results from a balance between the *production of heat* in the body and *heat loss* from the body. Think of it like the balance in the diagram on the right.

## Heat production

We produce heat in all our cells by respiration. You may have read about respiration in Chapter Five (Breathing and circulation). We can also take in heat from things around us, such as the Sun, a fire or hot food and drinks.

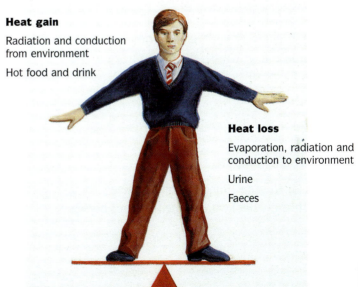

**Heat gain**

Radiation and conduction from environment

Hot food and drink

**Heat loss**

Evaporation, radiation and conduction to environment

Urine

Faeces

🔺 The temperature of a human body is generally in balance.

🔺 Daniel has raised his temperature.

▶ *How has Daniel tried to maintain his body temperature? Which of these ways could he control voluntarily?*

## Heat loss

We lose heat through our skin.

🔺 Chris has acted to lower his temperature.

Heat is lost from our bodies in other ways too. The air we breathe out is warm. Faeces and urine also carry heat from the body.

▶ *How has Chris tried to lose heat energy? Which of these could he control voluntarily?*

## Thermal imaging

Special thermal imaging can be used to take pictures which show the heat coming from our bodies.

▶ *Why is the rescue worker using a thermal imaging camera?*

🔺 A thermal imaging camera being used to locate trapped victims after a fire.

## Control of body temperature

The skin of all animals affects their body temperature because heat passes through it. Mammalian skin is especially adapted to control the amount of heat passing through it.

# Microscopical examination of the skin

You may be given a worksheet to guide you through an examination of the skin. Your teacher will help you use a microscope. You can also use the pictures below to help you identify different features.

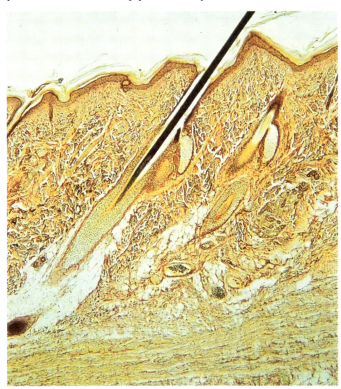

🔺 The microscopical structure of skin.

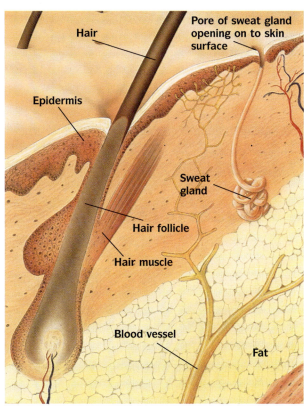

🔺 Drawing of a vertical section of human skin, magnified 20 times. Find the labelled parts on the photograph on the left.

▶ *Estimate the thickness of the fat layer in the section of skin shown in the photograph.*

▶ *Write down the route taken by sweat as it goes to the skin's surface.*

## Skin responses to cold

The skin has a layer of fat just underneath the surface. The fat is a **heat insulator**. It stops heat passing through the skin too easily and helps to keep heat in the body. Blood carries heat to the skin. In cold weather, blood is kept under the skin's layer of fat and so less heat is lost to the outside.

The hair on the skin is made to stand up by the **hair muscles**. This reaction traps a layer of warm air which insulates the body and so less heat is lost through the skin.

When we are very cold, we can **shiver**. Shivering is caused by very fast muscle movements in the skin and generates heat. This heat comes from friction. Also, some of the energy from respiration is given off as heat.

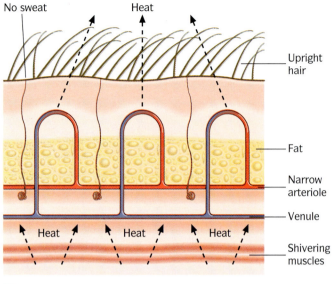

Skin response to cold.

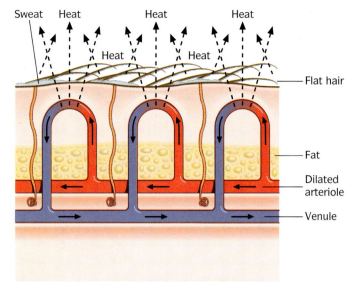

Skin response to heat.

▶ *Why do many mammals grow a thick coat of fur in the winter?*

▶ *Humans do not have very much hair.*
  *How do we compensate for this in cold weather?*

## Skin responses to heat

Blood flows easily to the skin's surface above the layer of fat. Heat leaves the blood and is lost through the skin.

The hair lies down flat on the skin and so heat leaves through the skin even more easily.

Heat can be lost by **sweating**. Sweat comes from small glands in the skin. As the sweat evaporates, it takes heat from the skin and blood.

▶ *Write some notes summarising our body's responses to changes in external temperature.*

▶ *Explain why you might feel cold on climbing out of a swimming pool, even on a warm day.*

## Heat receptors in the skin

The skin contains cells which are sensitive to different things like heat, touch, chemicals and pain. You may be given a worksheet to help you discover how sensitive your own heat receptors are.

## Skin area and body heat

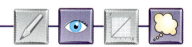

The purpose of this exercise is to investigate the effect of the area of skin on heat loss.

Some people lose heat more quickly than others because their skin has a larger **surface area** compared to their body mass. If you know your height and mass, you can find out your skin area by using the chart.

Place a ruler between the value for your height on the right-hand scale and your mass on the left-hand scale. You can now read off your skin area where the ruler crosses the middle scale. An example for a girl who is 160 cm tall and who weighs 48 kg is shown on the chart.

▶ *What is your height in centimetres?*

▶ *What is your mass in kilograms?*

▶ *What is the area of your skin in square metres?*

▶ *Calculate the area of your skin for every kilogram of your body mass.*

▶ *What is the skin area of a man who is 190 centimetres tall and who weighs 70 kilograms? Would he lose heat more quickly than you? Explain your answer.*

▶ *Elephants overheat easily, but very small mammals shiver a lot. Why is this so?*

## The thermoregulator

Just like the heating system in a house, your body has a **thermostat**. It detects whether the body is cold or hot and then directs the skin's responses accordingly.

The thermostat is located in the brain and is called the **thermoregulation centre**. The diagram summarises how the thermoregulation centre works.

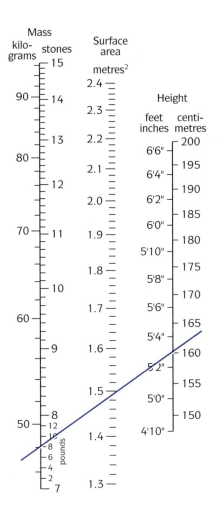

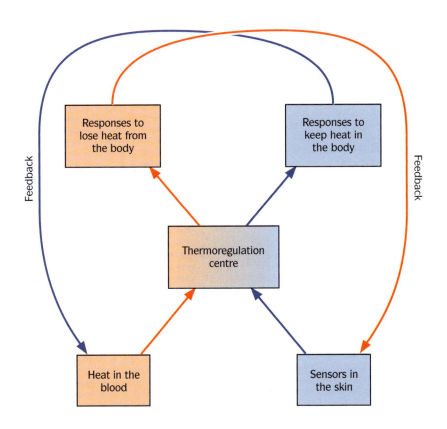

🔺 Mechanisms of thermoregulation.

▶ *If you go from a warm room to the cold outside, how does your thermoregulator detect the temperature change?*

▶ *What does your thermoregulator do when you return to the warm room?*

▶ *How else can heat leave the body as well as through the skin?*

BIOLOGY

## Fever

Sometimes your body temperature is not kept at a normal level. You have probably experienced overheating when you have been ill. This is called **pyrexia** or **fever**. Doctors believe that fever helps us by killing off the bacteria causing the illness. The bacteria grow best at our normal body temperature.

Substances called **pyrogens** raise the temperature setting of the thermo-regulation centre in the brain. The body's heat regulation mechanisms still work as before, but the body temperature is kept higher. Pyrogens are found in the walls of the bacteria which make us ill. These pyrogens are released when the bacteria are engulfed by phagocytes in the blood and tissues. You may have read about phagocytosis in Chapter Three (Health and blood).

▶ *Suggest a reason why the body usually overheats during an infection.*

## Hypothermia

**Hypothermia** results if the body temperature drops too far. The negative feedback mechanisms which usually make us warm when our body temperature drops stop working. This can happen if people are exposed to very cold conditions for a long time. Every winter in Britain, a number of old people die of hypothermia often because they have not got enough fuel for heating their homes.

▶ *Hypothermia is a common symptom in people who have suffered severe burns. They also dehydrate easily and are prone to infections. Explain how they get these symptoms.*

# Excretion of chemical substances

As well as controlling temperature, our bodies must control the amounts of all the chemicals contained in the blood. Any soluble substances which are present in too great a quantity must be excreted.

**Excretion** is the loss from the body of chemical substances that are present in the blood in higher levels than normal. These include the chemical waste products of the body's processes. For example, urea results from the breakdown of excess proteins.

Once we have stopped growing, our body cannot store protein. A high protein diet will not give you bigger muscles, unless you also exercise more.

There are several ways in which excess substances can be excreted from the body:

- Carbon dioxide is breathed out by the lungs. You may have read about this in Chapter Five (Breathing and circulation).
- Some substances are excreted by the liver. For example, bile pigments are produced by the breakdown of haemoglobin.
- Many waste substances are excreted in urine by the kidneys.

# The urinary system

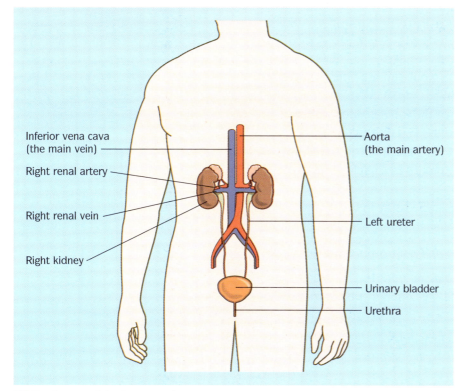

The layout of the human urinary system.

Labels on diagram:
- Inferior vena cava (the main vein)
- Right renal artery
- Right renal vein
- Right kidney
- Aorta (the main artery)
- Left ureter
- Urinary bladder
- Urethra

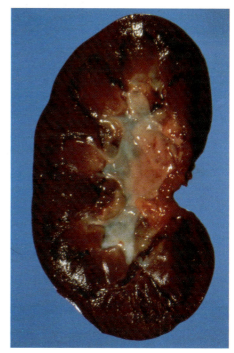

Photograph of a vertical section through a human kidney.

The **kidneys** take waste chemicals from the blood and excrete them as **urine**. Urine leaves the kidneys by tubes called **ureters** which empty the urine into a sac called the **urinary bladder** (usually just called the bladder). The bladder holds the urine for a few hours. After this time, the urine passes out of the body through a tube called the **urethra**. The passage of urine to the outside is called **urination** or **micturition**.

▸ *Which arteries take blood to the kidneys?*

▸ *Which veins take blood away from the kidneys?*

▸ *What other tubes are attached to the kidneys and what do they do?*

## Kidney dissection

Each of our kidneys is about 7 to 10 centimetres long and 2.5 to 4 centimetres across.

You may be given a worksheet to guide you through a dissection of a kidney. Alternatively, your teacher may demonstrate the dissection or show you an anatomical model. You can examine the internal features of a whole kidney and the microscopical features of nephrons.

## The production of urine

Inside each kidney there are about a million very small tubes called **nephrons**.

Each nephron has a round sac called a **capsule** at one end of a coiled **tubule**. Blood is taken to the capsule in a group of vessels called the **glomerulus** (the word for more than one of these is **glomeruli**).

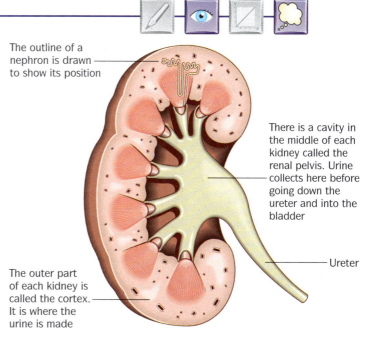

The outline of a nephron is drawn to show its position

There is a cavity in the middle of each kidney called the renal pelvis. Urine collects here before going down the ureter and into the bladder

Ureter

The outer part of each kidney is called the cortex. It is where the urine is made

A vertical section through a human kidney.

▶ *The nephron shown in the diagram has been magnified about ten times. Work out how long the nephrons really are.*

▶ *Where does the blood which is delivered to the glomeruli come from?*

Nephrons make urine. They do so in three main stages.

- *Stage 1.* Chemicals from the blood in the glomeruli are *filtered* into the capsules.
- *Stage 2.* The filtered chemicals pass down the tubules. Most of the chemicals are *reabsorbed* back into the blood so that the levels of chemicals in the blood remain constant. This stage is controlled by *hormones.* You may have read about hormones in Chapter Seven (Hormones).
- *Stage 3* The chemicals that are not reabsorbed stay in the nephrons and are *excreted*. They collect in the pelvis of each kidney and become urine.

▶ *In what parts of the nephron do filtration and reabsorption take place?*

▶ *All our nephrons filter about 120 cm³ of blood a minute. Our kidneys make about 1 cm³ of urine a minute. What percentage of the filtrate is not excreted? What happens to it?*

▶ *How much urine would an astronaut produce during a three-week space trip? What do you think happens to an astronaut's urine?*

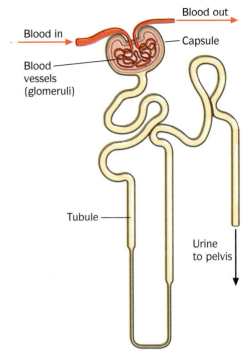

🔺 Drawing of a nephron.

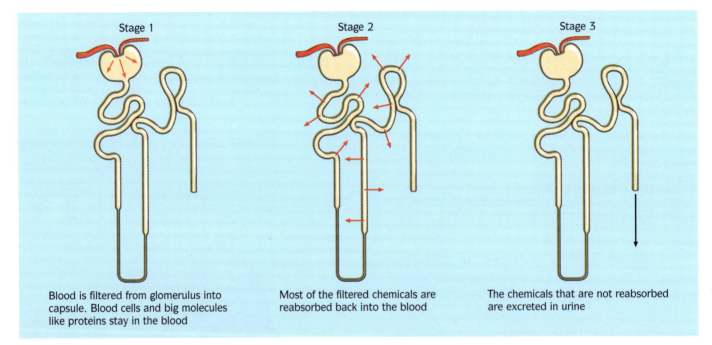

🔺 Nephrons make urine in three main stages.

## Kidney failure

One sign of the kidneys not working properly is that the chemicals that should be excreted stay in the blood. When the blood levels of these chemicals rise too high, they become poisonous. If the kidneys do not work at all, we say they have failed. People with kidney failure become very ill and die if they are not treated.

   The work of the kidneys can be replaced in one of two ways: artificial dialysis (kidney machines) or kidney transplantation.

## Artificial dialysis

A kidney machine removes poisonous chemicals from the blood, just like real kidneys. The blood is taken along plastic tubes into the machine where it runs over a large membrane. Some of the chemicals are filtered out of the blood through the membrane and into a liquid called dialysing fluid. Other chemicals stay in the blood. The process is called **dialysis** and it has to be carried out about twice a week.

The conditions inside a kidney machine must be carefully controlled so that the machine works like a real kidney. For instance, in order for the levels of chemicals in the blood to remain constant, just the right amount of waste chemicals must be filtered out. Blood must flow through the machine at the same speed as the heart pumps blood through the body. The tubes inside the kidney machine must be very smooth, so that the blood flows without being swirled around. The machine must also be sterile, so that micro organisms cannot enter the blood.

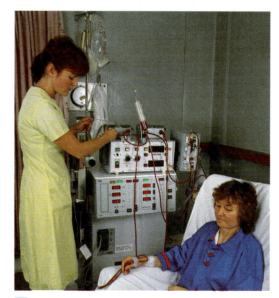

🔺 This woman is having dialysis.

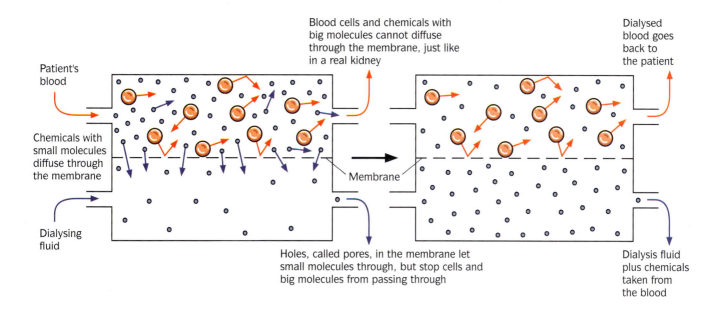

Patient's blood

Chemicals with small molecules diffuse through the membrane

Dialysing fluid

Blood cells and chemicals with big molecules cannot diffuse through the membrane, just like in a real kidney

Membrane

Holes, called pores, in the membrane let small molecules through, but stop cells and big molecules from passing through

Dialysed blood goes back to the patient

Dialysis fluid plus chemicals taken from the blood

🔺 The mechanism of dialysis in a kidney machine.

▶ *How do chemicals move from the blood into the dialysing fluid?*

▶ *Blood cells and big molecules like proteins do not go into the dialysing fluid. Why not?*

▶ *What effect does dialysis have on the levels of chemicals in the blood?*

▶ *A person using a kidney machine usually has dialysis twice a week. How does this compare with the action of normal kidneys?*

## Kidney transplants

A healthy kidney can be taken from one person and put into someone whose kidneys have failed. This is called **transplantation**. You may have read about this in Chapter Three (Health and blood). There are nearly two thousand kidney transplants in Britain each year.

Here are some facts about kidney transplants:

- Blood can still be cleared of poisonous chemicals if only half of one kidney is working properly.
- A transplanted kidney can be rejected by a reaction in the body. If this happens, the transplant fails to work, just like the kidney it replaced.
- Transplants are not rejected if the donor and the receiver have similar body tissues. Close relatives often have similar tissues.
- Surgeons can transplant kidneys fairly easily.
- Transplanted kidneys control the levels of chemicals in the blood much better than kidney machines do.
- Following a successful transplant operation, a patient has a good chance of leading a normal life.

▶ *Why might a kidney transplant fail?*

▶ *Why is a kidney transplant better than treatment with a kidney machine?*

▶ *How can a person give one of their kidneys for transplantation without suffering from kidney failure themselves?*

▶ *Sometimes, a kidney that is available for transplantation in a hospital cannot be given to a patient waiting for a kidney transplant in the same hospital. Why not?*

## Kidney function tests

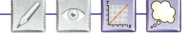

Doctors can measure kidney function. Look at the results of some tests and compare how diseased and healthy kidneys function.

Carol has diseased kidneys. She is in hospital having her kidneys examined by doctors using a **gamma camera**. You can read about this in Physics, Chapter Fifteen.

In the test, a radioactive substance which gives off **gamma rays** is injected into one of the patient's veins. The dose is carefully worked out so that the level of radioactivity does not harm her. The blood then carries the injected substance to her kidneys.

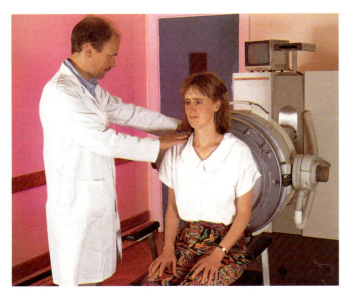

🔺 Carol having a kidney scan.

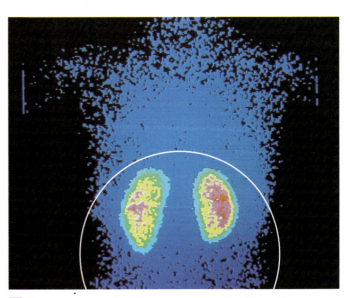

🔺 The area pictured by the gamma camera. Her urinary system is outlined.

The gamma camera detects the gamma rays coming from the patient, just as a photographic camera detects light. Unlike light cameras which use photographic film, the gamma camera has a computer which produces pictures. Doctors use these pictures to see how well the patient's kidneys can excrete the radioactive substance from her blood. The gamma camera is pointed towards the patient's back so the kidneys and bladder show up in the pictures.

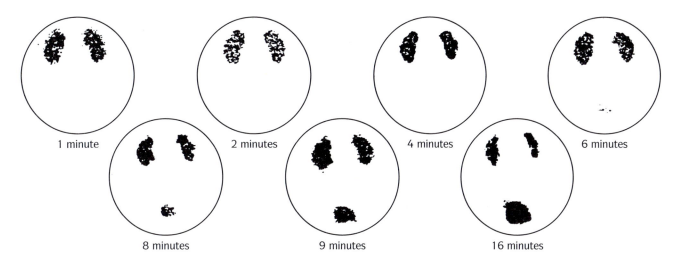

1 minute    2 minutes    4 minutes    6 minutes

8 minutes    9 minutes    16 minutes

🔺 Gamma camera pictures of Carol's urinary system taken over a period of 16 minutes.

▶ *How long does it take for the radioactive substance to start collecting in Carol's bladder?*

▶ *Why do the pictures of the kidneys become faint after 16 minutes?*

▶ *What will the pictures eventually look like if the patient does not go to the toilet for another hour?*

The gamma camera's computer can also plot graphs of the amount of radioactivity coming from the patient's kidneys, blood and bladder during the test. These graphs are called **renograms**. Here is a renogram for a person with healthy kidneys.

▶ *What is the highest radioactivity reading for each kidney?*

▶ *How long does it take each kidney to give off its highest level of radioactivity?*

▶ *Give a possible reason why the level of radioactivity in the left kidney is higher than in the right one. Remember, this patient's kidneys are working properly.*

▶ *What happens to the level of radioactivity in the bladder just after the highest levels are reached in the kidneys?*

▶ *Why does the level of radioactivity in the blood drop all the way through the test?*

▶ *What do the curves on the renograms tell you about the passage of the radioactive substance through the urinary system? Look at the gamma camera pictures as well as the renograms.*

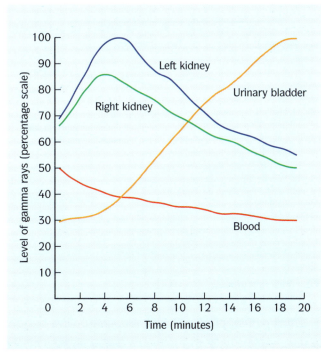

🔺 A normal renogram.

Here is a renogram from a person who has had one kidney taken out. The doctors suspect the other kidney is not working properly.

▸ *Which kidney has been taken out?*

▸ *Give a possible reason why gamma rays are detected from the area where the missing kidney used to be.*

▸ *Is the person's other kidney healthy? Explain your answer.*

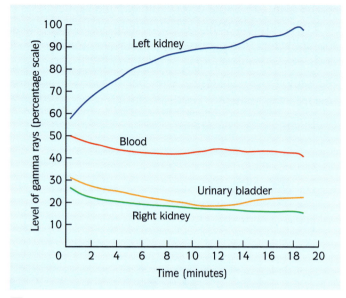

▲ Renogram from a person with only one kidney.

Here are renograms from three hospital patients. Underneath them are extracts from their medical notes and also from another patient.

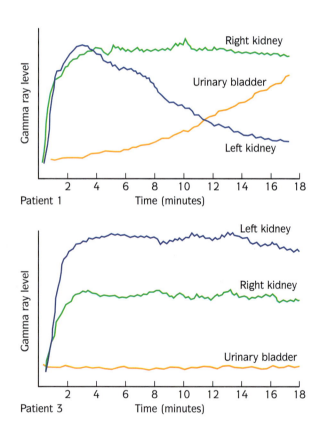

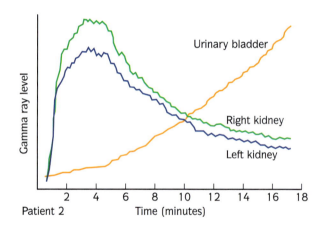

Mr Smith – both kidneys show normal function.

Mr Patel – left kidney removed two years ago. Right ureter blocked.

Mrs Collins – severe blockage in both ureters.

Miss Vincent – blockage in right ureter. Left side appears normal.

▲ Three renograms.

▸ *Which patient produced each renogram? Give reasons for your choices.*

▸ *What might the fourth patient's renogram look like? Draw a sketch of it with a brief explanation of its shape.*

# Summary

- Homeostasis is the maintenance of the body's internal environment, such as temperature and chemical constituents.
- The body temperature is kept fairly constant at 37°C.
- Body temperature is maintained by the balance between heat production and heat loss.
- Body heat is produced by cellular respiration. In emergencies, this is increased by shivering. Heat is absorbed from the environment.
- Heat is mainly lost through the skin. The bigger the skin's area, the more heat is lost.
- Heat loss is controlled by the skin: heat is lost from the blood at the skin's surface, hair traps a layer of warm air on the surface of the skin, sweating causes heat loss from the skin, shivering generates heat, fat provides insulation.
- Excretion is the loss of chemicals from the body in order to keep their concentrations in the blood normal.
- Kidneys are the main organs of excretion. Kidneys produce urine, which leaves the kidneys through ureters and enters the bladder for temporary storage. Urine is then passed to the outside via the urethra (micturition).
- Each kidney contains many nephrons which filter chemicals from the blood. Most of the filtered chemicals are reabsorbed into the blood. The remainder is excreted.
- Kidney failure results when the kidneys can no longer remove chemicals from the blood properly. Treatment is either by artificial dialysis (kidney machines) or by transplantation.

# Revision Questions

**1 a** What is meant by *homeostasis*?

 **b** Why is homeostasis important in the lives of animals?

 **c** State *three* examples of homeostasis in the human body. For each, say what might happen if homeostasis was not operating properly.

**2** Birds and mammals (including humans) can maintain a high and relatively stable body temperature. What advantage is this to birds and mammals compared to other animals such as fish and reptiles?

**3** Complete the following: Blood is brought to the kidneys in the _____ artery. Inside the kidneys, blood is filtered into the _____ of the nephrons. Most of the filtrate is _____ into the blood from the _____ . This is controlled by _____ which make sure the concentrations of chemicals in the blood are kept _____ . The material left in the nephrons is called _____ and is stored in the _____ . It is periodically eliminated from the body by the process called _____ .

**4** A friend of yours missed the first lesson on excretion and the kidneys. Write down the key points to help them catch up their work.

**5 a** Draw a sketch showing a vertical section of human skin. Label the main parts.

 **b** What changes take place in the skin when the body is exposed to the cold?

 **c** What changes take place in the skin when the body overheats?

 **d** Explain how these changes help to keep the body's temperature fairly constant.

**6 a** Explain why *homeostasis* and *excretion* are important to the lives of animals.

 **b** *i* Look back at the three diagrams on p118 illustrating how nephrons make urine. Explain how the processes shown represent homeostasis.

 *ii* What might happen if these processes do not work properly?

 **c** How can kidney function be replaced if the kidneys fail?

**7**

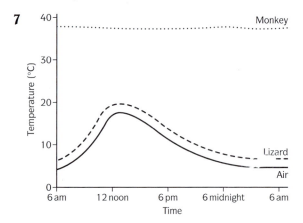

 ▲ The temperatures of a monkey, a lizard and the air over a 24-hour period.

Using the information shown by the graph,

 **a** How does the body temperature of the monkey differ from that of the lizard?

 **b** How do you account for this difference?

 **c** *i* At what time of day can the lizard be most active?

 *ii* Explain your answer.

 **d** During illness the monkey's body temperature rises. Explain how sweating can cool the body.

 **e** How can a monkey warm itself in cold weather?

**8 a** Explain what is meant by the term homeostasis, using human body temperature regulation as an example.

 **b** Describe how the human body temperature is regulated in hot and cold conditions.

 **c** Give *one* advantage and *one* disadvantage of human body temperature regulation.

# Genetics

**The forest is dark and cold. The smell of woodsmoke carries on the air, and a thin spiral of smoke rises from a clearing. In the centre of this clearing sits a tiny, tumbledown cottage. Standing next to the door of the cottage is a beautiful young woman. She is talking to an old crone who is offering her a basket of apples. The young woman takes the apple offered to her and raises it to her mouth.**

You may have heard the story of Snow White. Writers believe it is actually based on the tragic story of the children who used to work down coal mines in Northern Europe. Children were perfect for the work as they could fit through the small spaces underground and work the narrow coal seams. They were also very cheap to employ. They would have looked like dwarfs; little men and women.

Dwarfism is an inherited condition which means that it can be passed from one generation to the next. Dwarfs are unable to produce enough of the chemical responsible for growth, somatotrophin (growth hormone). This makes the individual grow more slowly, although they show normal intelligence and other characteristics.

A better understanding of genetics has allowed scientists to identify the gene that produces growth hormone, and to produce it artificially. Children who are unable to produce growth hormone can now be treated with human growth hormone produced by bacteria.

Snow White's wicked stepmother had a good understanding of genetics, too. She knew that in any basket of apples there would be apples of different shapes, sizes and colours. She knew that the poisoned apple would be only one amongst a variety of others, and so would not stand out.

# CHAPTER NINE

# Review

Before going any further, look at this page and attempt the tasks. Write the answers in your notes.

## CHECK NINE

**1** Write down all the ways that these apples differ. What might cause the differences you have recorded?

**2** Write down the features the apples have in common.

**3** How might a grower develop a new form of apple? How might she then produce many new trees very quickly?

# Differences

You might have noticed that the differences between the apples fit into one of two broad groups (**categories**). Some of the differences were of the type 'have got it' or 'have not got it'. You may have seen a stalk or not, or a scar on the surface, perhaps. This is called **discontinuous variation**. Other features might have shown a gradual change from one fruit to another. The size might have increased slowly, for example. This is called **continuous variation**.

If you plot continuous variation on a graph you get a typical 'top hat' shaped curve. This type of curve is called a **normal distribution curve**.

▶ *Which variations in humans are discontinuous? Which are continuous? Write a list under those two headings of all the examples you can think of. Share your ideas with other groups.*

🔺 Variation in apples.

# Inheritance

People are different. In any group, some will be taller than others. Others have different skin or eye colours. Even families show differences. Children often look a bit like mum or a bit like dad. They might even look like a mixture of their parents.

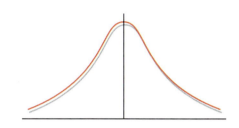
🔺 Normal distribution curve.

🔺 People vary in many ways.

🔺 Baby has his mother's nose and father's chin!

Children inherit features from their parents, but they do not inherit a nose or a chin. Rather, a child inherits coded information, or **genes**, for particular characteristics. Children get one set of codes from each parent and that is why they might look a bit like both parents. Characteristics showing discontinuous variation tend to be controlled by a single unit of code. Continuously varying features are usually controlled by several different units.

▶ *Look at your list of continuous and discontinuous variations in humans. Which are most likely to be controlled by a single code?*

## Gametes

Each child inherits one set of genes from mum, another from dad. The cells which carry mum's and dad's genes are called sex cells or **gametes** (**eggs** and **sperm**). They are made by **meiosis**. You may have read about gametes and meiosis in Chapter Two (Cells). Genes are carried on special structures in the nucleus called **chromosomes**.

▶ *How many chromosomes are there in the photograph?*

▲ Human chromosomes.

## Cloning

It is possible for some organisms to reproduce without using sex cells. This is called **asexual reproduction**. **Cloning** is a process of making a new organism from a part of an existing one – a type of reproduction without sex cells. You may be given a worksheet to help you carry out some cloning.

## Chromosomes

The number of chromosomes inside a cell is very important. Humans usually have 46 chromosomes in 23 pairs. In rare cases, the number of chromosomes passed on at **fertilisation** (when the sperm joins with the egg) might differ from this number. Instead of 23 chromosomes, an egg or sperm might carry 24, for example. This causes Down's syndrome. The extra chromosome seems to confuse the cell. Interestingly, alteration in chromosome numbers seems to have less effect on plants. Plants with multiple sets of chromosomes are said to be **polyploid**.

| Species | Number of chromosomes |
|---|---|
| Mosquito | 6 |
| Pea | 14 |
| Cat | 38 |
| Bread wheat | 42 |
| Human | 46 |
| Horse | 66 |
| Shrimp | 254 |

### DOWN'S SYNDROME

In Down's syndrome, the baby receives one extra chromosome. People with Down's syndrome have reduced resistance to infection and, like individuals with other chromosome differences, tend to have a lower than usual intelligence. Fortunately, modern drugs can reduce the risk from infection and Down's children can expect to lead a relatively normal life, surviving into their sixties in Great Britain. An alteration in chromosome number is called a **chromosome mutation**.

Father    Mother

Body cell
(46)

Body cell
(46)

Cell in testis divides to form sperm
(23)

Sperm (23) → ← (23) Egg

Cell in ovary divides to form eggs
(23)

(46) Fertilisation

(46) Fertilised egg (**zygote**)

| 46 | 46 |
|---|---|
| 46 | 46 |

Ball of dividing cells (**embryo**)

▲ Formation of the **zygote** (a fertilised egg).

BIOLOGY

After the sperm joins with the egg there are 46 chromosomes in 23 pairs, one of each pair coming from each parent. Each pair is different. However, the order of genes on each chromosome of a pair is the same. For example, the third gene on a pair might be for eye colour.

▶ *If the order of genes is the same on each of any particular chromosome pair, how can we inherit differences (hint: remember that a gene is a code)? What possible types of eye colour could be in the eye colour gene?*

The different codes of each gene are termed **alleles**. If we inherit two identical alleles we are said to be **homozygous** for that characteristic. If we inherit two different alleles, we are **heterozygous** for that characteristic.

▶ *Make a list of the possible alleles for eye colour?*

# Sex chromosomes

Girls and boys are different. These differences are due to two different causes. The first is the environment in which they are raised. Often parents, relatives and others expect girls to behave in one way and boys another. They might be dressed differently, have different toys or be allowed to follow different courses at school. These are **cultural** or acquired differences and occur as a result of influences that happen after birth.

The second cause of this variation is due to the features we inherited from our parents. There are clear physical differences between the sexes. Girls and boys have different sex organs, for example. We can explain how we become male or female just as we explain the inheritance of green eye colour; by studying the chromosomes and the genes on them. This is the science of **genetics**.

The sex chromosomes are called the X and the Y chromosome. In humans, males inherit one X and one Y. Females receive two X chromosomes.

▶ *Look at the drawing and then explain why a fertilised egg develops into a male or female baby.*

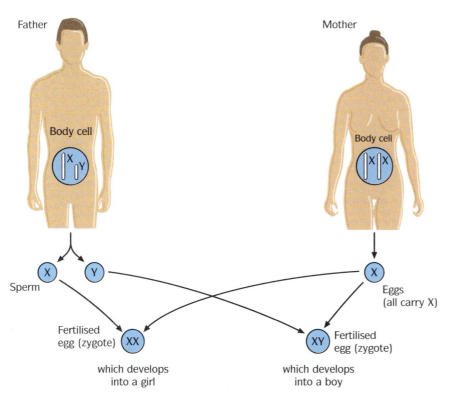

🔺 Both male and female humans have 46 chromosomes. 22 of those pairs are identical. The last pair are the sex chromosomes.

## XYY

Some years ago a North American scientist made a study of male prisoners in US jails. He discovered that a small number of the men had an extra Y chromosome, XYY. He concluded that this extra chromosome led to males being more likely to be criminal. Further studies then showed this conclusion was incorrect. It is now thought that his sample size was not big enough from which to draw conclusions. A cautionary tale for all scientists!

▶ *Draft a newspaper article explaining why the conclusions of his survey were suspect.*

▶ *What further work could be done to test the validity (value) of his conclusions?*

## The birds and bees

Not all animals are organised so that the males have XY chromosomes and the females have XX chromosomes. With birds, the situation is reversed. Male birds are XX, females XY. Many **social insects** (insects which live in groups and co-operate) have a system where the number of males in a community is closely controlled. In honey bees, females are still XX, but males develop from an unfertilised egg and so do not get a second set of chromosomes. This is described as XO, the O showing no paired chromosome.

🔺 The peacock is XX and the peahen is XY.

## Turner's syndrome

Turner's syndrome is the XO state in humans. Carriers of XO appear as sterile females. The X chromosome controls the development of the sex organs (**genitalia**). People with Turner's syndrome have underdeveloped genitalia, and tend not to be very tall.

## The history of genetics

Two thousand years ago, Lucretius, a Roman poet and philosopher, suggested that living things contained particles that were responsible for inheritance. This idea was a development of the ideas of Epicurus, an earlier philosopher. The ancient Romans were not experimental scientists. They used the power of argument instead to generate knowledge. One would put forward an idea or **thesis**. Another individual or group would reply with an **antithesis**, and a common agreement or **synthesis** might be arrived at. It was often the strength of conviction (and political connections) that drove advances rather than scientific reasoning. Consequently, ideas become fashionable and then less so. It was 1900 years before the ideas of Epicurus and Lucretius became fashionable again, and experimental proof was sought.

# Mendel's observations

Gregor Mendel, a monk and teacher, working in what was then part of Austria, discovered that certain characteristics of peas were always passed on in a way which he found he could predict. He made a number of observations in the mid 1850s based on discontinuous pea features such as seed coat, plant height and flower colour.

After his initial experiment Mendel prepared and tested several hypotheses based on his results. He stated that characteristics behave as if they are carried on factors or particles which cannot combine. He went on to explain that there were two particles for each characteristic but only one of the two could be passed to the next generation by each parent. For example, if blackness was on one particle and whiteness on the other, the offspring would be black or white, never grey.

▶ *Can you think of any examples where offspring get a* half-way *characteristic from their parents?*

# Mendel's experiments

🔺 Mendel carried out his experiments on pea plants.

**GENERATIONS**

The parent plants are called the $F_0$ or P generation. The offspring from the parent plants are called the first generation, or $F_1$. The offspring from the first generation are called the second generation, or $F_2$. An so on …

▶ *For each feature in the table use a calculator to divide the larger of the two numbers by the smaller. Round up the numbers to one decimal place. Is there a pattern? If you cannot see one, round up to one significant figure.*

Mendel noticed that when he did this sum the answer was usually about three. This means that for every three pea plants showing the commonest feature, the dominant characteristic, there was one showing the other recessive characteristic. He found a ratio of dominant feature to recessive of 3:1.

| Feature | Possible forms | Numbers in second generation | |
|---|---|---|---|
| Seed coat | Smooth Wrinkled | Smooth Wrinkled | 5474 1850 |
| Flower | Red White | Red White | 705 224 |
| Height | Tall Short | Tall Short | 787 277 |

🔺 Examples of Mendel's results.

| Feature | Possible forms | Numbers in second generation | |
|---|---|---|---|
| | | **Dominant** | **Recessive** |
| Unripe pods | Green Yellow | Green 428 | Yellow ____ |
| Seed coat | Grey White | Grey ____ | White 244 |
| Seed leaves | Yellow Green | Yellow 6022 | Green ____ |

🔺 Predicting Mendel's results.

# Applying Mendel's model

We can use Mendel's hypothesis to explain how the characteristic for height might be inherited in pea plants. Mendel used **pure** strains of peas in many of his experiments. Pure strains always give offspring identical to themselves when bred together. For example, pure tall pea plants will always produce tall peas if both parents were from families that always produced tall peas; short pea plants will always produce short plants. Mendel discovered that only the dominant characteristic was shown or expressed in the first generation when **cross-breeding** (or crossing) two pure strains.

If 'tall' is controlled by the allele (particle) T, and 'short' by the allele t, then, according to Mendel's hypothesis, pure tall parents would carry two cells from T's (TT): and short peas would carry two t's (tt).

The process of fertilisation is random, so an egg carrying a T allele is just as likely to be fertilised by pollen carrying the allele T as pollen carrying the t allele. You can show these chances in a probability or **Punnett square**:

Female gametes
|  | | T | t |
|---|---|---|---|
| Male | T | TT | tT |
| gametes | t | tT | tt |

Each box shows the alleles inherited by that offspring. In this case, 'tall' is the dominant feature, so we might predict that:
- In the first cross (TT × tt), all the peas will be tall.
- In the second cross (Tt × Tt), for every three tall plants, there will be one short plant.

In fact, after doing this experiment Mendel found all the first generation (F₁) plants were tall.

▶ *Work out the $F_1$ and $F_2$ generations for crosses between parent plant with red flowers (CC) and one with white flowers (cc). Use C for the dominant and c for the recessive allele.*

▶ *For each feature in the table, say which is the dominant and which is the recessive form.*

▶ *Predict the outcome of the following crosses using the number of the offspring showing the given feature in the second generation. Remember, dominant ÷ recessive should be about three.*

▶ *Mendel's answers were 152, 705 and 2001. Are they the answers you expected? If not, explain why they are different.*

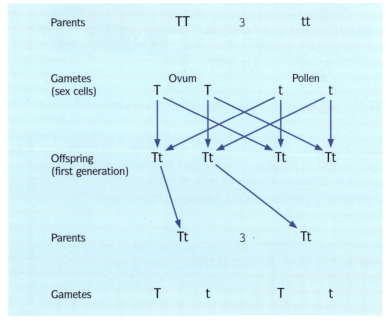

🔺 Working out crosses.

Look back at the table of Mendel's results. There were 787 tall peas to 277 short, a ratio of roughly 3:1. Mendel's results were, as a rule, so close to his predictions that his honesty has been questioned. However, most scientists believe that his results were not fixed, and that Mendel was one of the greatest experimental scientists.

Unfortunately he was not one of the most self-publicising and published his work in a local scientific journal, where it remained largely overlooked for nearly half a century.

## A scientific method

Mendel prepared and tested hypotheses by controlling variables (he controlled which plants were crossed). He measured his results as accurately as he could, always expressing them quantitatively. From his results he was able to produce generalised statements and to see patterns. He could then test the statements further until he found a model which predicted the behaviour of his observed features.

## Genome

**Genome** is the term used to describe all the genes in a cell. Even in humans, genes are found outside the nucleus, within the organelles known as mitochondria. (Plants also have genetic material in their chloroplasts. In yeast, a type of fungus, about 5 per cent of its total genome is contained outside the nucleus.)

Within 20 years it is hoped that we will have a complete genetic map of all 23 pairs of human chromosomes. This project involves scientists from all over the world and is called the human genome project.

▶ *Why do you think so many scientists are working on this one project?*

▶ *Which organelles contain genes?*

## Genetic fingerprinting

Amazingly, most of your genetic material, your **DNA** (**deoxyribose nucleic acid**) seems to code for nothing important. Perhaps as little as 5 per cent of your DNA actually codes for characteristics. Much of the rest consists of repeating sequences. By chance, it was discovered that these sequences, when sliced up in a particular way, are unique to each individual. We all have our own genetic fingerprint. The more complex the form of slicing, the less likely it is that two people have the same pattern.

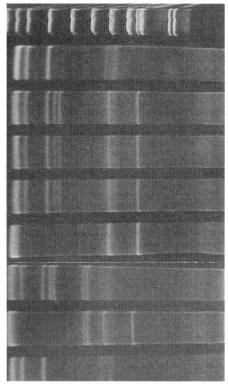

▲ The genetic fingerprint is a unique pattern.

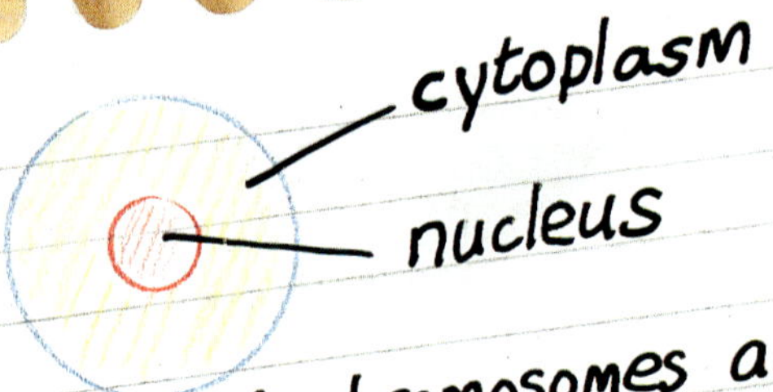

cytoplasm

nucleus

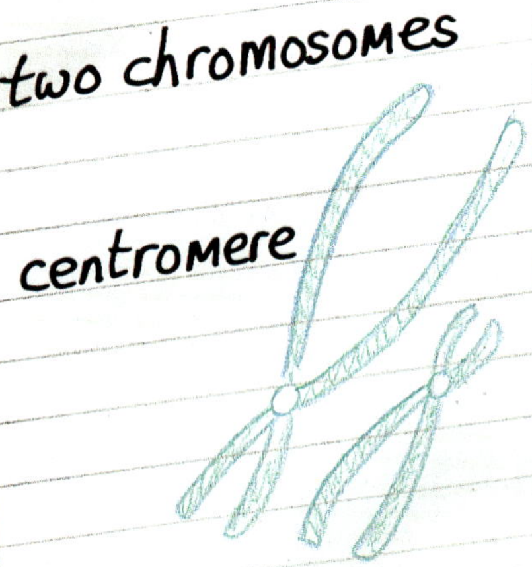

two chromosomes

centromere

Our 46 chromosomes are visible under a light microscope only during cell division. For division to occur the length of DNA must uncoil. This picture shows two chromosomes ready to divide. Each part of the 'X' is one copy of the chromosome.

Coils use less space so the chromosome can fit inside the nucleus.

Each chromosome is a long coiled ribbon-like structure. Of our 46, we received 23 from mum and 23 from dad. We have, then, 23 pairs of chromosomes.

On further magnification the ribbon is like a twisted ladder with three or four rungs in each twist. Together it looks like two helices twisted together, the double helix. This is DNA.

Straightened out we would see:

Only four chemicals form these rungs. These are bases and are called A, T, C and G.

A always pairs with T, and C with G.

The order of bases makes up the genetic code. The nucleus reads this genetic code and the cell converts it into proteins. This is the job of the endoplasmic reticulum.

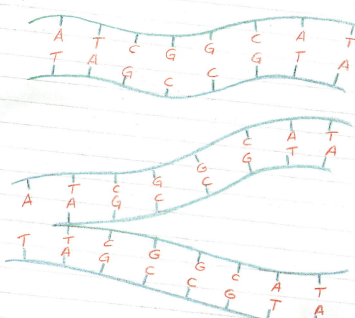

Before cells can divide their DNA has to be copied in a process called <u>replication</u>.

---

<u>Gene</u>

A gene is a length of DNA with a start and an end code. Genes code for individual units of protein.

Any errors that occur at this stage might alter the sequence, so changing the code. Ultraviolet light can affect this process. Such a change is called a <u>mutation</u>.

## Applying the new knowledge

Understanding the inheritance of flower colour in peas helps us to understand human inheritance. You have read in this chapter that many features shown by humans are inherited. Unfortunately, many diseases are also inherited.

Knowing that these diseases are genetic means that we can hope to cure them. If we could identify the gene that was damaged, we might be able to repair or replace it.

At the time of writing, trials had begun in which sufferers of cystic fibrosis were given **genetic therapy** to treat the disease. This involved using a puffer (**nebuliser**) similar to the kind used by asthmatics, but which delivered the repaired gene directly into the lungs in the hope that it would become part of the damaged cells.

| Disease | Dominant or recessive allele |
|---|---|
| Cystic fibrosis | Recessive |
| Albinism | Recessive |
| Huntington's chorea | Dominant |
| Achondroplasia dwarfism | Dominant |
| *Colour blindness | Recessive |
| *Haemophilia | Recessive |

*These features are carried on the sex chromosomes and are described as **sex-linked**. Both are found on the X chromosome.

▲ Some inherited diseases.

# CYSTIC FIBROSIS

In cystic fibrosis a single gene has been damaged. The job of this gene is to make an enzyme which thins the mucus made by your body. Mucus is your natural lubricating and cleaning fluid. If it is too thick your lungs and digestive system cannot work properly. It also causes your sweat to be saltier. It is seen in about one in three thousand live births.

Without this enzyme, breathing can be difficult and people with cystic fibrosis often have physiotherapy for several hours a day to keep their lungs clear and reduce the likelihood of bacterial infection.

**You can't spot the child with cystic fibrosis.**

## Mechanism of inheritance

Let A be the undamaged allele, a the damaged allele.

| | Father | Mother | |
|---|---|---|---|
| Parents | Aa | Aa | Each parent has a damaged allele. (They also carry the undamaged form and so do not have cystic fibrosis) |
| Gametes | A   a | A   a | |

Using a Punnett square:

|  | | Female gametes | |
|---|---|---|---|
| | | A | a |
| Male gametes | A | AA | Aa |
| | a | aA | aa |

AA  normal

Aa ⎫
aA ⎬ normal, carrier

aa  cystic fibrosis

So, if each parent carries a damaged allele, the probability that their children will have cystic fibrosis is one in four.

Increasingly, as we know more and more about the disease, sufferers are able to live longer and longer lives. Even 20 years ago, it was unusual for a child born with this condition to survive into his or her twenties. Today it is not unusual to see 30 year-olds living and coping with the disease, often requiring very little hospital support.

# Huntington's CHOREA

Huntington's chorea affects the nervous system. It is a **progressive disease** which means it gets worse with time. Huntington's chorea causes the progressive breakdown of the nervous system, and is associated with the loss of movement and speech and dementia. It is very rare.

## Mechanism of inheritance

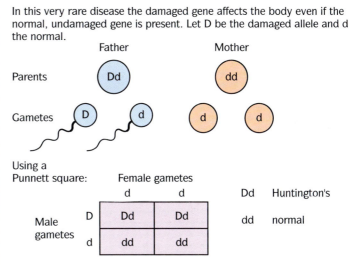

In this very rare disease the damaged gene affects the body even if the normal, undamaged gene is present. Let D be the damaged allele and d the normal.

In this case, half the offspring will have Huntington's chorea. The disease is often not apparent until early middle age.

## Mutation

Most children born do not suffer from one of these genetic diseases. They are all rare. However, things which causes damage to the cell may also damage one of our genes. Such damage is called a **mutation**. Mutation can be caused by many things, including radiation, ultraviolet light and chemicals in our environment. Even caffeine in very high doses can cause mutation. If this mutation takes place in a sex cell or gamete, we might pass that damaged gene on to our children. Fortunately, our cells have a way of dealing with most mutations, but occasionally one gets through.

# Haemophilia

## Mechanism of inheritance

The best studied mutation of all is probably that of the haemophilia gene in the Royal Family of Great Britain. It is thought to have begun with one of the pair of alleles from Queen Victoria, responsible for the production of the blood-clotting protein, factor VIII. It is the mutation of this gene which causes haemophilia, as without factor VIII your blood will not clot.

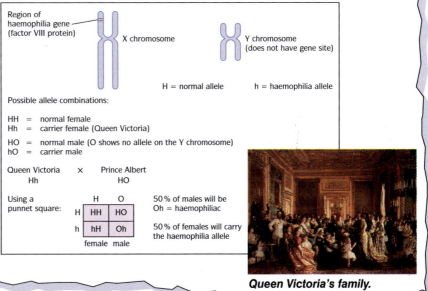

*Queen Victoria's family.*

▶ *Queen Victoria was not a haemophiliac even though she carried one damaged gene. How could this be possible?*

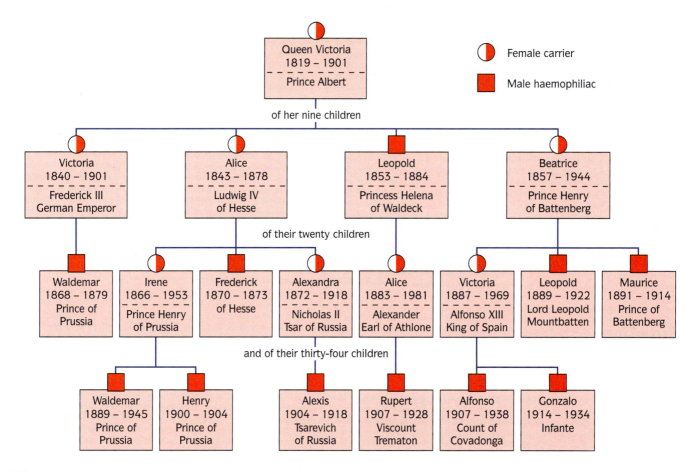

△ The life expectancy of males with haemophilia was relatively low. Today it is similar to the life expectancy of males without haemophilia.

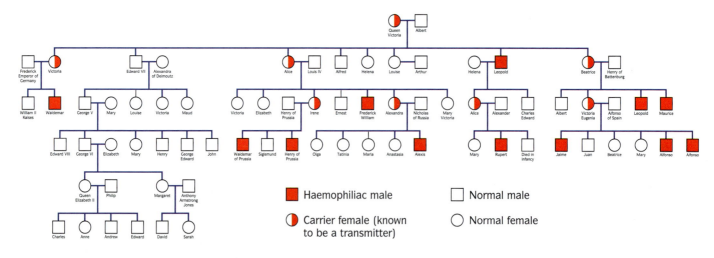

△ Family tree of Queen Victoria.

▶ *Estimate the average life expectancy of males with haemophilia in this family tree.*

# Summary

- Variation exists in natural populations and can be due to environmental or genetic factors.
- 'Have' or 'have not' characteristics are examples of discontinuous variation, for instance eye colour.
- Characteristics which change gradually across a population are examples of continuous variation, for instance height.
- Continuous variation is often shown on a normal distribution curve.
- Discontinuously varying features are probably controlled by a single gene; continuously varying features by several genes.
- Our gender is determined by the sex chromosomes inherited from our parents.
- A change in the DNA code of a gene can be very harmful. Such a change is called a mutation.
- We always inherit an X chromosome from our mother but can inherit either an X or a Y from our father.
- The DNA contained in our cells is unique to us. A pattern made from DNA is called our genetic fingerprint.
- A genetic or DNA fingerprint is the pattern of bands made when an individual's DNA is cut up with special enzymes. It is unlikely that two people have an identical DNA fingerprint.
- Females humans carry XX chromosomes. Males carry XY chromosomes. Other animals have different ways of determining gender.
- Any deviation from the normal number of chromosomes, 46, is generally harmful in humans.
- An alteration in the chromosome number is called a chromosome mutation.
- Different species may have a different number of chromosomes, but it is the content of the chromosomes, the genes, which determines whether we are human or hamsters.
- Mendel discovered that genes occur in pairs, only one of which is passed on to the offspring by each parent.
- A gene may exist in many different forms. These different forms are called alleles.
- If we carry two identical alleles for a characteristic we are said to be homozygous for the gene.
- If we carry two different alleles for a characteristic we are heterozygous.
- We inherit half our alleles from our mother and half from our father.
- Inherited diseases include Huntington's disease, cystic fibrosis and haemophilia.
- Some diseases are associated with the sex chromosomes including haemophilia and certain types of colour blindness.

# Revision Questions

1 Make a list of ten ways in which you are different from your best friend. How many of these differences are inherited?

2 How many chromosomes are there in the nucleus of one of your cheek cells? How many are there in one of your sex cells (gametes)?

3 List some of the ways in which our environment affects how we grow up.

4 Explain how sex is determined in humans. How is the system different in bees?

5 Look back at Chapter Two (Cells). Copy the diagrams on meiosis. Label the cell to show the nucleus.

6 Research some genetic characteristics in your class. How many people can roll their tongues, or have ear lobes which are detached? Guess which feature is dominant for each characteristic you investigate.

7 Identical twins are formed when the fertilised egg (ovum) splits into two, shortly after fertilisation. Use your knowledge of genetics to explain:
   a how identical twins are identical
   b why identical twins might not be identical.

8 Why do brothers and sisters tend to look more alike than unrelated individuals?

9 A class collected some data on the distribution of height. They then plotted those data on to a bar chart.

| Range (cm) | Number |
|------------|--------|
| 145 – 149  | 1      |
| 150 – 154  | 5      |
| 155 – 159  | 1      |
| 160 – 164  | 5      |
| 165 – 169  | 5      |
| 170 – 174  | 2      |
| 175 – 179  | 1      |

   a Plot these figures on to a bar chart.

b One of the students wrote: 'I don't think that height is an example of continuous variation. When you look at the graph, you do not get the "top hat" type of curve that you see with normal distribution.'

   Was he correct? Write a comment to go on this student's work.

10 Sally's grandmother (her mum's mother) has red hair. So does her dad's father but her mum has brown hair and her dad, grey (although it used to be brown). Tom, Sally's baby brother, has red hair. Sally's mum said it was what she expected because red hair skips a generation, just like Sally's blue eyes.

   Using your knowledge of genetics, explain how a feature can skip a generation.

11 Blood can be classified on the basis of the combination of proteins carried in the membranes of certain cells. Two particular proteins, A and B, are most commonly used in blood grouping. You can carry protein type A, type B, both or neither (OO).
   a List the four possible blood groups and all the combinations of alleles relating to them.
   b If a person carrying the type A allele has a child with a person carrying type B, what are the possible combinations of alleles carried by the child?
   c If a person with blood group O has a child with a person of group B, what are the possible combinations of alleles carried by the child?

12 You are a genetic counsellor. Your job is to discuss the possible outcomes of conception with couples who have a family history of genetic disorders. Prepare a leaflet for couples with a family history of cystic fibrosis. You should provide statistical evidence wherever possible to enable couples to make decisions for themselves.

13 Prepare a newspaper article on gene therapy.

# Evolution

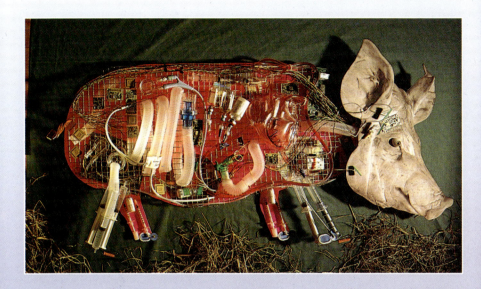

'When is a door not a door?'
'When it's a-jar!'
Hmm, not the best of jokes but when is a pig not a pig?
A strange question, perhaps, but one that is beginning to concern more and more people.

Although the pig in the photograph may not look like a human, the organs in its body are very similar in size to a human's. Pigs are also fast growing.

Scientists now see pigs as an ideal organism in which to *grow* human genes. The process of genetic engineering allows the transfer of genetic material from one organism to another. It is possible to isolate a human gene and to insert it into the cell of a pig embryo. Further work should ensure that this gene will work (**express**) in the pig itself.

## ■ Future choices

You may have read about insulin being produced from genetically engineered bacteria in Chapter Eight (Homeostasis). The insertion of a human gene into a bacterium now allows the production of insulin through an industrial fermentation process. Before this process was invented, pigs were slaughtered and the insulin extracted from their pancreases. Pigs were used because your body is not able to tell the difference between your insulin and pig insulin. This technique probably saved the lives of thousands of diabetic people, and enabled them to lead normal lives.

People are still unwilling to donate their organs for use in transplant surgery. For example, every year hundreds of people die in the United Kingdom because there are not enough donor kidneys available. Genetic engineering could allow scientists to grow a pig containing kidneys which your body might not reject. In two years, the pigs would be fully grown and their kidneys ready for use. The lowered likelihood of transplant rejection means that thousands of pounds could be saved on drugs and on further treatment. You might also have a spare heart, a set of lungs and a liver for later.

Tomorrow's donor?

# Review

Most scientists believe that all these living things can be traced back to a common ancestor, probably a single-celled creature which lived in a rock pool hundreds of millions of years ago. For convenience, scientists group living things together, based on how recently common ancestors were shared.

Before going any further, read this page and attempt the tasks. Write the answers in your notes.

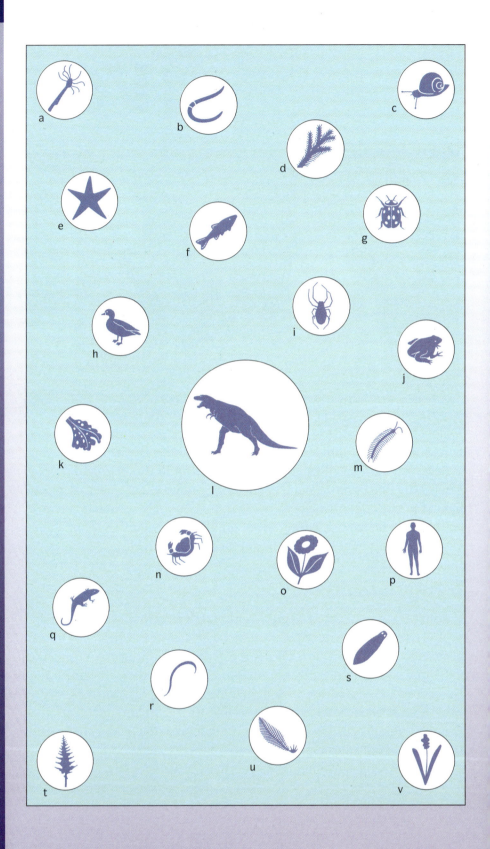

## CHECK TEN

**1** Place the creatures and plants shown above into groups. Say how you are classifying them.

**2** How many different ways can you group them together?

# The variety of living things

Apples come in many shapes and sizes. Some are red, others brown or green. Some have a sharp taste, others sweet. Some are crisp, others soft. Next time you go to a market, or to a greengrocer, count how many different **varieties** are on display.

# Darwin's pigeons

Charles Darwin was both a practical scientist and a pigeon fancier, collecting and breeding fancy pigeons, owning many thousands in his lifetime. He looked for particularly striking features and would breed from these birds. He tried to collect at least one of every recorded variety and was convinced that all his pigeons had a common ancestor, the rock pigeon. He thought that the variety he saw was present in *the blood* of this single species.

△ Apple varieties.

▶ *You might have noticed pigeons in the park, on the pavements or in the fields. How do the pigeons within a flock differ?*

△ These pigeons were bred for their different characteristics.

Fanciers selected birds with extreme features from which to breed, unconsciously mimicking the work of Mendel on genetics. The word **bloodline** was used (and still is) to describe birds showing particular features.

This form of **selection** has gone on since the beginning of human history.

▶ *Imagine you are a Neolithic (early human) farmer.*
  **a** *Which seed will you hold back to grow next year, the fattest or the smallest?*
  **b** *Which seed do you think will give plants with the greatest yield?*
  **c** *Now imagine this process occurring over many thousands of generations. How would the plant change?*
  **d** *What other features might be important in selecting the seeds for next year's crop?*
  **e** *Would these features help the plant survive if humans abandoned it?*

# Artificial selection

Farmers and growers work continually to improve their crop plants. Today this is big business, with the potential for massive rewards. Imagine you produced a new form of wheat, one which gave a high yield on poor soils and was resistant to disease. Or a variety of rice that grew faster than others, giving farmers four crops a year instead of two or three. Not just crop plants are developed in this way. Flowers of different colours can be grown, for instance a blue rose or a black tulip.

▶ *Some ideas for new varieties seem obvious, but suggest how breeders decide on a target for their breeding plans.*

At each stage, the breeder selects the plants nearest to what he or she is attempting to produce. We call this technique **artificial selection**.

## Variation

Artificial selection depends on the fact that there is a great deal of variation present in all species. This variation is due in part to sexual reproduction in which male and female gametes join together randomly. It is this randomness which produces the variation seen in the new generation. There is a second form of reproduction which does not depend on gametes joining. This is called **asexual reproduction** and it is of great economic importance.

# Species

A **species** is a group of plants or animals which can breed together successfully, but cannot breed successfully with members of another species. All breeds of domestic dog belong to the same species, a different species from wolves or foxes. Successful breeding means that not only are offspring produced but also that the offspring are fertile. Horses and donkeys are different species even though they can breed together. Their offspring, mules, are infertile.

# Improving artificial selection

Farmers and growers have been selecting for desired features in their crops for thousands of years, but the process of improvement is a gradual one. If we knew how, for example, flower colour was controlled in roses we might be able to speed up the process of artificial selection. To do this we would need to know which genes were involved in the process.

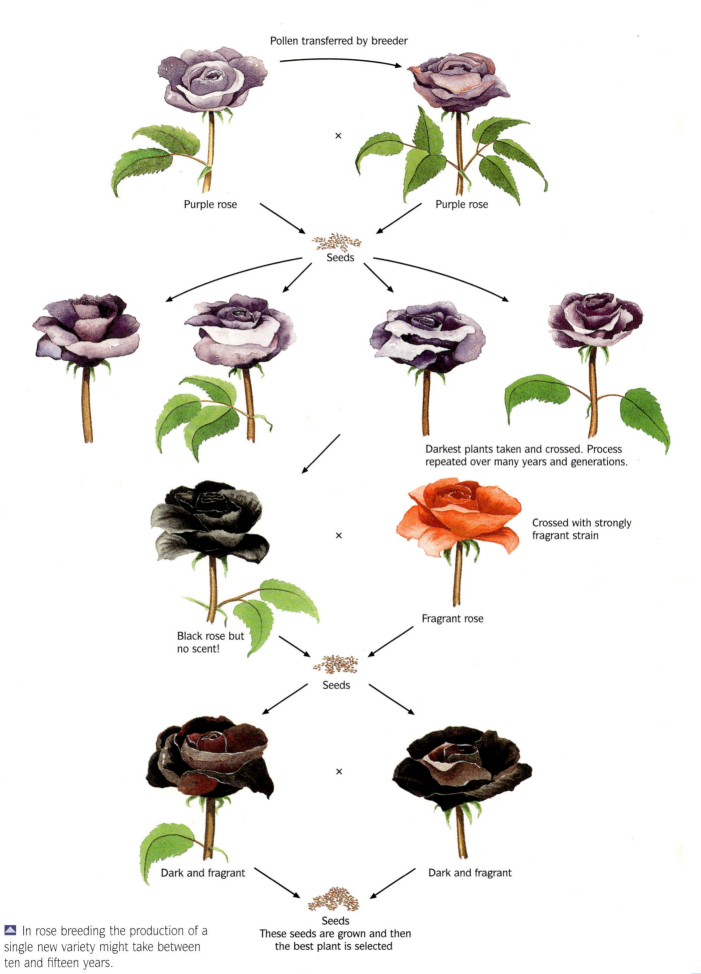

Pollen transferred by breeder

Purple rose  ×  Purple rose

Seeds

Darkest plants taken and crossed. Process repeated over many years and generations.

Crossed with strongly fragrant strain

Black rose but no scent!  ×  Fragrant rose

Seeds

Dark and fragrant  ×  Dark and fragrant

Seeds
These seeds are grown and then the best plant is selected

▲ In rose breeding the production of a single new variety might take between ten and fifteen years.

# Genetic engineering

Scientists all over the world are working on the new science of genetic engineering in the hope that they will be able to speed up artificial selection. Genetic engineers work to discover the precise site of a particular characteristic on a chromosome. If they can find the exact site of a gene for flower colour in roses and discover how it is controlled, they will be able to remove it and study it outside the rose. They might even be able to introduce a gene from another plant to produce a black rose.

▶ *Write down some of the advantages of genetic engineering over artificial selection. Can you think of any problems?*

# Genetic therapy

It is not just flowers that are being studied. You may have read about the diseases cystic fibrosis and Huntington's chorea in Chapter Nine (Genetics). Scientists have identified the gene responsible for causing cystic fibrosis. They have even found a way to replace the damaged gene with a healthy one, and have reported some success in achieving this inside otherwise healthy human cells.

Step 1   Identify the gene you are interested in.

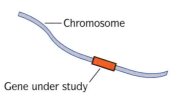

This can be done by looking for differences in the DNA when compared with the DNA of an individual lacking the feature under study.

This process can take years.

Step 2   Cut out the area of chromosome containing the gene under study.

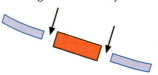

Special enzymes called **restriction endonucleases** chop up DNA into small pieces

Step 3   Produce many copies of the gene (**amplification**).

Step 4   Fix the gene under study into the DNA of a **host cell**. The host cell is often a bacterium.

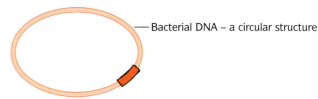

Step 5   The bacterium will multiply rapidly and with luck, produce the products of the gene under study.

🔺 Genetic engineering primer.

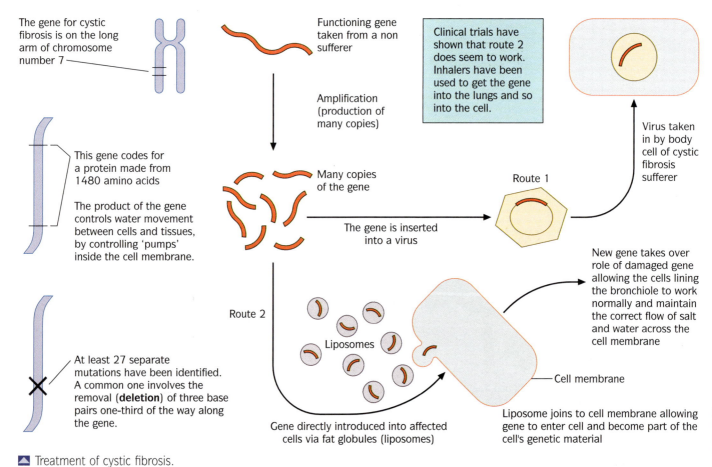

🔺 Treatment of cystic fibrosis.

## Transgenic animals

Genetic engineering could be used for many purposes. Scientists are exploring the possibility of producing faster-growing animals by introducing extra copies of the growth hormone gene into the cells of cows and sheep. Scientists have successively introduced antibiotic genes into cows so that they produce antibiotics in their milk. Scientists have even introduced genes from one species of farm animal into another, producing crosses between goats and sheep or even pigs and humans. Such animals are called **allophenes**.

## New sciences

Advances in science are linked closely to technological developments. Throughout the nineteenth century, new technologies were being applied to science in a way which had never before been possible. New discoveries were made frequently. Historians think that part of the reason for this was that improved communications meant that scientists could communicate their ideas very quickly to fellow workers. Criticism, a vital part of scientific progress, would have returned just as rapidly allowing techniques to be improved, or conclusions modified.

It is hard to share ideas if it takes a year to write to a fellow worker, and another year to receive a reply!

▲ The baboon is a collage of images from different places. Transgenic animals are genetic collages.

▶ *Make a list of those things you think essential for success in science today. How many of them were available to scientists in thc nineteenth century?*

### Linking ideas together

By the end of the last century, meiosis had been observed. You may read about meiosis in Chapter Two (Cells). New ideas on how species were formed had been published by Charles Darwin and Alfred Wallace. It was 16 years after Mendel's death that the importance of his work was recognised. A Dutch scientist, Hugo de Vries, is usually credited with the rediscovery of Mendel's work, although several research teams around the world were investigating different aspects of inheritance. You may have read about Mendel's work in Chapter Nine (Genetics).

Around 1914, all these ideas were synthesised into one big theory or **metatheory**, linking genetics and evolution. This was over fifty years after the initial work needed to make this theory possible had been published.

▶ *Why do you think the pace of scientific progress was so great in the latter half of the nineteenth century? Write down some of the reasons. Try to explain why it still took so long to link many of these great ideas together. Think about scientific research today. Is it as successful as in Victorian times? What is different?*

# Evolution

In the summer of 1858 a scientific paper arrived at Down House in Kent, the home of Charles Darwin, with a request that he should comment on it. The paper was from the Welsh naturalist Alfred Russel Wallace. It outlined his belief, with supporting evidence collected during his work in the Far East, that evolution through **natural selection** could explain the great diversity of species seen on the planet. Natural selection is the process by which animals within a species that are best suited to a changing environment survive and so their characteristics are passed on to following generations.

The choice of Darwin as a critic of this paper was not a coincidence. Darwin had received previous papers on similar topics from Wallace, but this one came as something of a shock. The views expressed by Wallace were an exact match to those in a book Darwin had spent twenty years writing but had not yet published.

# Science and society

Progress in science often needs more than just sound research. Darwin was aware of the importance of his theories, but he was also aware of the effect they could have on society. Not least, they could undermine the authority of the Church at a time when most British people believed in the Bible as a book of literal truths. It has been suggested that Darwin put off publication until his evidence for the theory was too strong to argue against. Certainly, the book he published (1859) was only a fraction of the size of the draft he prepared in 1856 and seemed to be published in a rush. Science does not exist in a moral or cultural vacuum and it can be impossible to separate the activities of scientists from the society in which they work.

Both Darwin and Wallace tried to explain how there are so many different plants and animals on our planet. They decided that a gradual process of change over many millions of years led to the diversity we see today. But there are other ideas.

| Idea | Explanation |
|---|---|
| Saltation | An abrupt change in the appearance of a species usually caused by genetic mutation |
| Special creation | Species created by a divine being |
| Natural creation | Species arising on Earth spontaneously |
| Steady state | Species have always existed – all we see are the numbers changing |

▲ Alternatives to evolution.

▶ *Say whether you agree or disagree with each of the ideas. Can any of them be proved or disproved?*

# The theory of evolution

Charles Darwin made many observations of the natural world. He was fortunate in travelling around the world as an unpaid naturalist aboard the survey ship HMS *Beagle*. This gave him the opportunity to observe plants and animals on different continents. He was also a keen geologist and made a large collection of fossils, particularly in South America. He made thousands of observations and was meticulous in collecting information. His interpretation of the evidence led him to publish *The Origin of Species*.

▶ *Fossils are the preserved hard parts of plants and animals, or the preserved evidence of their presence, such as footprints. Why do you think fossils of bacteria are so rare?*

▲ Charles Darwin.

## Examining the evidence

Darwin was greatly influenced by two authors. Thomas Malthus' *An Essay on the Principle of Population* tried to explain how human populations were kept in check by famine, disease, accident and war. Charles Lyell's *Principles of Geology* argued that fossil evidence suggested a succession of life forms. Lyell argued that fossils show how species changed with time.

Darwin also gave a catalogue of the strange fossils he found including several giant forms of existing mammals such as sloths, camels, rodents and elephant-like creatures, all of which were extinct. He noted too that although the grasslands of South America were far lusher than those of southern Africa, the herbivores living there were generally far smaller.

He noted a possible explanation for the development which was only confirmed in the twentieth century. The present theory is that the area now called Panama was submerged beneath the sea, dividing America into two. This was the first record of Darwin suggesting that a geographical barrier to **migration**, or the movement of large numbers of animals from one place to another, is needed for new species to evolve.

... we see beds of sand, clay and limestone containing sea-shells ... passing into the red clayey earth of the Pampas containing ... bones of terrestrial animals (and a tooth from a horse).

... if we divide America we shall have two zoological provinces strongly contrasting with each other ...

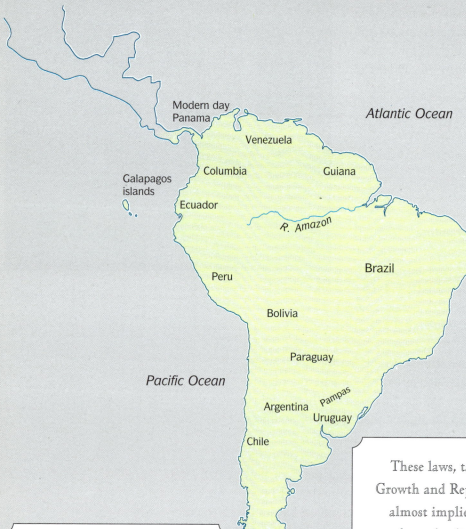

Modern day Panama

Atlantic Ocean

Venezuela

Columbia

Galapagos islands

Guiana

Ecuador

R. Amazon

Brazil

Peru

Bolivia

Paraguay

Pacific Ocean

Pampas

Argentina

Uruguay

Chile

Subsequently to this unusual drought (in which thousands of animals died) a very rainy season commenced, which caused great floods ... thousands of skeletons were buried ... the very next year. What would be the opinion of a geologist, viewing such a collection of bones ... would he not attribute it to a great flood ... rather than the common order of things?

These laws, taken in the largest sense, being Growth and Reproduction; Inheritance, which is almost implied by Reproduction; Variability from the direct and indirect action of the conditions of life, and from use and disuse: a Ratio of Increase so high as to lead to a Struggle for Life, and as a consequence to Natural Selection, entailing Divergence of Character and the Extinction of less-improved forms. Thus, from the war of nature, from famine and death, the most exalted object which we are capable of conceiving, namely, the production of the higher animals, directly follows.

Extracts from two of Darwin's most famous books.

- *Look at the map of South America, and read the extracts from Darwin's works. Try to explain:*
  - **a** *Why the animals of North and South America were so different;*
  - **b** *What causes natural selection;*
  - **c** *How Darwin was influenced by Charles Lyall.*

- *Find out where Darwin visited after leaving the South American mainland.*

## A natural selection model

You may be given a worksheet to help you with this practical.

You can find out about natural selection by examining what would happen if you dropped a handful of different-coloured cocktail sticks into a patch of grass.

You might expect that the colours which contrast with grass (for example, blue and red) were the easiest to find. A bird searching for insects would work in a similar way. Natural selection would tend to favour green insects if they lived in grass.

- *Why are grasshoppers green but woodlice brown?*

## Evolution by natural selection

Darwin's evidence for evolution was drawn from many sources. He was particularly puzzled by the horses' teeth he collected on his travels, suggesting horses had existed in South America before the arrival of the Spanish colonists. The modern evidence from fossils of horse-like animals suggests a gradual process of change, linked to alterations in habitat.

- *Examine the diagram on the next page. Try to explain why the fossil record of the horse changes.*

### Evolution of the horse

One explanation for the evolution of the modern horse might be that, as its environment changed from marshland to open grassland, those animals best suited to the changing environment produced more offspring. This might be simply because they lived longer. Being taller, for example, might allow the animal to find its food or to see predators more easily. Longer legs would also allow it to run faster so proportionally more shorter-legged animals would be killed, removing their genes from the **gene pool**.

In this way over several generations, there would be a drift towards a form best suited to that changing environment, as the genes for long legs become more common.

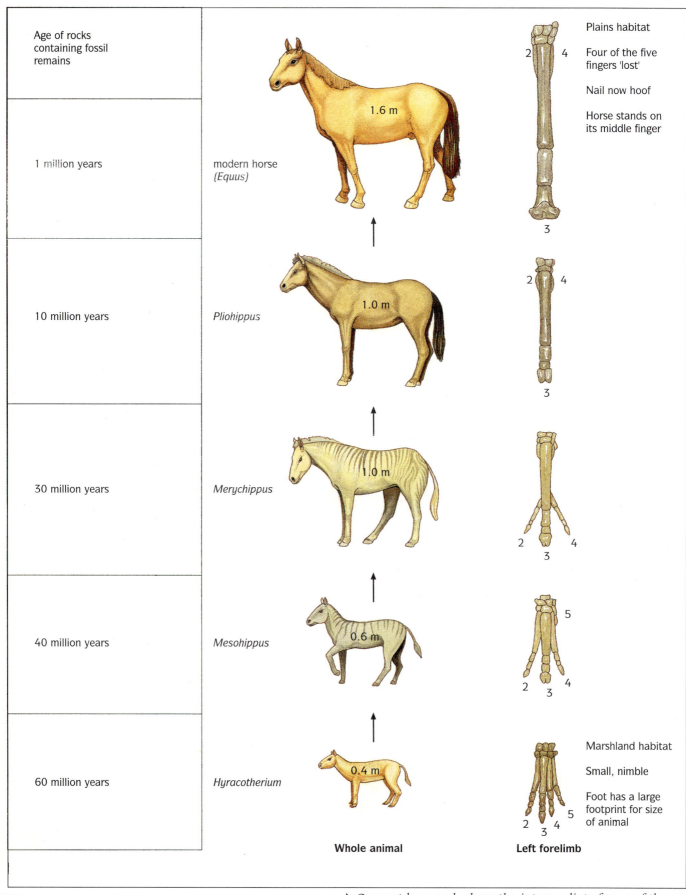

| Age of rocks containing fossil remains | | |
|---|---|---|
| 1 million years | modern horse (*Equus*) | Plains habitat |
| | | Four of the five fingers 'lost' |
| | 1.6 m | Nail now hoof |
| | | Horse stands on its middle finger |
| | | 2  4 |
| | | 3 |
| 10 million years | *Pliohippus* | 2  4 |
| | 1.0 m | 3 |
| 30 million years | *Merychippus* | 2    4 |
| | 1.0 m | 3 |
| 40 million years | *Mesohippus* | 5 |
| | 0.6 m | 2    4 |
| | | 3 |
| 60 million years | *Hyracotherium* | Marshland habitat |
| | 0.4 m | Small, nimble |
| | | Foot has a large footprint for size of animal |
| | | 2  4  5 |
| | | 3 |
| | **Whole animal** | **Left forelimb** |

◤ The possible evolution route for the horse. Fossil specimens were found in successive rock strata.

▶ *Suggest how and where the intermediate forms of the horse might have lived.*

# A synthesis of ideas

Scientists in the twentieth century linked the idea of natural selection to Mendel's work on genetics, suggesting that changes in the genetic code (mutations) become common through selection. This leads to the formation of new species.

This **Neo-Darwinian theory** suggests that evolution is a dynamic process, with each change in the environment placing new pressures on the organisms living there. Mutations in the genetic make-up of an individual are more likely to be passed on to successive generations if these changes give it an advantage over its competitors.

# The survival of the fittest

This process of adaptation and change has been described as the survival of the fittest. Here *fittest* means *fit like a key* rather than healthy. The better the fit of a particular set of genes to the demands of an environment, the greater the likelihood of the organism surviving. The longer an organism lives, the greater chance there is of a particular set of genes being passed on to the next generation. This idea suggests that if the environment changes, any organisms which no longer *fit* will tend to die out.

▶ *Use this part of the theory to explain the extinctions seen in the fossil record.*

▶ *If extinctions are part of the natural scheme of things, why should we worry if plants and animal become extinct?*

# Isolation

Darwin recognised that only if a group of organisms was isolated could these various pressures lead to the evolution of new species. Isolation prevents outbreeding, concentrating the characteristics found in a particular group of organisms. Groups can be isolated by mountains and valleys, rivers and seas, or by their courtship behaviour. On his voyage around the world Darwin spent some time on the Galápagos Islands. This helped him to come to this conclusion about isolation.

▶ *Find the Galápagos Islands on the map on page 150. How are they isolated?*

▶ *Why do you think isolation is so important in the formation of a new species?*

## Other sources of evidence

It is important that scientists look for more than one source of evidence for their theories. There is other evidence for the theory of evolution. **Biochemistry** is the study of chemicals made by living things. Recent work shows that there are families of chemicals found in living things that can be used to reveal relationships between organisms. Also, animals can be placed in related groups using evidence from their **anatomy**, the structure of their bodies. Studies of embryos (**embryology**) also show relationships, as do studies of plant and animal distribution.

▶ *Go back to the table of alternative theories (page 148). Do these additional forms of evidence make one particular alternative more likely than another?*

On its own, no one source of evidence can prove evolution to be true. In fact, scientists can prove nothing to be true. The job of a scientist is to provide models which help us understand our Universe. Darwin's theory of evolution is just that – a model which helps us to understand the world in which we live – but next year, somebody might come up with a better theory.

## Modern alternatives

Darwin's idea of gradual change leading to the formation of new forms does not have it all his own way. Many scientists believe that evolution is not a gradual process, but takes place in fits and starts, a model called **punctuated equilibrium**. This model can be used to explain the rapid extinction of the dinosaurs. Scientists supporting this model believe that the rate of mutation seen in living things is simply too low to account for the vast number of species seen on our planet.

▶ *Can science ever prove evolution, or is it destined to remain a theory forever?*

🔺 *Tyrannosaurus rex.*

# Summary

- The variety of food plants and domestic animals we see on our planet is due to artificial selection.
- Pigeons, cereal crops and roses are examples of organisms where human intervention has produced new forms.
- A species is a group of organisms which can breed successfully only with other members of that group.
- Successful breeding means producing fertile offspring.
- Asexual or vegetative reproduction produces offspring which are identical to the parent.
- Now genetic engineering is being used commercially.
- In 1858 Charles Darwin and Alfred Russel Wallace published a paper describing how pressures on species in their environment leads to natural selection. This idea was developed by Darwin and others into the theory of evolution by natural selection.
- Evolution requires selection pressures and a degree of isolation.
- Selection pressures include predation (being caught by predators), lack of space, food and competition for mates.
- Isolation may be by barriers such as the sea or mountain chains.
- Evolution suggests that those individuals which fit their environment best will be the most likely to pass on their genes (the survival of the fittest). Over many generations this process may lead to the formation of new species.
- The evolution of the horse is one example of where Darwin's theory has been used to explain changes in the fossil record.
- This interaction of a species with its environment is called natural selection.
- Modern theories of evolution link natural selection with changes to an organism's chromosomes called mutations.
- Evidence for evolution comes from fossils, biochemistry, anatomy, embryology and from distribution studies of selected species.
- Not all scientists believe that Darwin's theory, and its modern equivalent, Neo-Darwinism, explains the variety of living things seen on our planet. One alternative theory is punctuated equilibrium, which suggests that evolution proceeds in fits and starts, with long periods of no change punctuated with short intervals of rapid change.
- Punctuated equilibrium can be used to explain the rapid extinction of the dinosaurs.

# Revision Questions

1 Make a list of plants and animals produced by artificial selection. Do they have anything in common?

2 Look back at the photographs of the pigeons.
   a Can they be grouped together into types?
   b Are your types separate species? How would you find out for sure?

3 List the things needed for a new species to occur according to the Neo-Darwininan theory of evolution. Imagine that you have just seen a news report about a new species. Would you guess that it had evolved recently or that it had only just been discovered?

4 What is your appendix? Some scientists say that the appendix is evidence for evolution. They say it is a *vestigial structure,* which means that it no longer has a useful function. Why do vestigial structures provide evidence for evolution?

5 Many people object to the use of animals in experiments and treatments – for example, the genetically engineered pigs with organs for transplanting into humans. Prepare two letters to your Member of Parliament. One should argue for the use of animals in medical research, the other against. Which one would you be most likely to send?

6 Thomas Malthus wrote that human populations were kept in check by famine, disease, accident and war. His book was written two centuries ago. Write an essay with the title, 'Malthus – as true then as now?'

7 A present-day animal, the rock hyrax, is said by many objectors to evolution to be identical to the supposed early ancestor of the horse, Hyracotherium. What evidence would you want to collect before coming to a conclusion about this controversial issue?

8 Darwin and others stated that fossils provide some of the best evidence for evolution. Fossils of the horseshoe crab have been dated to be 350 million years old. They can be found alive today living in the same conditions as we think they lived in all that time ago. Fossils of our human ancestors on the other hand can rarely be dated older than five million years. Try to explain why the horseshoe crab has not evolved but humans have.

# Water for life

Water is a solvent that can dissolve thousands of chemicals.

Water has a high specific heat capacity. This means that there has to be a relatively large change in the surrounding (ambient) temperature to change the temperature of the water. Because of the fairly constant temperature, watery places can be good to live in.

Water behaves strangely when it freezes. Ice has a lower density than liquid water. This means that ice floats on liquid water – a very important fact if you live in a pond.

**Water has many remarkable properties.**

Water cannot be compressed and so containers of water can have great strength.

Water molecules are very *sticky* and can stick tightly to one another. This property is called cohesion.

Water is the stuff of life. Cells are full of it. Your blood is made up of chemicals dissolved in water with large proteins, cells and cell fragments. About one-third of blood is water, not counting the water inside the blood cells. In total, you are about two-thirds water. Plants, and especially their fruits, can contain even more.

Water is needed for most of the chemical reactions occurring in your body, and is used to transport everything from food to the chemical waste produced by its use.

# Review

**Before going any further, read this page and attempt the tasks. Write the answers in your notes.**

Living on land means that you can never be sure where your water supply will come from. Plants and animals which have made their home away from water have special mechanisms for finding and conserving water.

Survival on the Earth's surface can depend on keeping the water held in your body, or finding a source of fresh water.

▲ Beavertail cactus (*Opuntia basilaris*) survives in dry, hostile conditions.

## CHECK ELEVEN

**1** Imagine you have a pen-pal a few years younger than yourself. Your pen-pal is just about to start a topic on plants but wants a head start and has asked you for some notes on plants. Use what you have learnt already about plants to write some notes for your pen-pal using the following headings:

Photosynthesis

Healthy plant growth – include some information on what plants need to remain healthy

Plants and water

Plants and animals

You might find it helpful to look back at earlier chapters.

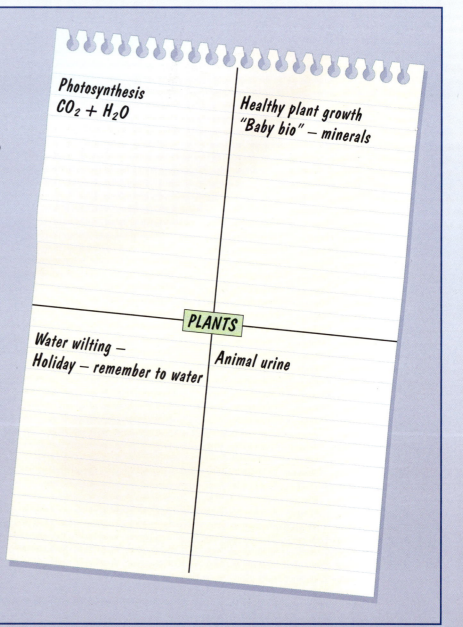

Photosynthesis
$CO_2 + H_2O$

Healthy plant growth
"Baby bio" – minerals

PLANTS

Water wilting –
Holiday – remember to water

Animal urine

# Water for life

Think of all the ways in which you make use of water. You need it to drink, but what about for all those other things you take for granted? Washing and cooking food, keeping clean and growing food. It is needed by industry. Plants also need it as a raw material, for photosynthesis, for support and for the transport of materials.

▶ *List the ways you depend on water. Compare your list to a friend's, add any ideas you missed.*

# Water for strength

Plants are more water than anything else. Water is taken in from the soil, then passes through the plant before being lost to the atmosphere. Eventually this water will fall from the skies as rain or snow, allowing the process to start again. This process is called the **water cycle**.

🔺 Ways of using water.

| | % water | | % water |
|---|---|---|---|
| lettuce | 94 | beetle | 60 |
| strawberry | 89 | humans | 60 |
| potato | 77 | peanut | 5 |

🔺 Percentages of water in a range of living things.

🔺 Litres and litres of water help to hold up these trees.

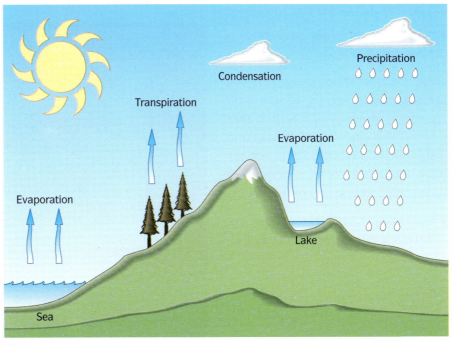

🔺 The water cycle.

BIOLOGY

# How plants use water

Plants need water for three purposes. First, it is the raw material used in photosynthesis as a source of hydrogen. You may read about this in Chapter Twelve (Photosynthesis). This hydrogen is combined with simple carbon compounds to make glucose. As a useful by-product of this process, plants release oxygen into the air.

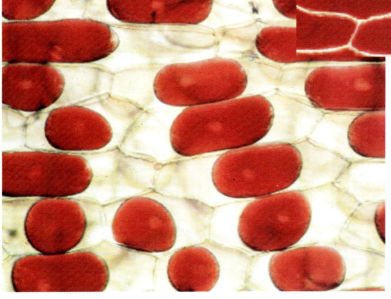

▲ Fully turgid red onion cells, magnified 600 times.

▲ Plasmolysed cells from a red onion, magnified 600 times.

Second, plants use water for support, a bit like a skeleton. Growing upright means a plant has to overcome the force of gravity pulling it back to Earth. The stems of many plants are full of special packing cells called **parenchyma**. These cells are modified to contain water and as long as they are full (**turgid**), the plant will remain upright but if a plant gets too little water, it might wilt or shrivel. This is called **plasmolysis**.

▶ *What happens to the cells when a plant wilts?*

Third, because water is such a good solvent, plants use it to transport chemicals. Minerals such as iron salts and nitrates, and sugars dissolved in water are moved rapidly about the plant through a complex network of tubes called **xylem** and **phloem**.

▶ *List three ways plants use water. Explain why each is so important to the plant.*

▲ In a wilting plant parenchyma cells are no longer turgid.

# Water from the soil

The amount of water in soil depends on many factors. You may read about soil structure and its importance to plants in Chapter Thirteen (Farming and cycles). Soil consists of minerals and decaying plant matter (humus) separated by 'air' spaces. These spaces can contain air or water.

Too much air, and the plants will not be able to take in enough water. Too much water, and the plants will not be able to get enough oxygen into their roots to support respiration. This means the roots will not have enough energy to grow healthily.

▶ *List some of the factors controlling the size and quantity of the spaces between soil particles.*

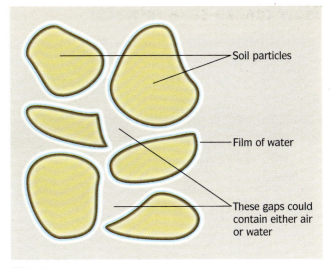

Soil particles.

# Estimating water in a soil sample

You may be given a worksheet to help you with this practical.

To discover the amount of water in a soil sample is relatively easy. You heat carefully a known mass of soil and discover its loss in mass.

▶ *Before you begin the practical, carry out a risk assessment for this activity. What particular safety precautions should be taken to prevent accident or injury?*

▶ *Estimate the percentage of water in this sample.*

| Mass of soil before drying | 12.4 grams |
|---|---|
| Mass of soil after drying | 9.8 grams |

▲ Results obtained by a group doing a similar experiment.

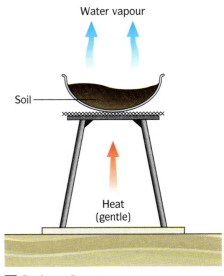

▲ Drying soil.

## Humus

The percentage of water in a particular soil sample depends on a number of things. The amount of water received by the soil is important but so is the soil type. Soils rich in sand drain quickly and so water passes through them rapidly. This process can be slowed down by increasing the percentage of organic material in the soil. This organic matter is called **humus**. The percentage of humus in soil can be determined by roasting a dried soil sample in a crucible and discovering the loss of mass. You may carry out this practical in Chapter Thirteen (Farming and cycles).

# Investigating plants and soils

You may be able to develop this into an investigation. Some possible questions might include:

▶ *At what percentage of soil water does a certain houseplant begin to wilt?*

▶ *Does the type of soil influence the water content?*

▶ *How can you reduce the number of times you have to water your houseplants?*

# How plants take in water

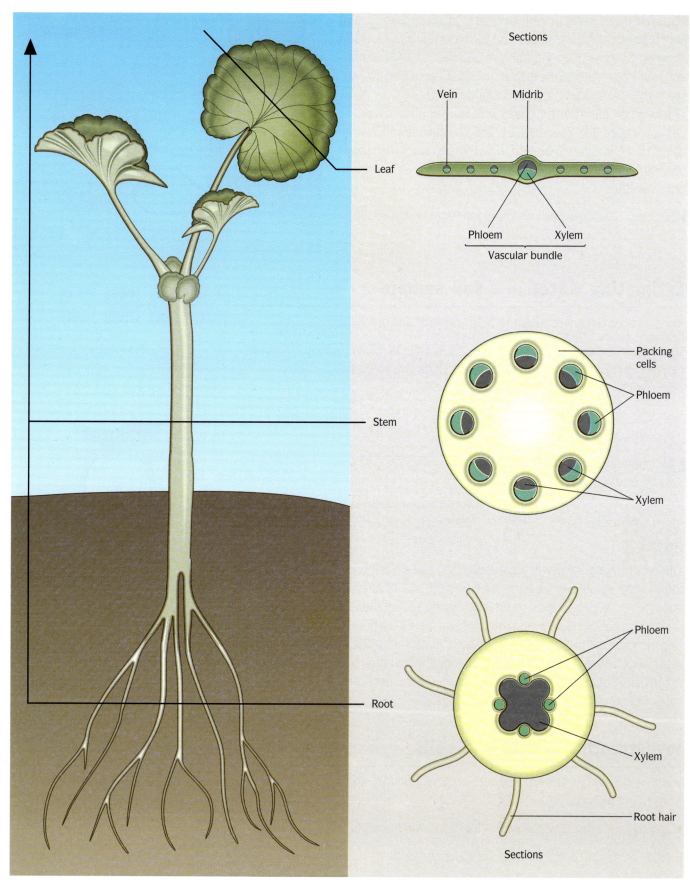

Sections

Vein    Midrib

Phloem    Xylem

Vascular bundle

Packing cells

Phloem

Xylem

Leaf

Stem

Root

Phloem

Xylem

Root hair

Sections

▲ Water enters through the roots, moves up through the stem and passes out from the leaves.

# Roots

The many branches of a plant's roots anchor it in the soil. The roots of a large tree will occupy a soil volume of many hundreds of cubic metres. Roots also have the ability to detect and grow towards water. The ability to grow towards water is called a **hydrotropism**. You may read about other plant growth responses in Chapter Seven (Hormones).

Plants need little more than light, carbon dioxide, water and a good supply of minerals to grow healthily. Roots have many special features which allow them to collect water, and the minerals dissolved in it, from the soil.

> This fact has been taken advantage of in the process called **hydroponics**. Plants are grown without soil in a solution that contains everything they need.

## Roots and osmosis

You may have read how water moves into plant cells by osmosis in Chapter Two (Cells). Root cells are rich in salts and sugars and so water tends to enter from the soil by osmosis. Scientists are still not entirely clear as to how water and the salts dissolved in it reaches the water-transporting tissue, the **xylem**.

🔺 There is probably more of a tree below the soil than above!

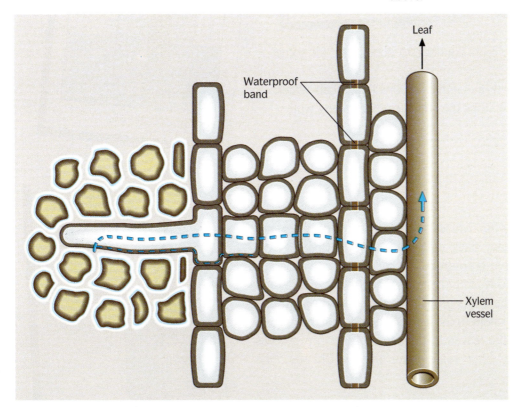

🔺 One possible route for water entering the xylem.

> ▶ Copy the drawing of the root cells. Use different coloured crayons or felt-tip pens to show the possible routes for water to take from the soil to the water-transporting tissues of the xylem.

# The evidence

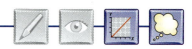

Here are some extracts from an investigation undertaken by a group of students. They were investigating how water passes from the soil into the xylem. Read the extracts and write down your conclusion to each observation.

1 A cut stem will still ooze water from its top if the roots are placed in water.

2 This process continues if the water is aerated – for example, by using an air pump from a fish tank – but will eventually slow and then stop as the oxygen level drops.

3 The process is affected by the temperature. Up to a point, the higher the temperature, the faster the process.

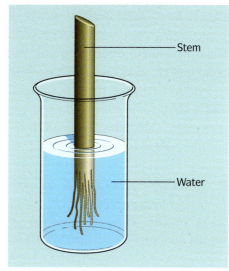

▲ Cut stem in water.

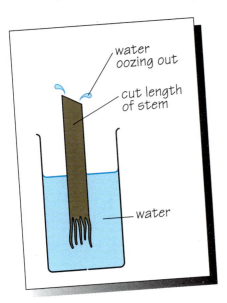

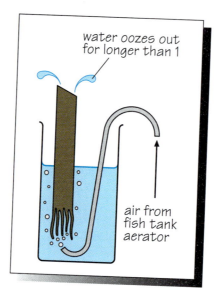

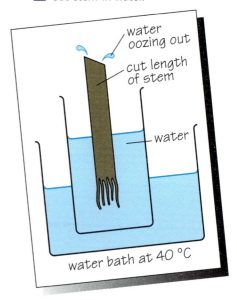

4 Dead lengths of stems with no roots continue to ooze water for some time.

5 Treating the roots of a plant with metabolic poisons (chemicals which stop the process of respiration) stops the stems from pumping water.

▶ *Can you think of any other experiments which might help solve the problem?*

## Active transport

These results suggest that energy is involved in the transport of water and minerals through a plant. You may have read about this in Chapter Two (Cells). The process is called **active transport**.

Scientists believe that water passes into the roots along the root hairs and towards the centre of the root where it is probably actively pumped into the xylem. Water moves through the xylem to the leaves where it may be used in photosynthesis or lost through the leaves to the atmosphere in a process called **transpiration**. You may have read about this in Chapter One (Experiments and investigations).

▶ *Why do plants have root hairs?*

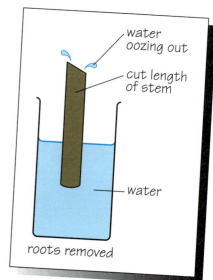

# Xylem

If you have ever eaten a piece of celery and got stringy bits caught between your teeth you know how tough xylem can be! Those stringy bits are the xylem, the woody part of a stem.

Xylem is dead tissue. Plant cell walls consist mostly of a chemical called **cellulose**. The cellulose cell wall of a plant cell is **porous**, full of microscopic holes. This means that chemicals, including water, can pass freely through it into the cell, keeping it alive. Cells which are destined to form the xylem produce a second chemical, **lignin**. Lignin is very hard and waterproof and fills in these tiny pores. The cell wall becomes waterproof and so chemicals can no longer reach the cell. It dies, forming a hollow structure called a xylem vessel.

This process occurs in chains of cells from the roots to the leaves forming hollow strands of dead, waterproof material reaching from the root of the plant to just below the growing point. This network of tubes, called xylem vessels, connected end to end forms the xylem. Pores develop in the vessel walls allowing water to enter and exit. Extra lignin may also be laid down in the vessel walls to help the xylem support the plant.

▶ *Write down why you think xylem vessels are arranged in different ways.*

▲ Water-based dye flowing through the xylem.

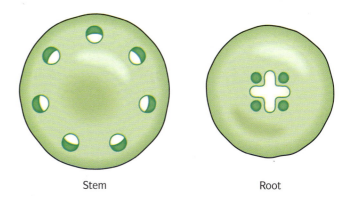

Stem             Root

▲ The arrangement of xylem in the root and stem.

# Wood

Some plants may contain threads of solid lignin or cellulose in their stems for extra support. These threads are called **fibres**. This mixture of vessels and fibres, with the associated packing cells and other stem materials, is better known as wood. It has been an important building material for millions of years and not just for humans.

▲ Rooks build their nests from woody twigs.

# Transpiration

Unlike conifers, which are evergreen, deciduous trees shed their leaves in the autumn. This reduces the amount of water they lose, even though it also prevents them from photosynthesising. Leaves are the organs of photosynthesis. You may read about this in Chapter Twelve (Photosynthesis). As well as needing light and chlorophyll, they need a supply of water and carbon dioxide. Leaves are able to control the flow of water through a plant by opening and closing special pores called **stomata.** Usually, these are found on the underside of the leaf.

▶ *Marram grass is specially adapted to live in very harsh conditions. Its stomata are buried away inside its rolled leaf. How might this reduce water loss?*

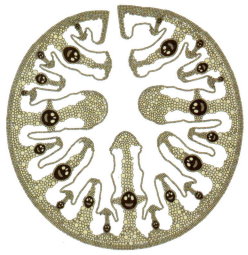

▲ Marram grass grows on sand dunes where fresh water is very scarce.

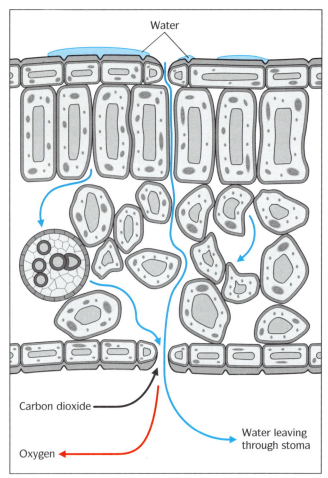

▲ Water reaches the leaf through the xylem. Carbon dioxide enters and oxygen exits via the stomata. It is these stomata that play such a vital role in the transport of water and minerals through the plant.

# Investigating stomata

Investigate the distribution of stomata on a leaf. You may be given a worksheet to help you with this practical.

▶ *If you compare the numbers and distribution of stomata from either side of the leaf, what do you notice?*

### Stomata distribution

You might have discovered that the distribution of stomata is unequal with many more being observed on the underside of the leaf, if you used a land or terrestrial plant.

▶ *Look back at the diagram of the leaf*
   **a** *What do you see on the upper surface of the leaf?*
   **b** *What does this tell you about the regulation of water loss from a leaf?*

By now, you should have discovered that water enters a plant through its roots, is moved through the xylem to the leaf, and leaves through the stomata, the process called transpiration.

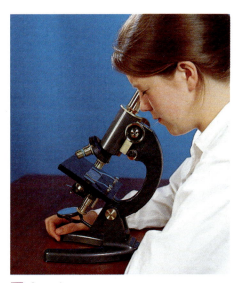

▲ Counting stomata.

# How stomata work

Scientists are still not clear as to exactly how stomata work. These are some of the facts discovered so far:

It is known that stomata contain chloroplasts and that they can photosynthesise. You may read about photsynthesis in Chapter Twelve (Photosynthesis). This would increase the amount of sugar in the stomata cells during the day. An increase in sugar content would also increase the water content of the cell as water would enter by osmosis.

It can be observed that the cell wall on the inner surface of stomata is much thicker than the wall on the outer surface. This would make the guard cells bend as they took in water, so opening the pore.

It has also been demonstrated that certain mineral ions from certain minerals can be moved into and out of the guard cells by active transport. This would also control the opening and closing of the pores, by altering the osmotic potential of the guard cells.

▶ *Write a step-by-step account explaining how stomata work.*

▶ *Scientists have shown that temperature, number of leaves and air flow rates (wind) all have significant effects on the rate of transpiration. Explain why each of these factors should affect the rate of transpiration.*

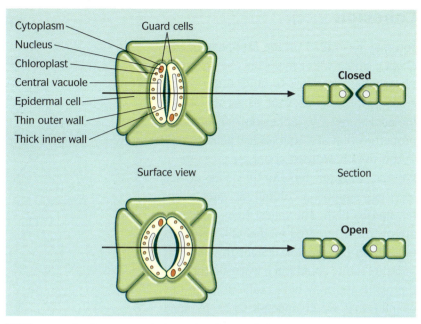

Cytoplasm
Nucleus
Chloroplast
Central vacuole
Epidermal cell
Thin outer wall
Thick inner wall

Guard cells

Closed

Open

Surface view

Section

▲ The guard cells open and close, thereby regulating the amount of water lost.

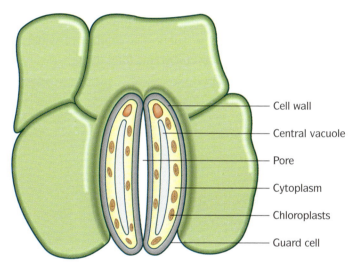

Cell wall
Central vacuole
Pore
Cytoplasm
Chloroplasts
Guard cell

▲ Chloroplasts inside the guard cells produce sugars by photosynthesis.

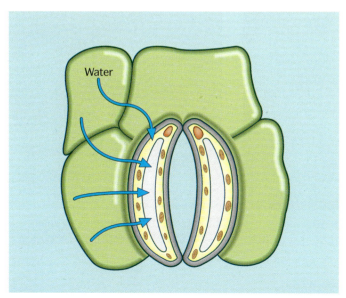

Water

▲ Water enters the guard cells by osmosis causing them to swell. The pore opens.

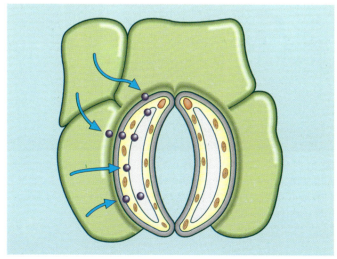

▲ Ions move into the cells causing more water to enter by osmosis. The pore opens further.

## Cohesion

You may have read on the first page of this chapter about water molecules being *sticky*. Water molecules stick to other water molecules (cohesion) as well as to any other molecules nearby (adhesion). It is these properties that are exploited by plants.

You may have read about air pressure in Physics, Chapter Ten. Air pressure at sea level will support a column of water about ten metres high. The tallest trees, however, are over one hundred metres tall, ten times taller than the greatest height to which air pressure alone could force water up through the plant. You may have read earlier in this chapter that water appears to be pumped into the base of the xylem by active transport. The 'push' of water entering the xylem, along with the 'pull' from transpiration, must be great enough to support a column of water of over 100m. This would have a mass of several grams (and the downward force it applies).

### STICKY WATER MOLECULES

Water molecules

O — Strong bond (covalent bond)

Weak bond (hydrogen bond)

Popper beads

▲ In 1895 a Douglas fir was cut down with a reported height of 129 metres. Although not confirmed, this is the tallest tree ever recorded.

▲ Giant sequoias can have a circumference of 30 metres, 1.2 metres above their base.

▲ A bristlecone pine in the Arizona desert has been dated at four thousand years old.

# Investigating water loss

When stomata are open, water evaporates from the underside of the leaf. Investigate what affects the rate of water loss from the underside of a leaf.

Possible things to consider include the type of plant, the number of stomata, the temperature and air movement near the underside of the leaf.

## Transpiration stream

You can estimate the rate of water flow through a plant, the **transpiration stream**, by using a water-soluble dye (such as eosin) and timing how long it takes to move between two points.

Another way is to allow uptake from a capillary tube and to measure the rate of movement of a bubble along that tube.

▶ *What assumptions have to be made when using a potometer?*

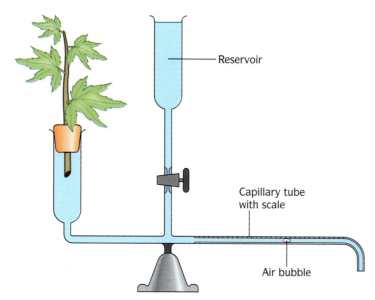

Reservoir

Capillary tube
with scale

Air bubble

🔺 A potometer.

# Evapotranspiration

The term **evapotranspiration** is used to cover more than just water loss from plants. Every second of every day millions of litres of water evaporate from rivers, lakes and seas to add to the total amount of water vapour in the air. This vapour will condense, fall as rain or snow (**precipitation**) and find its way back, possibly into plants and animals. This process is called the water cycle. You have read about the water cycle earlier in this chapter.

# Summary

- Water is used by plants for photosynthesis, strength and support, and for transport.
- Water is taken in through the roots of a plant.
- Root hairs are tiny extensions in the surface of root cells. Root hairs increase the surface area of the roots.
- The greater the surface area, the greater the rate of water uptake into the plant.
- Scientists believe that water enters plant roots by a mixture of diffusion and active transport.
- Evidence for active transport comes from observations that oxygen is needed for uptake and that the rate of water uptake is temperature-dependent.
- Water is transported through the plant in special tissues called xylem vessels.
- Vessels and other tissues make up the xylem.
- Xylem is dead. It adds great strength to a plant.
- Water is a sticky (cohesive) molecule and can form chains many metres long inside a vessel.
- Deciduous trees lose their leaves in winter. This helps water conservation. Other plants conserve water by having rolled leaves, or leaves which are reduced in size.
- The flow of water through a plant is called transpiration.
- Pores called stomata in the leaf regulate the rate of transpiration. Scientists are unsure how stomata work but know that they are able to open and close in response to changes in their environment.
- The rate of transpiration is also affected by temperature, air movements, the rate of air flow across the underside of the leaf and the type of plant.
- The constant recycling of water in the environment is called the water cycle.

# Revision Questions

**1** List some reasons why water is needed for life.

**2** A book on gardening for beginners suggests that it is best to water plants last thing in the evening so that the water has a chance to soak into the soil.
  **a** What might happen to the water if you watered in the morning?
  **b** Write a section for the Beginner's Gardening Book called 'Why your plants might wilt'.

**3** Some celery was prepared for tea. To keep it fresh, the cut ends of the leaves were placed in water. By tea-time the celery appeared to have grown in size.
  **a** Explain what had happened.
  **b** What might have happened if the water was salted?

**4** Write notes for a friend who missed this chapter through illness. Your notes should detail the key points under what you think are the most important headings. Use no more than one side of A4 paper.

**5** A student had a great idea. She added blue food colouring to the water containing a bunch of white carnations. The next morning, the flowers had turned blue. Explain what had happened.
(You might be able to try this experiment at home, but ask permission first.)

**6 a** Make a large copy of the water cycle.
  **b** How does human activity interfere with the water cycle?

**7** How does the layout of the xylem in the root differ from the pattern seen in the stem? Why do you think there is this difference?

**8** Draw three different types of plant cell. Say how each is adapted to its particular job.

**9** A student made the following observations when investigating transpiration. He measured how far a bubble moved along a scale on a potometer containing a plant cutting under different conditions.

Analyse his results for him, attempting to explain each one.

| Conditions | Movement (cm) |
|---|---|
| Hair dryer (cold) | 6.4 |
| Hair dryer (hot) | 9.7 |
| Radiant heater | 5.5 |
| Bright light | 4.9 |
| Control (bench top) | 3.2 |

▲ Student's results.

**10** A student collected data over 24 hours relating to the movement of water through a plant.
  **a** Look at her results and plot them on a suitable graph.
  **b** Analyse them, attempting to explain the pattern.

| Time | Relative rate of water flow |
|---|---|
| 3 a.m. | 2 |
| 6 a.m. | 5 |
| 9 a.m. | 15 |
| 12 noon | 30 |
| 3 p.m. | 24 |
| 6 p.m. | 15 |
| 9 p.m. | 7 |
| Midnight | 1 |

▲ Date of experiment: 22 June

  **c** Draw a second line on your graph representing the pattern you would expect to see for 22 December.

**11** A student counted the stomata on either side of a leaf using a microscope. On the top surface of the leaf, an average of one per field of view was seen. On the underside there were so many he decided to divide his field of view into four and count all the stomata in a quarter of the field. He counted 120. He compared this count to a friend's. The friend saw 134. The field of view was approximately $3\,mm^2$.
  **a** Estimate the number of stomata on each side of the leaf if the leaf had a surface area of $5\,cm^3$. Show all the stages in your calculations.
  **b** Comment on the way he tried to ensure his results were fair.

**12**

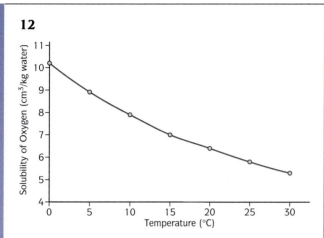

🔺 The relationship between the oxygen content of water and its temperature.

A student measured the concentration of oxygen in distilled water at different temperatures using an oxygen probe connected to a computer. She then plotted the graph shown above.

    **a** What general pattern can be seen from this graph?

    **b** She was investigating a stream near her school. A local factory had started discharging warm water into the stream. Predict some of the effects of this discharge on the stream.

**13** Why is water wet? Answer in as much detail as possible.

# *Photosynthesis*

All living things need a supply of energy to allow them to move, grow and reproduce. Some scientists believe that the very first living things on this planet were blue-green algae. They were simple single-celled organisms with a very special ability. They were able to trap the Sun's light energy and use it to make food.

## ■ Energy for life

It is thought that all other living things on this planet eventually evolved, over millions of years, from simple algae. Some living things lost the ability to trap the Sun's energy. These organisms had to get their energy by eating others. This group of organisms is called animals. Others retained the ability to use the Sun's energy and are called plants.

Plants play a vital role in all our lives. They provide the food we need to move, grow and reproduce. They also provide the oxygen that we need to turn the chemical energy in food into energy that we can use.

In this chapter you will look in detail at the process of photosynthesis and see how scientists have discovered more about it. You will find out how plant growers can control a plant's environment to maximise photosynthesis and so produce more food. You will also look at how some very recent research into the process of photosynthesis could lead to the production of a non-polluting renewable fuel.

# Review

## CHECK TWELVE

**Before going any further, read this page and attempt the tasks. Write the answers in your notes.**

**1** Look at the diagram below of a typical plant.

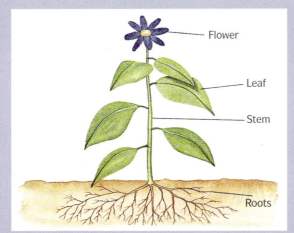

Copy and complete this table showing the job done by the different parts of the plant.

| Part of plant | Job done |
| --- | --- |
| Leaf | |
| Stem | |
| Roots | |
| Flower | |

**2** The diagram of a leaf below shows some important features which allow the leaf to do its job. Look at each feature in turn and explain why it is important.

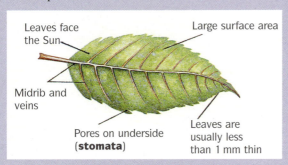

**3** Copy the diagram below of a plant cell and label the following parts:

nucleus   cell wall   cell membrane
chloroplast   cytoplasm   cell vacuole

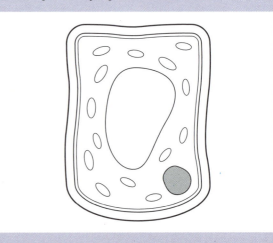

**4** Photosynthesis can be summarised by the following word equation:

$$\text{water} + \text{carbon dioxide} \xrightarrow[\text{chlorophyll}]{\text{light energy}} \text{glucose} + \text{oxygen}$$

Explain in your own words what this word equation tells you about photosynthesis.

**5** Copy and complete the sentences below. Choose words from the following list to fill in the gaps:

sound   light   heat   energy
electrical   potential   chemical

Plants perform a very important _____ transfer. They take in _____ energy from the Sun and convert it to _____ energy in glucose.

# Photosynthesis

Plants are able to use the light energy from the Sun to convert simple, readily-available chemicals into energy-rich compounds which they can use as food. Water from the soil and carbon dioxide from the air are combined to produce glucose. The light energy needed for this reaction is captured by the green pigment in the leaves called **chlorophyll**. This process is called **photosynthesis**.

Energy from the Sun is essential for photosynthesis. The glucose made in photosynthesis is important as it can be broken down to provide energy or it can be converted into more complex substances such as starch, fats or protein. Reactions like photosynthesis which take in energy are called **endothermic** reactions. Photosynthesis is the most important endothermic reaction on Earth. You may have read about endothermic reactions in Chemistry, Chapter Twelve.

## The role of starch

A starch molecule is made up of hundreds or thousands of glucose molecules linked together in a long chain. This long chain then curls up on itself forming a very compact molecule which looks a bit like a spring. Glucose molecules are very small, soluble and quite reactive. If there is excess glucose in a leaf it is turned into starch. Starch is insoluble and very compact and therefore an ideal way of storing glucose. The starch forms microscopic grains which can be seen inside cells. This store of glucose can be broken down and used when energy is needed.

## Testing a leaf for starch

This is a fairly simple procedure. This is why you test leaves for starch rather than glucose if you want to find out if the leaf has been photosynthesising. If starch is present the leaf will go blue-black when iodine solution is added.

You will probably test a leaf for starch. The basic method is outlined below.

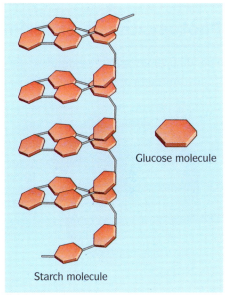

Glucose molecule

Starch molecule

▲ Glucose and starch molecules.

▶ *Explain why each of the steps shown is necessary.*

⚠ Ethanol is flammable.

1  Boil the leaf in water until it is limp

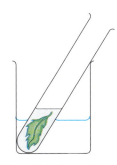

2  Turn off the heat. Place a test tube of ethanol in the beaker of hot water. Add the softened leaf

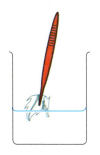

3  Gently remove the leaf from the ethanol when the green colour has disappeared. Rinse it in the water to soften it.

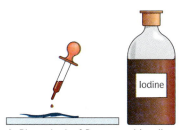

4  Place the leaf flat on a white tile and add iodine solution

▲ Starch test on a leaf.

# Investigating photosynthesis

Scientists have researched the process of photosynthesis for hundreds of years. The basic facts are now taken very much for granted. Using the latest technology scientists can now investigate what happens during photosynthesis at a molecular level. Early scientists did not have modern technology to help them. They had to use simple experiments, careful observation and logic to help them understand photosynthesis. The experiments they did are still of great value today.

## Photosynthesis experiments

The diagrams below summarise three experiments which tell you some important facts about photosynthesis.

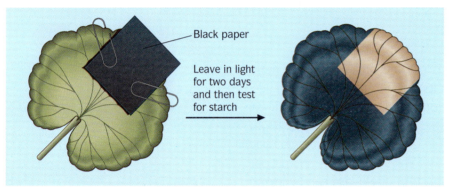

▲ Experiment one.

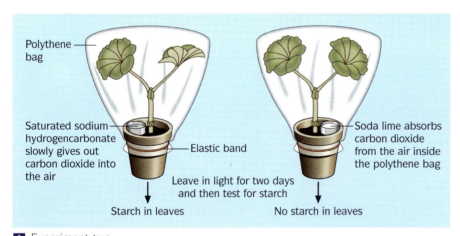

▲ Experiment two.

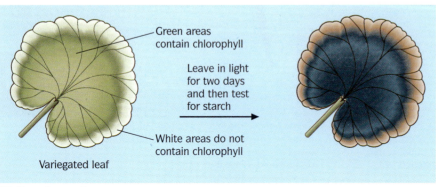

▲ Experiment three.

▶ Look carefully at how each experiment was set up and examine the results that were obtained.

▶ Try to explain what each experiment is designed to prove.

▶ Before the start of these experiments the plants are kept in the dark for two days. Why?

▶ Write a few sentences summarising what these experiments reveal about photosynthesis.

# Products of photosynthesis

The products of photosynthesis are oxygen and glucose. Starch is present in leaves that have been photosynthesising. Starch is made from glucose.

Joseph Priestley (1771) was the first scientist to demonstrate that plants give out oxygen.

| A lighted candle in the jar quickly goes out | A sprig of mint is put in the jar and left in the light for about a week | A lighted candle will burn inside the jar |

🔺 Priestley's experiment.

▸ *Look carefully at the diagram. Can you work out how this experiment proves that oxygen is produced?*

Priestley did not know about oxygen. In his account of this experiment he explained that plants were able to 'restore' the air which had been 'injured' by the burning of candles.

▸ *Imagine that you have travelled back in time and Mr Priestley has just presented you with the results of his experiment. Write a note to him explaining:*
   **a** *the difference between 'restored' and 'injured' air*
   **b** *the plant's role in this transformation.*

The pondweed, *Elodea*, can also be used to show that oxygen gas is produced in photosynthesis. A piece of *Elodea* in water will produce bubbles of gas when a light is shone on to it. These bubbles can be collected.

▸ *How can you prove that the gas collected is oxygen?*

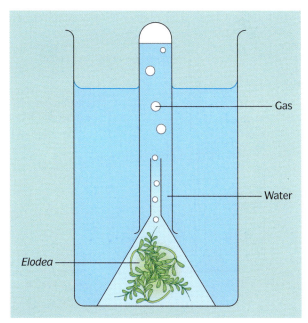

Gas

Water

Elodea

🔺 Apparatus for the *Elodea* experiment.

# An equation for photosynthesis

Photosynthesis can be summarised in this equation:

$$\text{carbon dioxide} + \text{water} \xrightarrow[\text{chlorophyll}]{\text{light energy}} \text{glucose} + \text{oxygen}$$

$$6CO_2 + 6H_2O \longrightarrow C_6H_{12}O_6 + 6O_2$$

Carbon dioxide and water are the raw materials and glucose and oxygen are the products. The energy needed to combine the raw materials comes from the Sun. Chlorophyll's job is to trap light energy from the Sun so that it can be used in photosynthesis.

The amount of light, the concentration of carbon dioxide and the temperature can all affect the rate of photosynthesis.

Animals are dependent on plants for food and oxygen. They break down sugars using oxygen. Plants use our waste products – carbon dioxide and water – and turn them back into sugars and oxygen. This is the basis of the **carbon cycle.** You may read about the carbon cycle in Chapter Thirteen (Farming and cycles).

## Investigating the rate of photosynthesis

As oxygen is a product of photosynthesis, the rate at which *Elodea* produces oxygen bubbles can give you an idea of how fast photosynthesis is occurring. If you compare the rate of bubble production in different conditions, you can find out what factors affect the rate of photosynthesis. Think about what is needed for photosynthesis and what factors might affect its rate. The diagram below may give you some ideas. Plan and carry out an investigation to test one of your ideas. Check your plan with your teacher before you start.

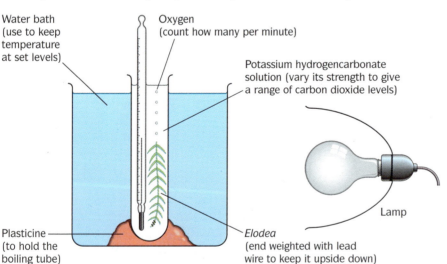

Water bath (use to keep temperature at set levels)

Oxygen (count how many per minute)

Potassium hydrogencarbonate solution (vary its strength to give a range of carbon dioxide levels)

Lamp

Plasticine (to hold the boiling tube)

*Elodea* (end weighted with lead wire to keep it upside down)

Ruler (use to measure distance of light from *Elodea*, convert to light intensity using a light meter)

🔺 The basic experiment with hints on how to change different variables.

The chemical equation for photosynthesis shows that:

- carbon dioxide ($CO_2$) contains carbon (C) and oxygen (O)
- water ($H_2O$) contains hydrogen (H) and oxygen (O)
- glucose ($C_6H_{12}O_6$) contains carbon, hydrogen and oxygen.

The carbon in the glucose must come from carbon dioxide. The hydrogen must come from water but the equation does not reveal where the oxygen comes from.

Scientists can now label atoms and follow their path through a chemical process, like photosynthesis, using very sensitive instruments. If a plant is given water which contains **labelled oxygen**, the labelled oxygen appears in the air around the plant. If it is fed with carbon dioxide containing labelled oxygen, the labelled oxygen is found in the glucose and starch inside the plant. These experiments show that the oxygen in the glucose molecule comes from carbon dioxide. The oxygen which is released comes from water.

| | unlabelled | | | |
|---|---|---|---|---|
| water containing + | carbon | $\longrightarrow$ | glucose + | labelled |
| labelled oxygen | dioxide | | | oxygen |

$$6H_2O^* \quad + \quad 6CO_2 \longrightarrow C_6H_{12}O_6 + \quad 6O_2^*$$

| unlabelled + | carbon dioxide | $\longrightarrow$ | labelled + | unlabelled |
|---|---|---|---|---|
| water | containing labelled | | glucose | oxygen |
| | oxygen | | | |

$$6H_2O \quad + \quad 6CO_2^* \longrightarrow C_6H_{12}O_6^* + \quad 6O_2$$

> There is a rare form of oxygen whose atoms are slightly heavier than normal oxygen atoms. We call this form of oxygen an **isotope** and it can be detected using a instrument called a **mass spectrometer**. The oxygen is referred to as *heavy* or labelled oxygen. An isotope of carbon which is radioactive has been used to follow the path of carbon atoms in plants.
> You can read about isotopes in Physics, Chapter Fifteen.

## Using radioactive isotopes to study photosynthesis

You may be given a worksheet to help you look closer at the process of photosynthesis.

## Two stages of photosynthesis

Photosynthesis occurs in two stages. In the first stage water is split into oxygen and hydrogen. This process can only occur if light *and* chlorophyll are present. This is called the **light stage**.

In the second stage the hydrogen is combined with carbon dioxide to produce glucose. This stage can happen without light so it is called the **dark stage**.

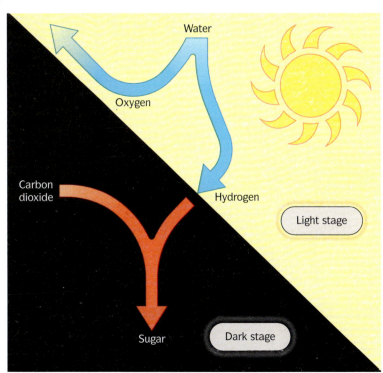

Light and dark stages of photosynthesis.

# Chlorophyll

To understand more about chlorophyll you have to know a little about light. White light can be split into a spectrum of colours by passing it through a triangular prism. The colours you see are the colours of the rainbow; red, orange, yellow, green, blue, indigo and violet.

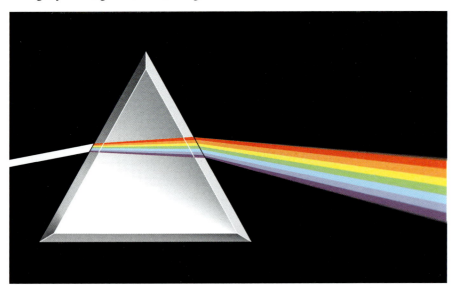

▲ The colours of the spectrum.

If you pass white light through a solution of chlorophyll and then split it into a spectrum, some colours are missing. These are the colours which the chlorophyll molecule has absorbed. This allows you to produce an **absorption spectrum** for chlorophyll.

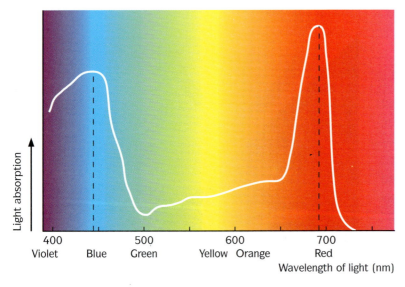

▲ Absorption spectrum of chlorophyll.

1 nm = 1 nanometre
= $10^{-6}$ millimetre

▶ Look carefully at the absorption spectrum of chlorophyll.
  **a** Which colours does chlorophyll absorb?
  **b** Which does it reflect?
▶ Why do leaves look green?

# Investigating plant pigments

You may be given a worksheet to help you extract and analyse chlorophyll from different plants.

BIOLOGY

The diagram shows some of the possible fates of a glucose molecule produced in photosynthesis. The path taken will depend on the plant's requirements at the time.

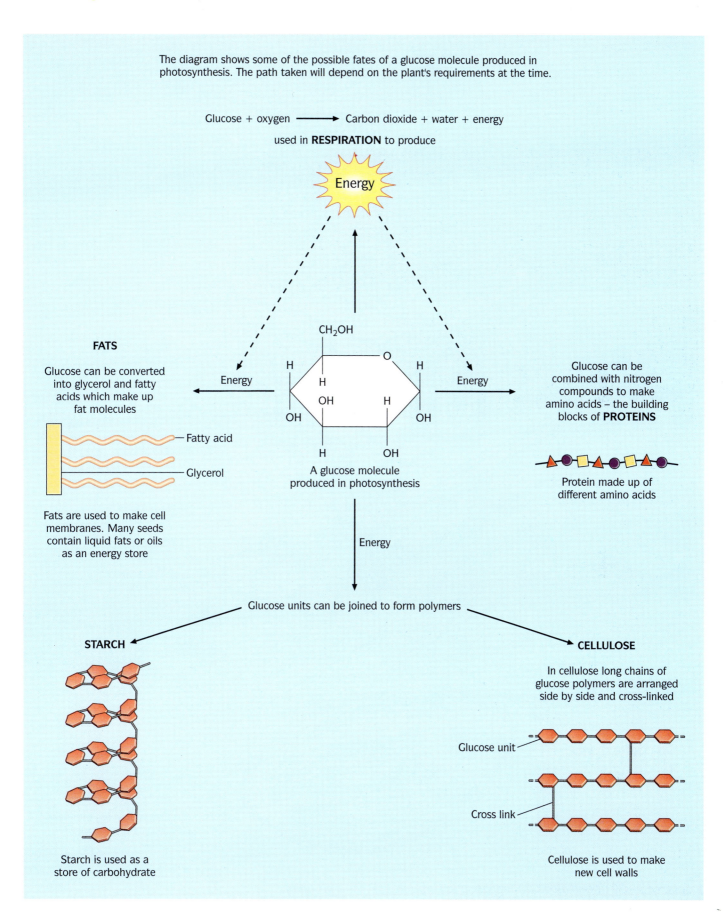

Glucose + oxygen ⟶ Carbon dioxide + water + energy

used in **RESPIRATION** to produce

Energy

**FATS**

Glucose can be converted into glycerol and fatty acids which make up fat molecules

Fatty acid

Glycerol

Fats are used to make cell membranes. Many seeds contain liquid fats or oils as an energy store

CH₂OH

A glucose molecule produced in photosynthesis

Energy

Energy

Glucose can be combined with nitrogen compounds to make amino acids – the building blocks of **PROTEINS**

Protein made up of different amino acids

Glucose units can be joined to form polymers

**STARCH**

Starch is used as a store of carbohydrate

**CELLULOSE**

In cellulose long chains of glucose polymers are arranged side by side and cross-linked

Glucose unit

Cross link

Cellulose is used to make new cell walls

▶ *Use the information in this diagram to draw up a table showing what might happen to a glucose molecule produced during photosynthesis.*

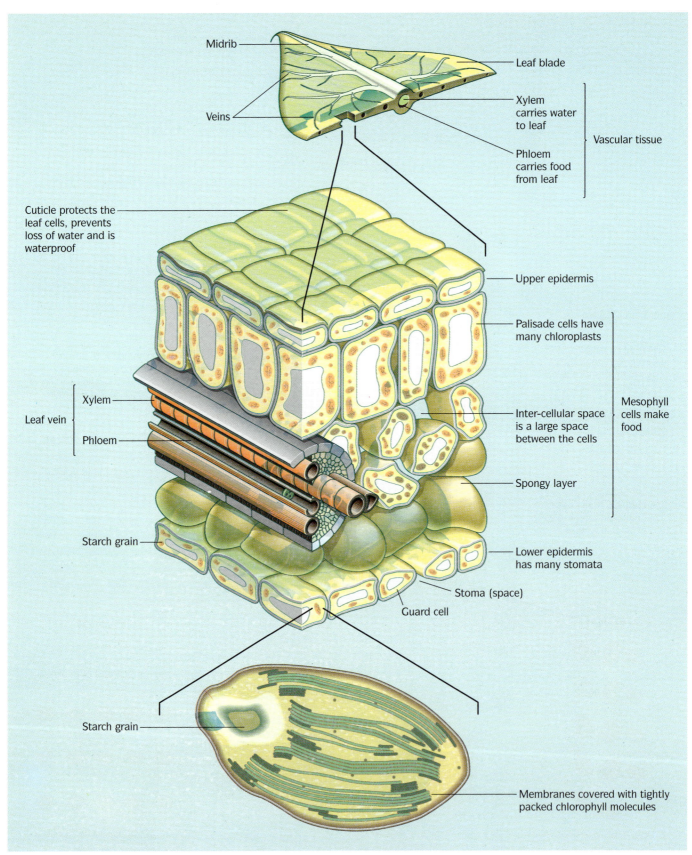

Midrib

Leaf blade

Veins

Xylem carries water to leaf

Phloem carries food from leaf

Vascular tissue

Cuticle protects the leaf cells, prevents loss of water and is waterproof

Upper epidermis

Palisade cells have many chloroplasts

Leaf vein

Xylem

Phloem

Inter-cellular space is a large space between the cells

Mesophyll cells make food

Spongy layer

Starch grain

Lower epidermis has many stomata

Stoma (space)

Guard cell

Starch grain

Membranes covered with tightly packed chlorophyll molecules

▶ *Look carefully at this diagram. Prepare a ten-minute talk for a group of 12-year-olds who are studying photosynthesis. In your talk you need to use simple language and simple pictures to explain how leaves are perfectly adapted for photosynthesis.*

# Rate of photosynthesis

Sarah Bennett grows lettuces to sell to supermarkets. The supermarkets demand that the lettuces have large heads with plenty of leaves. To grow high-quality lettuces as quickly as possible Sarah has to ensure that her plants photosynthesise at the maximum rate whenever possible. To photosynthesise efficiently plants need to have a good supply of raw materials – water and carbon dioxide – plenty of light and a suitable temperature.

## Light

In the summer there is usually plenty of bright sunlight. Sarah has installed fluorescent lights to provide artificial sunlight at night and in the less sunny winter months.

▲ Sarah Bennett is able to control the environment in her greenhouses.

## Investigating light

You may have read about or even carried out an investigation into the factors which affect the rate of photosynthesis, using the water plant called *Elodea*, earlier in this chapter.

▸ *How could you use* Elodea *to find out how light levels affect the rate of photosynthesis?*

Here are some results that students obtained when they did an experiment using a lamp and *Elodea*.

| Distance of lamp from *Elodea* (cm) | 100 | 80 | 60 | 40 | 20 | 0 |
|---|---|---|---|---|---|---|
| Number of bubbles/minute | | 13 | 12 | 31 | 41 | 55 | 76 |

▲ Students' results.

▸ *Plot a graph of these results.*

▸ *What does the graph tell you about the rate of photosynthesis?*

▸ *One of the results does not fit in with the general pattern.*
   **a** *Can you think of a reason for this?*
   **b** *How could check to see if you are right?*

## Temperature

Look back at the results of the *Elodea* experiment. When the light gets very close to the boiling tube the rate of photosynthesis increased dramatically.

▸ *Apart from the light from the lamp what other factor(s) could explain this big increase?*

Up to a certain point, the higher the temperature, the faster a plant will photosynthesise. In living things a 10°C rise in temperature will double the reaction rate of most processes. If the temperature rises above 40°C, the rate of reaction starts to decrease. This is because the enzymes, which help photosynthesis to happen, are destroyed at higher temperatures.

When it is cold Sarah heats her greenhouse so that the plants are at the ideal temperature. She uses a system similar to household central heating. A gas-fired boiler heats water which is then circulated around the greenhouse in metal pipes. Some glasshouse growers prefer to use heaters which burn paraffin, which is made from crude oil.

▸ *Apart from heat what else might burning paraffin produce which could encourage photosynthesis?*

## Carbon dioxide

The concentration of carbon dioxide in the air is very low, about 0.03 per cent. Experiments show that the more carbon dioxide there is in the air, the faster the rate of photosynthesis. Sarah pumps carbon dioxide into her greenhouse to encourage photosynthesis.

▶ *Why might talking to plants improve their growth?*

## Water

Water is also needed for photosynthesis. A plant which is short of water may begin to wilt. Wilting plants may only photosynthesise at half the normal rate. However, because water is needed for many other things in the plant it is difficult to determine the exact effect of water shortage on the rate of photosynthesis.

## Limiting factors

▶ *Look at the graph on the right.*
**a** *What does line A tell you about the effect of light intensity on photosynthesis? Why does the graph level out?*
**b** *What do lines B and C show you?*

From studying these results you can see that the rate of photosynthesis is controlled by various factors. The actual rate is determined by the factor which is in shortest supply. This factor is referred to as the **limiting factor**. In summer, when there is plenty of bright light, carbon dioxide is usually a limiting factor. In the winter, light is often a limiting factor.

# Greenhouse effect

You may read about the greenhouse effect in Chapter Thirteen (Farming and cycles). One of its main causes is an increase in the amount of carbon dioxide in the atmosphere.

▶ *How might the greenhouse effect affect the rate of photosynthesis in plants?*

## Atmospheric carbon dioxide

Plant growers like Sarah Bennett use elevated (raised) carbon dioxide levels to increase the rate of photosynthesis. Some scientists have argued that we do not need to worry about the greenhouse effect because the higher the carbon dioxide content of the atmosphere, the faster plants will remove it.

Diana Wilkins is a researcher at the International Horticulture Research Centre, Littlehampton, West Sussex. She is trying to find out how increased carbon dioxide levels will affect plant growth in the long term.

The plants are grown for a specific period of time and then leaves are removed and carefully analysed. Diana measures leaf areas, dry mass, **rubisco** (an important enzyme needed for photosynthesis) activity and the chlorophyll content of plants grown in ambient (normal) and elevated carbon dioxide levels. The table on the next page shows some results Diana obtained after growing seedlings for 62 days. One set of seedlings were watered with a low nutrient solution and the other with a high nutrient solution.

▲ Talking to plants might make them grow faster.

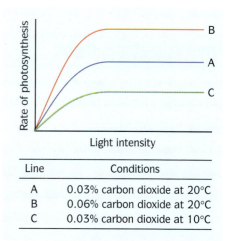

| Line | Conditions |
|------|------------|
| A | 0.03% carbon dioxide at 20°C |
| B | 0.06% carbon dioxide at 20°C |
| C | 0.03% carbon dioxide at 10°C |

▲ Limiting factors of photosynthesis.

▲ Diana grows her plants in controlled environment cabinets. Inside these cabinets the exact temperature, light intensity and carbon dioxide concentrations can be carefully controlled.

BIOLOGY

| | Low nutrient treatment | | High nutrient treatment | |
| --- | --- | --- | --- | --- |
| | A | E | A | E |
| Total chlorophyll ($\mu$g/cm$^2$) | 13.7 | 15.7 | 33.4 | 27.5 |
| Rubisco activity (relative units) | 12.6 | 17.8 | 15.3 | 12.9 |

▲ Diana's experimental results.

*A = ambient carbon dioxide concentration*
*E = elevated carbon dioxide concentration*
*$\mu$g = microgram*

▶ *What conclusions would you draw from these results?*

▶ *What experiments would you like to do to investigate this further?*

## Controlling photosynthesis

The control of photosynthesis is a very complex process. Diana's (and other researchers') findings seem to show two things:

- Elevated carbon dioxide does increase the rate of photosynthesis in the short term.
- After a period of time plants seem to adapt to the increased carbon dioxide levels and the amount of chlorophyll and photosynthetic enzymes declines.

▶ *What does Diana's research seem to show about the long-term effects of increased carbon dioxide levels on the rate of photosynthesis?*

▶ *Do Diana's results suggest that plants can compensate (make up) for the greenhouse effect, or not?*

## Negative feedback

Diana's research suggests that the products of photosynthesis control the rate of reaction. As the concentration of the products increase, the reaction is slowed down. This maintains a relatively constant rate of photosynthesis and is called *negative feedback*. The concentration of glucose in your blood is controlled using the same principle. You may have read about this in Chapter Seven (Hormones).

## Photosynthesis and fuel

Plants are expert at doing what scientists have been trying to do for years. Using free, readily available sunlight, they convert carbon dioxide and water into the sugars they need for energy and growth. Chlorophyll plays a vital role in this reaction, trapping light energy from the Sun so that it can be used to split water molecules. Chemists can now produce synthetic molecules which are able to trap light energy. If this trapped energy could be used to split water molecules into hydrogen and oxygen, the possibilities are very exciting. Hydrogen is an ideal fuel as it burns producing just water vapour and heat. If successful, this research could result in chemical factories powered by sunlight producing an unlimited supply of hydrogen gas for fuel.

Other scientists are using similar synthetic molecules to turn light energy into electrical energy. Although in its early stages, it is possible that future research into the process of photosynthesis could result in an unlimited supply of clean fuel and electricity.

🔺 Cars powered by sunlight and water might be a reality in the future.

## Summary

- Green plants make their food using a process called photosynthesis. Carbon dioxide and water are combined to make glucose.

$$\text{water} + \text{carbon dioxide} \xrightarrow[\text{chlorophyll}]{\text{light energy}} \text{glucose} + \text{oxygen}$$

$$6H_2O + \quad 6CO_2 \quad \longrightarrow \quad C_6H_{12}O_6 \quad 6O_2$$

- The light energy needed for photosynthesis is absorbed by chlorophyll in the chloroplasts. Chlorophyll absorbs blue and red light but reflects green light.
- Oxygen is given off as a waste product of photosynthesis.
- Plants are well adapted for photosynthesis by having broad thin leaves and cells packed with chloroplasts.
- Glucose made in photosynthesis may be used for respiration and building new molecules such as starch, cellulose, protein and fats.
- Light, temperature, carbon dioxide concentration and water can all affect the rate of photosynthesis. If any of these are in short supply they will limit the rate of the reaction.

# Revision Questions

**1** The diagram below shows a simplified section through a leaf.

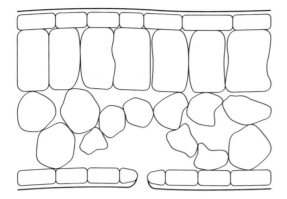

**a** Make a large copy of the diagram and label the following:

stoma      spongy mesophyll cell
palisade mesophyll cell      waxy cuticle

**b** Write a C inside the cells you would expect to contain the most chloroplasts.

**2** Why are most leaves flat and thin?

**3** Harvinder and Susan decide to have a competition to find out who can grow the biggest sunflower. Harvinder plants his seeds in a shady area and Susan plants hers in a sunny area. Which sunflower would you expect to grow the biggest? Why?

**4** The rate of photosynthesis can be monitored using the aquatic plant *Elodea*. It produces bubbles of oxygen which can be counted.

**a** Draw a diagram to show how you would set up an experiment to find out how light intensity affected the rate of photosynthesis.

**b** A group of students obtained the following results when they did this experiment.

| Distance of plant from light (cm) | 10 | 20 | 30 | 40 | 50 | 60 |
|---|---|---|---|---|---|---|
| Number of bubbles/minute | 62 | 34 | 17 | 8 | 3 | 1 |

Display these results in a clearer way and then write a few sentences to explain what the results show.

**c** When the experiment was repeated using the same piece of *Elodea* and the same apparatus the plant stopped producing bubbles even when the light source was very close. Suggest a reason for this.

**5** Imagine that an alien plant virus has been released on Earth. The virus infected every single plant and they all died. Describe in detail the effects you think this might have.

**6** Copy and complete the following passage about green plants and the way they feed. Use the words from the list below.

Plants make their own food using a process called _____ . This process uses _____ energy from the _____ . The energy is trapped by _____ in the _____ . The process requires two raw materials, _____ from the air and _____ from the soil. The _____ products of this process are _____ and the gas _____ .

two      chlorophyll      light      water
leaves      oxygen      photosynthesis
carbon dioxide      glucose      Sun

**7** Write down a word equation to summarise photosynthesis. Write the chemical equation underneath it if you can.

**8** Leaves are tested for starch to find out if they have been photosynthesising.

**a** Match the stages of the starch test with the correct reason for it.

**b** Arrange the stages in the right order.

| Stage | Reason |
|---|---|
| Cover with iodine | Kills leaf |
| Boil leaf in water | Removes chlorophyll |
| Wash leaf in water | Softens leaf |
| Boil leaf in ethanol | Stains starch |

**9** A geranium plant had one of its leaves covered with tinfoil as shown in the diagram. After a day in bright sunshine the leaf was removed and tested for starch.

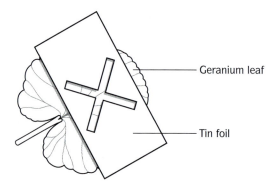

Geranium leaf

Tin foil

**a** Draw a diagram to show what this leaf would look like when the starch test was complete.
**b** What is this experiment designed to prove?
**c** The geranium was put in a dark cupboard for 24 hours before the experiment. Explain why.

**10** Tomato growers in the south of England produced a very early crop of greenhouse tomatoes in 1978. In February that year, there was a heavy snowfall and although the Sun shone brightly afterwards it took two weeks for the snow to melt. Explain how the weather conditions:
**a** helped the tomato growers
**b** caused them problems.
**c** How might the farmers have overcome the problems caused by the weather?

**11** Write down three factors which can affect the rate of photosynthesis.

**12 a** Glucose is converted to starch for storage. Why?
**b** Describe two other things which could happen to a glucose molecule produced during photosynthesis.

**13** Inside chloroplasts, chlorophyll molecules are tightly packed together on folded membranes. Why is this arrangement useful?

**14** The percentage sugar content of the leaves of a plant were measured over a 24-hour period.

| Time | Percentage sugar content |
|---|---|
| 12 midnight | 0.4 |
| 3 a.m. | 0.3 |
| 6 a.m. | 0.4 |
| 9 a.m. | 0.9 |
| 12 noon | 1.7 |
| 3 p.m. | 1.9 |
| 6 p.m. | 1.4 |
| 12 midnight | 0.4 |

**a** Draw a line graph to show these results.
**b** Describe and explain the changes in the sugar content of the leaves over the 24 hours.
**c** The data were collected on a warm, sunny summer day. Draw a second line to show what you would expect to find on a cool, dull autumn day.

**15** 'On a bright summer's day carbon dioxide can be a limiting factor for photosynthesis.' Explain what this statement means.

**16 a** Describe an experiment you could do to show how different-coloured light affects the rate of photosynthesis.
**b** What colour(s) would you expect to produce the fastest rate of photosynthesis? Explain why.

# Farming & cycles

You may have read about photosynthesis in Chapter Twelve (Photosynthesis). It seems strange that plants need fertilisers if they can make their own food. The process of photosynthesis provides plants with a constant supply of carbohydrates (glucose and starch) but just like us they need a variety of other substances to keep them healthy. You can get the different minerals and vitamins you need to keep you healthy by eating a variety of foods or by taking vitamin and mineral supplements. Fertilisers could be regarded as a plant's dietary supplements.

**Plants are able to make their own food using the process called photosynthesis. Plants grow better if they are fertilised. Farmers add fertilisers to their land to improve the growth of their crops.**

Baby Bio is a common houseplant fertiliser. The Baby Bio label tells you that it is made from humus and seaweed. Humus is a soil substance made from rotted plants, and seaweeds are plants that come from the sea.

A more detailed look at the ingredients gives you a clue about why plants benefit from humus and seaweed. The specific amounts of certain chemicals are shown. Presumably these particular chemicals must be the ones which are important to plants.

In this chapter you will find out why some substances are so important for healthy plant growth and how farmers can use this knowledge to improve their crop yields. You will also look at some of the environmental problems that the overuse of manufactured fertilisers can cause.

**Add only 5 drops to each pint of water when you water your houseplants, and see the difference.**

# Review

Before going any further read this page and attempt the tasks. Write the answers in your notes.

⏢ Farmers can use fertilisers to produce high yields of healthy crops year after year.

## CHECK THIRTEEN

**1** These two plants have been treated in exactly the same way except that A has been grown in garden soil and B has been grown in thoroughly-washed sand. How can you explain the difference in the appearance of the plants?

A                              B

**2** A student set up an experiment to find out under what conditions bread would go mouldy fastest. He tested four different conditions:

**a** warm and dry
**b** cold and dry
**c** cold and moist
**d** warm and moist.

Under which conditions will the bread go mouldy fastest? Explain your answer.

**3** What are the processes labelled X and Y in this simple diagram of the carbon cycle?

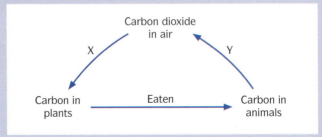

## Aquatic plants

You might have seen plants growing in ponds and rivers. If these **aquatic** plants are removed from their natural environment and placed in distilled water they do not grow very well. After a few weeks their leaves may turn yellow, growth will slow down and eventually the plants that were initially very healthy may begin to die.

🔺 Some plants grow very well in ponds and rivers.

## Thinking about pond water

▶ *Make a list of the differences between pond water and distilled water.*

▶ *Which of these differences might affect plant growth?*

▶ *What experiments could you do to prove that there is a difference between the two types of water?*

Wai Lin and Sandra carried out an experiment to find out if there is a difference between pond water and distilled water. One of them suggested heating a small sample of each type of water in a clean watch glass. The photograph shows what happened.

▶ *What does this experiment say about the different types of water? What does it tell us about the aquatic plants growing in pond water?*

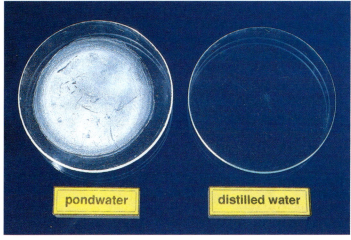

🔺 Wai Lin and Sandra heated samples of pond water and distilled water.

## Artificial pond water

It seems that pond water has substances dissolved in it which the plants need for healthy growth. By making artificial pond water with different chemicals dissolved in it you can find out exactly what substances plants do need.

## Macronutrients

One of the first people to realise that plants need these dissolved substances was a German scientist called Willhelm Knop. Knop experimented with various substances and eventually produced a solution in which plants flourished. He discovered that the elements nitrogen, phosphorus, sulphur, magnesium, potassium, calcium and iron were needed in quite large amounts. These elements are called **macronutrients**. If any one of them is missing from the solution the plant is grown in, it will show symptoms of deficiency. There are a variety of ways of growing plants in solutions. The diagram on the next page shows some possibilities.

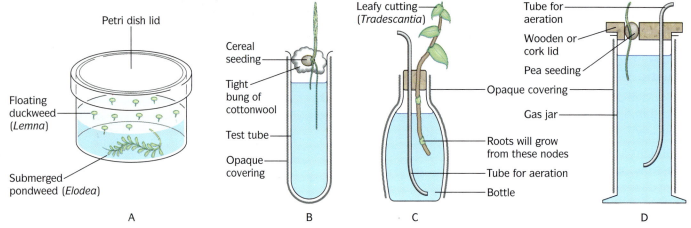

Different ways of culturing plants in solution.

▶ *What sort of observations would you make to compare plant growth in different solutions?*

▶ *Why do you think the containers are covered in methods B, C and D? Why do C and D have aeration tubes?*

## Nutrients and plant growth

▶ *Why is it important to set up 'control' experiments?*

▶ *Study the diagram carefully, looking at the roots and shoots of each plant. Draw a simple diagram of each plant which clearly shows the effects of the deficiency of each element tested.*

▶ *If you have carried out this experiment in class, compare these results with any you may obtain yourself.*

▶ *Which substances seem to have the greatest effect on plant growth?*

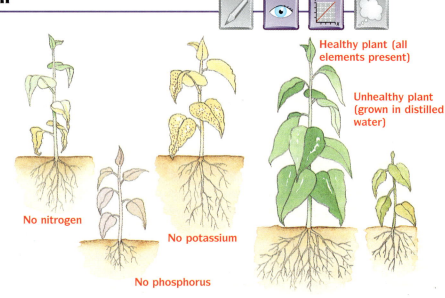

The results of an experiment growing plants in solutions in which one important element is missing. The last two plants are used as controls.

## Micronutrients

The elements mentioned so far are needed in quite large amounts (macronutrients). However, this is not quite the full story. Plants also require boron, zinc, copper, molybdenum, sodium, chlorine, silicon, manganese and cobalt. We call these elements the **trace elements** or **micronutrients** as they are only needed in tiny amounts. Absence of any of these elements in the soil will also result in poor growth.

Some soils are totally deficient (lacking) in certain micronutrients. Farmers can dramatically increase the yield of crops in these soils by spraying with a very dilute solution of the missing micronutrient mineral.

All the essential elements are dissolved in soil water in the form of mineral ions. For example, nitrogen is taken in through plant roots as nitrate ions, phosphorus as phosphate ions and potassium as potassium ions.

You may read about mineral ions in Chemistry, Chapter Nine.

# Uses of elements in plants

Nitrogen is needed to make proteins and to make chlorophyll. Lack of nitrogen results in poor growth and yellowing of leaves. Phosphorus is essential for the release of energy and is particularly important in actively growing root and shoot tips. Plants which are short of phosphorus will withdraw it from leaves and transport it to growing points causing dead patches on leaves. Potassium is needed for chlorophyll formation and is also essential for actively growing tissues. If deficient, it is transported away from leaves causing leaf scorch, when the leaves wither at edges turning first brown then yellow.

▶ *Use the above information and the diagram on the previous page to construct a table showing:*
   **a** *why nitrogen, potassium and phosphorus are each needed*
   **b** *what happens if the plant does not get enough of a particular mineral.*

# Recycling elements

Some living things may only survive a few days or weeks. Others may live for tens or even hundreds of years. Eventually, however, all living things will die. In the last ten thousand years millions and millions of plants and animals have lived and died. The reason you are not knee deep in dead bodies is that all of these organisms have been recycled.

Just as children's building blocks can be used over and over again to make a huge variety of different things, from cars to aeroplanes, atoms which make up living things can be used over and over again. Some of the atoms that you are made of may once have been part of a plant, a bird, a rock or maybe all three.

# Decomposers and detritivores

When an organism dies it is broken down and recycled by a variety of organisms in the soil. Fungi and bacteria in the soil cause plants and animals to decay in the same way that they make your food rot. They are **decomposers**. **Detritivores**, such as earthworms, swallow soil, digesting the **organic matter** (remains of living organisms) it contains. The soil travels through the earthworm's gut and any undigested material is egested as worm casts. Earthworms are very helpful in the recycling process as their burrowing and formation of casts helps to mix the different layers of soil.

The job of the decomposers and detritivores is to take the building bricks of the organism apart so that they can be used to build something else.

As the decomposers get to work on animal and plant remains they release the elements they were made from back into the environment where they can be used for plant growth. Animals may then eat the new plants and so a cycle is set up.

▶ *Explain in your own words how the atoms that were once part of hairy mammoths could now be part of you.*

Each of the elements mentioned in the first part of this chapter has to be recycled as the Earth is a closed system with a finite supply of resources. Two of the most important elements in all living organisms are carbon and nitrogen.

▲ Building blocks can be used over and over again to make many different things ...

▲ ... and recycled to make something else.

▲ Decomposers at work.

BIOLOGY

# The carbon cycle

You may be given a worksheet to help you understand how carbon and nitrogen are recycled.

The nitrogen and sulphur which also made up the organisms which eventually turned into coal, oil and gas now cause serious environmental problems. When these fuels are burned the sulphur and nitrogen combine with oxygen forming acidic gases. These gases dissolve in water vapour causing acid rain.

The carbon compounds in coal, oil and gas combine with oxygen when they are burned. In this way the carbon which has been trapped under the Earth for millions of years is finally released back into the atmosphere as carbon dioxide

Combustion

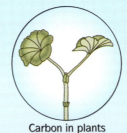
Carbon in plants

Plants take in carbon dioxide from the air and use it in **photosynthesis**. The carbon atoms are combined with other atoms and become part of the molecules which make up the plant.

Carbon in coal and oil

Decomposers can only do their job successfully if they are supplied with oxygen. In the absence of oxygen decomposition may be incomplete and some of the carbon compounds in plant or animal remains do not get broken down. When plants died millions of years ago they sank to the bottom of the water. There they gradually became squashed and compressed. As there was very little oxygen available under these conditions, the decomposers were unable to complete their job. The plants eventually turned into **coal**. **Oil** and **gas** were formed in a very similar way from the remains of tiny animals.

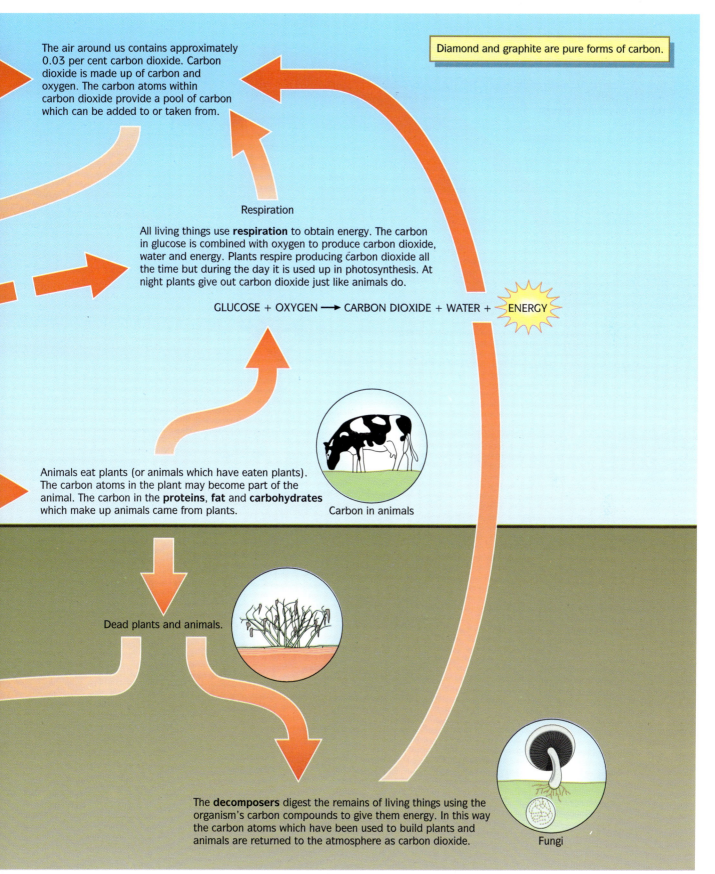

The air around us contains approximately 0.03 per cent carbon dioxide. Carbon dioxide is made up of carbon and oxygen. The carbon atoms within carbon dioxide provide a pool of carbon which can be added to or taken from.

Diamond and graphite are pure forms of carbon.

Respiration

All living things use **respiration** to obtain energy. The carbon in glucose is combined with oxygen to produce carbon dioxide, water and energy. Plants respire producing carbon dioxide all the time but during the day it is used up in photosynthesis. At night plants give out carbon dioxide just like animals do.

GLUCOSE + OXYGEN ⟶ CARBON DIOXIDE + WATER + ENERGY

Animals eat plants (or animals which have eaten plants). The carbon atoms in the plant may become part of the animal. The carbon in the **proteins**, fat and **carbohydrates** which make up animals came from plants.

Carbon in animals

Dead plants and animals.

The **decomposers** digest the remains of living things using the organism's carbon compounds to give them energy. In this way the carbon atoms which have been used to build plants and animals are returned to the atmosphere as carbon dioxide.

Fungi

# The nitrogen cycle

All living things need as source of nitrogen to make proteins. Plants get their nitrogen from the soil in the form of nitrates. Animals get their nitrogen by eating plants or by eating animals which have eaten plants.

The energy from a bolt of lightning is sufficient to break down the highly stable nitrogen gas in the air and convert it into a very reactive form. This readily combines with oxygen to form nitrogen oxide. The nitrogen oxide dissolves in rain water and falls to the ground. Here nitrates are formed.

Nitrogen in plant protein.

There are bacteria in the soil which can absorb nitrogen gas and combine if with other elements. These organisms are called **nitrogen-fixing bacteria**. Some are found living in the the soil but more often they are found in small swellings (**root nodules**) on the roots of certain types of plants, for example, peas, beans and clover. Both the bacteria and the plant gain from this relationship. The plant gets a continual supply of nitrogen compounds and the bacteria get a supply of carbohydrates. Nitrogen fixation requires a lot of energy. It takes six units of carbohydrate to fix one unit of nitrogen.

Dead plants and animals.

Nitrogen in soil nitrates.

When plants and animals die they deca The proteins that they were made of ge broken down into **ammonia** by microbe in the soil (the decomposers). Ammonia is also produced when microbes break down animal waste products such as ur and faeces. **Nitrifying bacteria** in the s convert ammonia into **nitrates**.

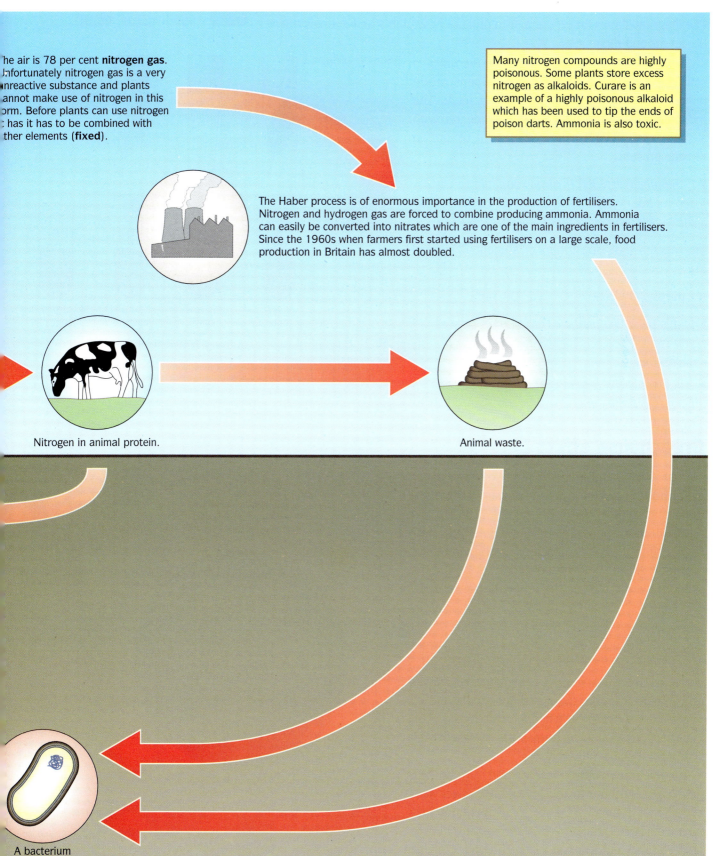

The air is 78 per cent **nitrogen gas**. Unfortunately nitrogen gas is a very unreactive substance and plants cannot make use of nitrogen in this form. Before plants can use nitrogen it has it has to be combined with other elements (**fixed**).

Many nitrogen compounds are highly poisonous. Some plants store excess nitrogen as alkaloids. Curare is an example of a highly poisonous alkaloid which has been used to tip the ends of poison darts. Ammonia is also toxic.

The Haber process is of enormous importance in the production of fertilisers. Nitrogen and hydrogen gas are forced to combine producing ammonia. Ammonia can easily be converted into nitrates which are one of the main ingredients in fertilisers. Since the 1960s when farmers first started using fertilisers on a large scale, food production in Britain has almost doubled.

Nitrogen in animal protein.

Animal waste.

A bacterium

# Demonstrating the carbon cycle

The diagram shows an experiment to find out how plants and animals affect the air around them.

The hydrogencarbonate indicator in the tubes is sensitive to carbon dioxide levels. When carbon dioxide dissolves, it makes the solution acidic. The indicator is purple with no carbon dioxide, red with a small amount and yellow with a lot of carbon dioxide present.

▶ *If the tubes were left in strong sunlight for several hours what do you predict will happen to the indicator in each tube?*

The results that one group of students obtained are:

A – purple,  B – yellow,  C – red,  D – red.

▶ *Is this what you predicted? Explain as fully as you can the reasons for the colour change in each tube.*

▶ *What would the results be if all four tubes had been left in the dark?*

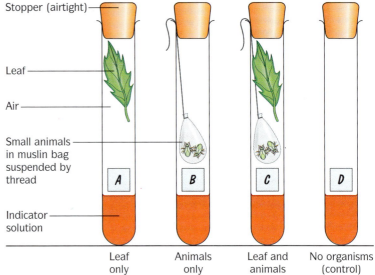

An experiment to find out how plants and animals affect the air around them. The colour of the indicator will change as carbon dioxide levels decrease or increase.

# Greenhouse effect

Carbon dioxide and methane are two of the major **greenhouse gases**. Carbon dioxide is removed from the atmosphere by photosynthesis and returned by respiration and burning. These processes naturally balance each other so the amount of carbon dioxide in the atmosphere stays about the same. However, humans have now begun to upset this balance. Life in the developed world requires large amounts of electrical energy. Nearly all of this energy is produced by burning fossil fuels. Large-scale deforestation in tropical areas causes further problems. Trees which are cut down may be used as timber, burned, left to rot or perhaps used as fuel.

Methane is produced when bacteria digest plant material. Thousands of tonnes are released each year from the guts of herbivores.

The diagram shows how carbon dioxide and methane contribute to the greenhouse effect. It is feared that a small increase in temperature may melt ice in the Arctic and Antarctic causing the sea levels to rise and low-lying land to flood. Climatic change may have disastrous effects on crop growth because of changes in temperature and rainfall.

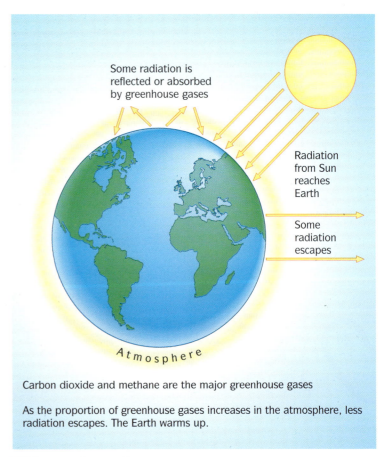

Carbon dioxide and methane are the major greenhouse gases

As the proportion of greenhouse gases increases in the atmosphere, less radiation escapes. The Earth warms up.

The greenhouse effect.

BIOLOGY

# Soils and farming

In a natural plant community, such as a forest or meadow, plants die and rot away. The minerals and other substances they were made from are broken down by microbes and become part of the soil humus.

When a farmer ploughs a previously uncultivated area (fallow land) and plants a crop there will usually be a very good yield in the first year. If the same crop is planted and harvested year after year, the yield will gradually go down. Eventually the crop may even fail. This happens because each time a crop is harvested the nitrates and the other minerals the plant has taken from the soil are also removed. Eventually the level of nitrates and other minerals becomes too low to sustain healthy plant growth.

▶ *Look back at the diagram of the nitrogen cycle. Suggest some ways a farmer could replace the nitrates which have been removed by cultivation.*

🔺 A fallow field (left) and newly ploughed field.

🔺 Some crops remove nutrients from the soil.

🔺 Some crops such as peas (right) fix nitrogen and replenish the soil.

## Crop rotation

Some crops take more substances from the soil than others. Crops like peas and clover which have nitrogen-fixing bacteria in their root nodules actually make the soil richer in nitrates. If a different crop is grown in a field each year and this crop rotation includes peas, beans or clover the nitrogen levels in the soil can be maintained without adding fertilisers. Many farmers in developing countries still rely on crop rotation to keep their soil healthy, but the pressure on farmers to grow more and more of one type of crop has led to a move away from such traditional methods. Farmers in developing countries cannot always afford to replace nitrates using artificial chemical fertilisers.

### CARNIVOROUS PLANTS

Carnivorous plants like the Venus fly-trap exploit soils which are low in nitrogen. They get their nitrogen by digesting the proteins in the insects they catch.

🔺 Venus fly-trap.

# Fertilisers

There is a wide variety of fertilisers available. There are two basic categories; organic and inorganic.

## Inorganic fertilisers

Some inorganic fertilisers are naturally occurring and can be extracted from the Earth. Others are manufactured: we call these synthetic fertilisers. You can read about this in Chemistry, Chapter Thirteen. Inorganic fertilisers contain minerals which can be absorbed easily by plants and therefore have an immediate effect. Most fertilisers contain nitrogen (N), phosphorus (P) and potassium (K) and are sometimes referred to as NPK fertilisers.

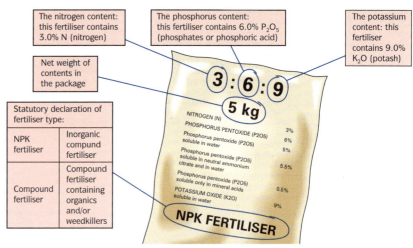

The nitrogen content: this fertiliser contains 3.0% N (nitrogen)

The phosphorus content: this fertiliser contains 6.0% $P_2O_5$ (phosphates or phosphoric acid)

The potassium content: this fertiliser contains 9.0% $K_2O$ (potash)

Net weight of contents in the package

3 : 6 : 9
5 kg

NITROGEN (N)                                        3%
PHOSPHORUS PENTOXIDE (P2O5)
Phosphorus pentoxide (P2O5)                         6%
soluble in water
Phosphorus pentoxide (P2O5)                         5%
soluble in neutral ammonium
citrate and in water                                5.5%
Phosphorus pentoxide (P2O5)
soluble only in mineral acids                       0.5%
POTASSIUM OXIDE (K2O)
soluble in water                                    9%

NPK FERTILISER

| Statutory declaration of fertiliser type: | |
| --- | --- |
| NPK fertiliser | Inorganic compund fertiliser |
| Compound fertiliser | Compound fertiliser containing organics and/or weedkillers |

By law the manufacturer of a product described as a 'fertiliser' must declare the nitrogen, phosphates and potash content on the package. The content of most other nutrients must also be declared if they have been added to the product.

🔺 The percentage of each mineral is usually shown on the fertiliser packaging.

## Organic fertilisers

You can buy organically grown versions of most vegetables in our supermarkets these days. Food which has been grown organically has not been exposed to manufactured chemicals, such as fertilisers and pesticides. You may read about this in Chapter Fourteen (Adaptation and competition).

Organic farmers have a number of fertiliser options. Animal waste can be added directly to the soil. Farmyard manure which is a mixture of dung, urine and straw can be applied. Sometimes crops such as clover, peas or beans are ploughed back into the soil. However, all these substances need to rot before their nitrates and other minerals are released into the soil. This means that they do not have the same immediate effect as inorganic fertilisers but they release nutrients slowly and over a longer period.

▶ *Using information from this chapter try to explain why Baby Bio, mentioned at the start of the chapter, can make your houseplants so much healthier.*

**Organic compounds** are also referred to as carbon compounds because they always contain carbon. For example, proteins are organic compounds which also contain the element nitrogen. All living things are made up of organic compounds.

## Humus and soil structure

Soil is a mixture of rock particles and partly-rotted plant and animal remains called **humus**. The rock particles are stuck together in clumps called soil crumbs, and it is humus that sticks them together. Soils with a good crumb structure have larger and more frequent spaces than soils with a poor structure. These spaces are important as they allow the air needed by soil organisms and plant roots to circulate easily. They also provide space for water, and allow soils to drain so that they do not get waterlogged.

▶ *What problems might arise if a soil became waterlogged?*

▶ *How might organic fertilisers have beneficial effects on soil structure?*

▶ *High levels of inorganic nitrates in soils can stimulate microbial activity. If there is not much organic matter in the soil the microbes may start to break down soil humus. What effect could this have on plant growth?*

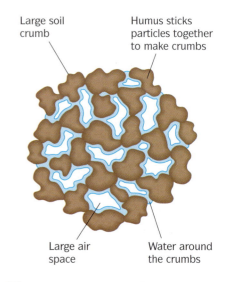

Large soil crumb

Humus sticks particles together to make crumbs

Large air space

Water around the crumbs

🔺 Soil crumbs provide space for air and water.

# Testing soils

You may be given a worksheet to help you measure soil humus and soil air content. You may be able to do an investigation to find out if there is a relationship between the two.

## Compost

Gardeners who do not want to use inorganic fertilisers may build a compost heap. Compost is partially decomposed vegetable waste. The diagram below shows how a garden compost heap can be made.

▶ *Look at the features labelled on the compost heap and explain why each is needed.*

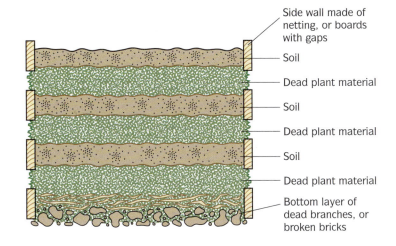

Side wall made of netting, or boards with gaps

Soil

Dead plant material

Soil

Dead plant material

Soil

Dead plant material

Bottom layer of dead branches, or broken bricks

▲ Compost heap.

## Denitrifying bacteria

Unfortunately, as well as bacteria which add nitrates to the soil there are others which do the opposite. These are called **denitrifying bacteria** and they convert nitrates back into nitrogen gas. The breakdown of nitrates also releases oxygen which the bacteria use to release energy from sugars. Farmers can discourage the activities of denitrifying bacteria by ensuring that the soil is well drained and well aerated.

▶ *Denitrifying bacteria are particularly active in poorly aerated, waterlogged soil. Why?*

## Nitrate pollution

All rivers have algae and other plants growing in them. Algae are microscopic plants and, just like all plants, they need nitrates. Nitrates are very soluble in water. If too much nitrate fertiliser is added to the soil it can be quickly washed away (leached out) when it rains. A good proportion of these nitrates will therefore end up in nearby ditches and eventually in local rivers. Here they can cause a number of problems.

If the level of nitrates in a river increases, the number of algae and other plants can rapidly increase. This is called **eutrophication**. The plants stop light from reaching the lower parts of the river. When the plants die they are decomposed by bacteria. The bacteria use large amounts of oxygen as they respire. This **deoxygenates** (decreases the oxygen content of) the water. Fish and other organisms suffocate and die. As their bodies are decomposed by bacteria the dissolved oxygen content of the water is reduced even more. Water pollution is often measured as **BOD** (**biological oxygen demand**).

This is the amount of oxygen that has been removed by the bacteria.

▶ *Explain how nitrate fertilisers can cause eutrophication.*

▶ *How can fertilisers kill fish?*

High levels of nitrates in drinking water are also a health concern. High levels of nitrates can cause 'blue-baby' syndrome and there could be links with cancer in animals and humans.

🔺 Fish suffocate when water becomes deoxygenated as a result of eutrophication caused by nitrate pollution.

## Fertilisers and plant growth

The graph shows how increasing the amount of nitrate fertiliser affects the yield of crops. Study the graph and answer these questions.

▶ *What quantity of fertiliser would you recommend the farmer uses to get the maximum yield from the field?*

▶ *Is it possible to use too much fertiliser?*

▶ *What might happen to the excess nitrates? (Clue: nitrates are very soluble in water.)*

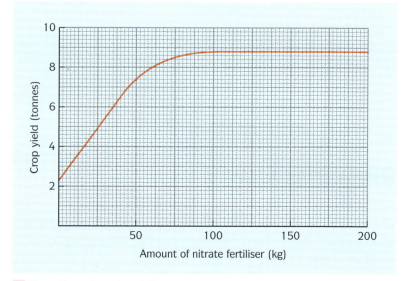

🔺 The effect of putting different amounts of nitrate fertiliser on a field.

## Rothamsted experimental station

Scientists at Rothamsted have been monitoring yields of grain on plots of land for over 100 years. Some plots have never had any fertiliser added. Other plots have been treated with different kinds of fertiliser. The results for the period 1852–1967 are shown in the table.

▶ *Use the information in the table together with what you have learnt about fertilisers in this chapter to do one of the following:*
  **a** *Produce a poster showing the pros and cons of inorganic and organic fertilisers.*
  **b** *Write a letter to a farmer explaining whether you support the use of organic or inorganic fertiliser. Why do you think your choice is best?*
  **c** *Write a short report on fertilisers for a gardening magazine.*

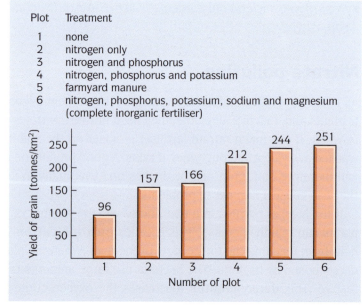

🔺 Rothamsted data.

# Summary

- Plants require a variety of different elements to grow healthily.
- Plants obtain these elements from the soil in the form of dissolved mineral salts.
- Elements which are required in fairly large amounts are called macronutrients and include nitrogen, phosphorus and potassium.
- Nitrogen, phosphorus and potassium are taken in as nitrate, phosphate and potassium ions.
- Other elements are needed in tiny amounts; these are called micronutrients.
- Plants obtain the element carbon from the air in the form of carbon dioxide. All living things are based on carbon compounds so it is a very important element.
- Photosynthesis removes carbon dioxide from the air and incorporates it into plant tissues.
- Respiration releases carbon dioxide into the atmosphere.
- Combustion and decomposition also release carbon dioxide into the atmosphere.
- Nitrogen is an essential element needed by all living things to make proteins.
- Plants can only make use of nitrogen in the form of nitrates which are absorbed through plant roots.
- Nitrogen can be fixed in three ways: by nitrogen-fixing bacteria, the Haber process and by lightning.
- Decomposers convert waste products from animals and plants into ammonium compounds.
- Nitrifying bacteria convert ammonium compounds into nitrates.
- Denitrifying bacteria convert nitrates into nitrogen gas.
- Fertilisers can be used to replace minerals such as nitrogen which have been removed from soil by crops.
- Excess nitrates can cause pollution in the environment.

# Revision Questions

1 Look back at the picture of the carbon cycle and then answer these questions:
   a What is photosynthesis and why is it important in the carbon cycle?
   b What is respiration and why is it important in the carbon cycle?
   c What role do microbes play in the carbon cycle?
   d What happens to the carbon in coal when it is burned?

2 Why is it a good idea to open the windows in a crowded classroom whenever possible?

3 Many gardeners go to a great deal of effort building compost heaps. Explain why this is a good idea.

4 Plants such as beans and peas often have special structures called root nodules on their roots.
   a What kind of organisms live in these nodules?
   b How do these organisms help the plant?
   c Farmers often plough the roots of beans into the soil. Why is this a good idea?

5 Explain why the organisms which cause decay are important:
   a to plants
   b to animals.

6 Sometimes farmers plant and harvest crops in the same fields year after year. If they do not add manure or fertilisers the crop yields gradually decrease. Eventually the crops may even fail.
   a Why does the yield of crops gradually decrease?
   b Why are manure or fertilisers needed for good crop growth?

7 Which of the following increase the amount of carbon dioxide in the air and which decrease it?
   animals    green plants    decomposers
   burning fossil fuels    cutting down forests
   planting trees

8 a Suggest two reasons for the increased concentration of carbon dioxide in the air over recent years.
   b Explain why such increases are a cause for concern.
   c What can be done to reduce the release of carbon dioxide?

9 Describe two ways (excluding bacteria) in which nitrogen gas can be converted into nitrates.

10 Some tomato plants were grown in sand in the laboratory. They were given plenty of light, carbon dioxide and water but few survived the first two months and none produced tomatoes. Explain why as fully as you can.

11 A farmer's 11-year-old daughter saw bags of fertiliser stored in a shed. She asked what 'NPK' on the fertiliser bags meant. Imagine that you are the farmer; how would you explain what an NPK fertiliser is and why it is important?

12 Pollution of water by inorganic fertilisers can lead to the death of fish and other aquatic animals. Explain fully how this can happen.

13 Large areas of tropical rainforest are being cut down in various parts of the world. This may be to provide timber for building or fuel or it may be to clear land for agriculture. Explain why environmentalists are worried about this.

# Adaptation & competition

**S**outh Africa, under the government of President Nelson Mandela, wants to sell elephant meat and hides.

But some conservation groups fear this would lead to the reopening of the ivory trade, which led poachers to slaughter hundreds of thousands of elephants in Africa in the 1970s and 1980s. The trade was banned in 1989.

Food for thought: cans of elephant meat.

Rearguard action: a South African National Parks Department worker with elephants' tails.

South Africa says its elephant population is growing, despite regular culling, putting pressure on land and resources. President Mandela's government is also under pressure to improve the lot of the black population after years of apartheid. People and politics . . . somehow, conservation must fit into this equation.

'Let us eat elephants.' Elephants have for many environmentalists become symbols of the natural world, to cherish and conserve. All are agreed about the importance of conserving species and their habitats, but they are divided over whether individual animals should be killed and traded, if this can be done sustainably.

Workers with a huge tusk at the Kruger National Park.

# CHAPTER FOURTEEN

# Review

The study of how plants and animals live in their natural surroundings is called *Ecology*.

Before going any further, read this page and attempt the tasks. Write the answers in your notes.

These animals can be found living in fresh water. They are not drawn to the same scale.

▲ Freshwater organisms.

Billions of organisms live on Earth. They all have needs which they must meet if they are going to survive. The organisms must find all these requirements from their surroundings. If they cannot they must move and search for them in other places or die. Only successful individuals will be able to survive, reproduce and carry on their species.

## CHECK FOURTEEN

**1** Use the key below to identify the animals shown above.

**1** Legs present go to 2
Legs absent go to 5

**2** Six legs go to 3
More than six legs go to 4

**3** Hairs on two legs   water boatman (*Notenecta*)
No hairs on legs   dragonfly nymph (*Libellula*)

**4** Flat body   water louse (*Ascellus*)
Curled body   freshwater shrimp (*Gammarus*)

**5** Shell present go to 6
Shell absent go to 7

**6** Curled shell   great pond snail (*Lymnaea*)
Pyramid-shaped shell   freshwater limpet (*Ancylastrum*)

**7** Rounded body, two antennae   water flea (*Daphnia*)
Flat body, no antennae, sucker at each end   leech (*Hirudo*)

**2** Why is the size of organisms rarely used in keys?

**3** Animal F is a parasite.

**a** What is meant by the term *parasite*?
**b** Suggest one feature which could help it to survive as a parasite.

# Environments

An organism's environment is all those things around it which affect its way of life. The Earth has many types of environment with huge differences in their conditions: cold in the Arctic and Antarctic; hot, steamy tropical rainforests in Brazil; and dry, dusty deserts in Egypt.

▶ *Choose two of the environments shown in the photographs. Write down the advantages and disadvantages they have for the plants and animals that live there.*

▲ Cold in the Arctic.

▲ Hot, steamy rainforests.

▲ Dry, dusty desert.

You may have considered factors such as the weather, temperature and the availability of water and shelter. These are the non-living, physical things in an environment and are called **abiotic factors**. You may also have considered other living organisms which are called **biotic factors**.

▶ *List any biotic factors you can think of in the two environments you chose.*

## Biotic factors

One of the more important biotic factors is the supply of food organisms. These provide nutrients and energy for other organisms. The organism which is eaten is called the **prey**, the organism which eats it, the **predator**. You may read about these relationships in Chapter Fifteen (Energy flows). Sometimes a predator may be eaten by another organism. For example, ladybirds which prey on aphids (greenfly) are preyed on in turn by another predator (the blue tit).

Living organisms also affect each other in other ways, for example:

- plants compete with each other for light, water, minerals and space
- insects pollinate flowers
- flowers may need pollen from other flowers
- animals disperse seeds
- animals may need a mate
- humans clear land for housing, farming and quarrying and pollute the environment.

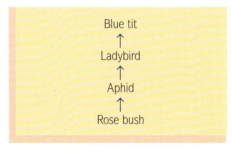

Blue tit
↑
Ladybird
↑
Aphid
↑
Rose bush

▲ A simple food chain showing the flow of nutrients from a rose bush to a blue tit.

▶ *List all the ways you can think of in which one organism may affect another. How many items on your list involve people?*

BIOLOGY

# Habitats

The place where an organism lives is called its **habitat**. Within that habitat the organism must find all it needs to survive and reproduce.

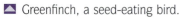
▲ Greenfinch, a seed-eating bird.

▲ Eagle, a bird of prey.

▲ Wood anemones.

▶ *Name the habitat of the organisms shown in the pictures and describe how they are adapted to survive in their habitats.*

Sometimes you can identify very specialised conditions within the main habitat. For example, the conditions on top of a rock or a rotting log are very different from those underneath it where it will be darker and damper. These specialised conditions are called **microhabitats**.

**Garden habitat**

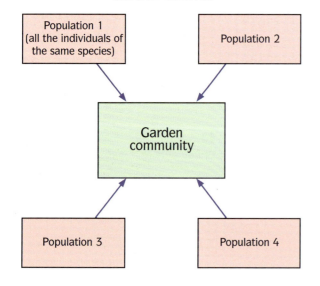

▲ Organisms in a garden habitat community.

▲ A polar bear.

## Populations and communities

All the individuals of a particular species in a habitat at a particular time are called a **population**. There are usually several species living in a habitat, each with its own population. All the populations which share a habitat make up a group known as a **community**.

▶ *Name four populations which could be present in a garden community.*

# Ecosystems

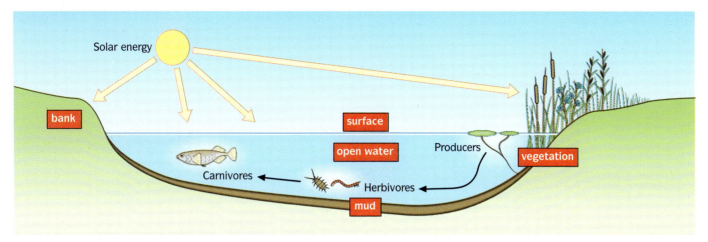

🔺 A pond is a small, simple ecosystem, but they can be much larger, such as a forest or an African plain.

An **ecosystem** is all of the biotic (living) and abiotic (non-living) things in a particular habitat and how they interact with each other. An ecosystem must have a supply of energy for its organisms. You may read about this in Chapter Fifteen (Energy flows).

▶ *What is the ultimate source of energy in most ecosystems?*

▶ *Suggest how conditions vary in the different habitat zones shown in the pond ecosystem.*

An organism's **ecological niche** is how it fits into the ecosystem, that is, how it behaves and finds its food or shelter. Simple plants like liverworts, for example, need very moist conditions. A niche may involve more than one habitat; for example, a frog may spend most of the year on damp land searching for food but in the spring it must return to water to breed.

# Investigating habitats

It is possible for you to investigate habitats using some of the same ideas and equipment as professional scientists. You could make a nature film, for example, or study the activities of one particular organism over a whole day. You could do simple studies with home-made equipment, or more ambitious investigations at school or with a local conservation group.

You may be given a worksheet to help you with this practical.

# Investigating a population

You might carry out an investigation to measure the size of a population, for instance a population of dandelions on a school field. If you do this, you may find it useful to refer to the worksheet for the previous investigation.

▶ *You might think of walking over the whole area counting every dandelion plant. What would be the advantages and disadvantages of doing this?*

It is even more difficult to count animals. You may be given a worksheet to help you *estimate* the population size of woodlice in an area of woodland.

# Changes in the environment

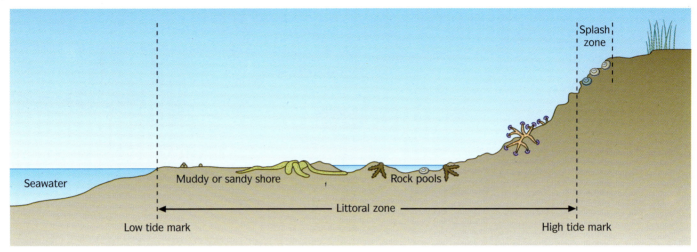

🔺 A beach habitat.

Habitats do not stay the same forever. Changes may occur regularly on a daily basis, or over longer periods of time – for example, in a beach habitat. It is very difficult for organisms to live in the **littoral** zone between the high and low tide line. They must be able to survive wave action, being exposed to air when the tide is out and being covered by salt water when the tide is in.

▶ *Suggest how the conditions in a beach habitat may change during:*
   **a** *one day*
   **b** *one month*
   **c** *one year*
   **d** *one hundred years.*

You may have suggested factors such as light intensity, temperature, wind, rain, height of the tides, availability of food and oxygen, erosion or deposition of new beach, and the formation of sand dunes.

Plants and animals are affected by changes in conditions, but they are also able to cause changes in the environment.

## Biological succession

Plants would **colonise** (move into) the area and eventually cover the surface of the soil. Over a longer period of time the plant species living there would change.

**Biological succession** involves a series of slow changes which provide different conditions, one after the other, in the same habitat. Each time the environmental conditions change new types of plants and animals can **immigrate** to or colonise the habitat and survive.

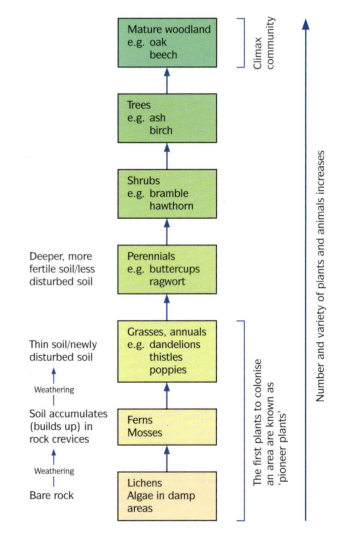

🔺 Succession. Examples of plant species which can succeed each other on land.

▶ *What changes would you expect to see if a patch of soil was dug over and then left for a year or longer?*

However, these organisms may cause further changes in the habitat. The change in conditions may be so great that some organisms can no longer survive there and they have to **emigrate** (move out), adapt or die.

Succession can start with bare rock, soil in a garden or even when plants manage to break through the tarmac of pavements. Eventually stable conditions are reached which are known as the **climax community**. On land this will usually be woodland.

▶ *Why do you think dandelions and thistles are often among the first plants to colonise an area?*

⬆ Dandelion fruits. Each seed has its own 'parachute'.

# Adaptation

Both dandelions and thistles have fruits that are spread by the wind. They have special adaptations which make their fruits float on the wind.

## Parasites

**Parasites** are good examples of well-adapted organisms. They must be able to find a host to provide food and perhaps also shelter. They must not kill their host or they may die themselves. Their offspring need to find a new host to avoid overburdening their parent's host and causing its death.

▶ *Write a list of the ways in which the pork tapeworm (*Taenia*) is adapted to the life of a parasite. Explain why these adaptations are useful.*

# Population size

The size of a population can change over time, increasing or decreasing depending on a number of biotic and abiotic factors in its environment. These can include:

- climate
- food supply
- number of sexually mature individuals present
- space
- waste products
- disease
- predation
- migration.

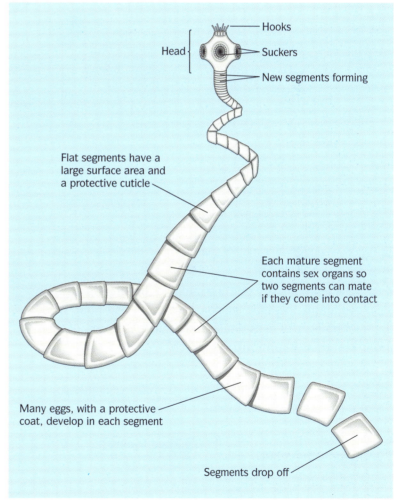

⬆ A pork tapeworm (*Taenia*). This can grow to a length of 3–4 metres inside a pig's intestine.

The amount of resources available in a particular area limits the size of the populations there. The maximum size of a population that can survive there is called the **carrying capacity** of that environment.

▶ *Construct a table to show how each one of these factors might affect the size of a population.*

# Population growth

When population increase is measured, the *population size* (number of individuals in the population) is plotted against *time* and a growth curve is produced. It is usually a characteristic 'S'-shaped (**sigmoid**) curve, consisting of three phases known as the **lag**, **log** and **stationary** phases. It is easiest to see these clearly if you study a simple, single-celled organism such as yeast or bacteria growing by themselves under laboratory conditions.

## Yeast growth

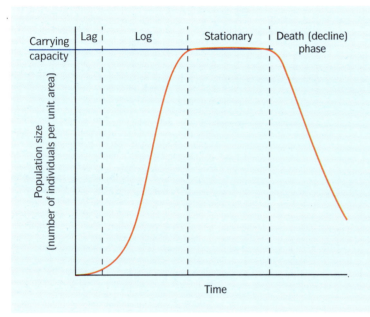

| Lag phase : | individuals adjust to environmental conditions. Reproduction rate low: little change in the population size |
| Log phase : | good environmental conditions allow individuals to grow and reproduce rapidly. Reproduction rate high, mortality (death) rate low: population size increases. As the carrying capacity of the environment is reached population growth slows because there is more competition for the resources |
| Stationary phase : | environmental factors, such as the amount of food available, limits growth and reproduction. Reproduction and mortality rates are the same: population size remains the same |
| Death (decline) phase : | environmental resources available decrease. Reproduction rate low, mortality rate high: population size decreases |

🔺 A population growth curve for yeast showing the changes which can occur in population size over a period of time.

Yeast cells reproduce by splitting into two (**binary fission**). In ideal conditions this may happen once every half hour. When the total number of cells doubles at regular intervals of time, this is known as **exponential growth**.

| Minutes | 0 | 30 | 60 | 90 | 120 | 150 |
|---|---|---|---|---|---|---|
| Number of yeast cells | 1 | 2 | 4 | 8 | 16 | 32 |

🔺 Exponential increase in cell number.

▸ *Use the information in the table below to plot a growth curve following the introduction of 100 yeast cells into a sealed container of fresh broth.*

▸ *Label the following phases on your graph and explain what is happening in the yeast culture during each of them.*
   **a** *lag phase*
   **b** *log phase*
   **c** *stationary phase.*

| Time (hours) | 0 | 2 | 4 | 6 | 8 | 10 | 12 | 14 | 16 | 18 | 20 | 22 | 24 |
|---|---|---|---|---|---|---|---|---|---|---|---|---|---|
| Number of yeast cells (per 10 cm³ broth) | 100 | 110 | 125 | 160 | 260 | 400 | 540 | 680 | 800 | 880 | 905 | 910 | 910 |

🔺 Numbers of yeast cells in a nutrient broth culture over a 24-hour period.

▸ *If the experiment continued you would observe a decrease in yeast cell numbers.*
   **a** *Explain why the population size would decrease.*
   **b** *Suggest what might be done to prevent this decline.*

# Population growth in nature

Although most organisms do not live in enclosed containers like the yeast, the same phases of population growth can be seen. Good conditions cause increased survival and rates of reproduction. If there is a reduction in resources, population growth slows and may even decline (decrease). Because environments are constantly changing, population size often fluctuates (varies up and down) with the availability of resources.

▶ *Would you expect the number of moths living in a tree to be exactly the same over ten years? Say what you would expect and why.*

# Interactions between populations

In a community, the size of one population can directly affect the size of another. This might be due to both species competing for the same resource (**interspecific competition**), for example food, or one species feeding on the other in a predator – prey relationship.

▶ *Write down two examples of interspecific competition.*

▶ **Intraspecific competition** *occurs when members of the same species compete for the same resource. Write down two examples of intraspecific competition.*

# Predator–prey relationships

If the size of a prey population increases there is more food available for its predators, so the predator population may increase. However, the increased predator population will need more food to survive and this will result in a decrease in prey population size. This in turn means that too little food is available for the predators and some of them will starve. The drop in predator population allows the prey population size to recover. This cycle can repeat many times.

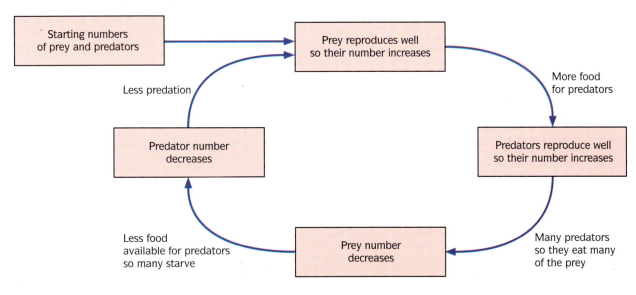

🔺 Stages in the predator–prey cycle.

A well-known example of a predator–prey relationship is that of the snow-shoe hare and lynx in Canada.

▶ *Draw a predator–prey cycle diagram for the snowshoe hare and the lynx.*

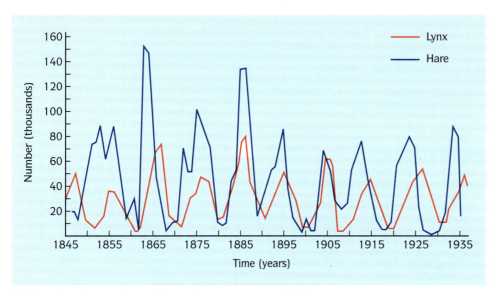

The changing numbers of snowshoe hare and lynx in Canada.

Snowshoe hare.

Lynx.

▶ *Describe the link between the changes in numbers of predator and prey.*

## Biological control

Humans have used predator–prey relationships to control pest populations.

A natural predator of the pest species is deliberately introduced into the place which contains the pest. The predator preys on the pest and reduces its numbers.

One of the earliest examples of biological control was the use of cats to reduce the number of rats or mice in a barn or aboard a ship.

## The control of whitefly

Biological control can work very well in an enclosed space such as a greenhouse. A common pest in agricultural glasshouses growing tomatoes is the whitefly. Growers used to spray a chemical insecticide on the plants but this contaminated the food. Nowadays they introduce a small parasitic wasp called *Encarsia formosa* into their glasshouses. These lay their own eggs into the whitefly eggs and prevent young whitefly being produced.

Scientists have not always got it right. Of all the biological control systems tried, only about one third have worked and another third made no difference! In the final one third of attempts, something unexpected happened which often made an extra problem!

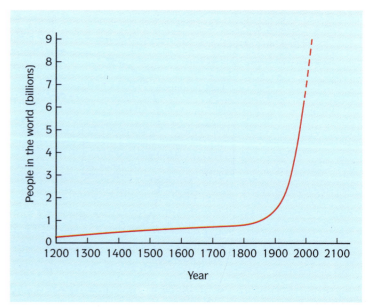

Graph showing world human population size.

# Human population size

▶ *Most of the numbers in the graph on page 214 have been estimated from historical records. Why?*

The human population has grown very rapidly during the last two hundred years. This is because of great advances in agricultural and industrial techniques.

▶ *Write down factors which tend to prevent the increase in population size.*

You might have thought of factors such as droughts and floods which can cause famine and wars, as well as the use of contraception.

| Factor | Result | Effects |
|--------|--------|---------|
| Better housing, sanitation and hygiene | Less overcrowding Clean water supplies Better sewage disposal | These mean that infectious diseases such as tuberculosis and dysentery cannot spread as easily |
| Better medical treatment | Antibiotics e.g. penicillin Vaccination Medical machinery such as X-rays, body scanners | These mean that if people become ill they are more likely to recover |
| Better agriculture | Mechanisation Chemicals: fertilisers, pesticides | More food is available. Well-nourished people grow better and have more resistance to disease |

🔺 Important factors which have led to an increase in population size.

## Population structure

In addition to knowing the total number of people in a population it is also useful to know whether they are male or female and their ages. This information can be presented as **population pyramids**. These show the relative number of people in each male and female age group of the population.

> **CENSUS**
>
> In Great Britain information is collected about the population every 10 years in a census.

▶ *What proportion of the female population was aged 60–64 in:*
**a** *1891*
**b** *1956?*

▶ *Suggest why a larger proportion of the population is older in 1956 than in 1891. What problems may occur in countries with an ageing population?*

▶ *Changes in the age structure of a population are known as* **demographic trends**. *Why is it useful for a government to know what demographic changes are taking place?*

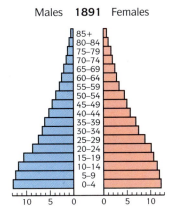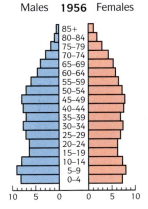

The horizontal bars represent the percentages of the male and females in the population, according to their age

🔺 Population pyramids for Great Britain in 1891 and 1956, showing how the age distribution has changed.

# World population

Population growth is slowing down in the wealthy, industrialised nations. Their populations are well fed and have good health care. Families limit the number of children they have so they can improve their standard of living and enjoy good health and leisure time.

In 1842 there were six or seven children in the average North American family. By 1900 it was more usual to have just three or four children. Now, most women do not have more than two children.

# Human influences on the Earth

Our present numbers place great demands on the planet. The environment has been changed dramatically and is not allowed to return to its natural state.

Only a few hundred years ago, the world human population was much smaller and lived a very different form of lifestyle. Many people were nomadic (wanderers) and travelled around to find food. They did not stay in one place for long and so did not cause much damage.

To provide enough food, housing and roads for todays population more land has been cleared of its natural vegetation. This has often destroyed the habitat of plants and animals. The mixed plant species of grasses, flowers and trees are removed by cutting, burning and ploughing. They are replaced by a dense population of one crop species such as wheat or rice. This is called a **monoculture**.

Resources are any materials we need to survive. They include food, water, land for agriculture and building, building materials and energy supplies. To fill their leisure time people demand consumer goods such as televisions, hi-fi's and training shoes. These all use up resources, many of which are non-renewable.

Photochemical smog occurs in warm urban environments due to the gases produced by traffic and industry. Sunlight causes nitrogen oxides, hydrocarbons and ozones to combine. A white mist is formed which irritates people's eyes, noses and throats.

Some species like the dodo have become extinct, which means that all the members of that species are dead and will never live on Earth again.

Lead tetraethyl is added to petrol to make engines run more smoothly. Lead is released in car exhaust fumes. If large quantities are absorbed into the body the nervous system is damaged. High concentrations of lead have been shown to cause brain damage in young children.

As human population size and standard of living increase, so does the amount of waste we produce. This is often referred to as pollution.

Domestic rubbish is one of our biggest problems. Some of the rubbish is biodegradable (can be broken down by living organisms) and rots down. This can take a long time. Toxic chemicals can be released which may poison organisms.

Some of the rubbish is non-biogradable and will be unchanged in hundreds of years' time – for example, plastic lemonade bottles.

When human wastes are treated the breakdown products include phosphates and nitrates. These cause eutrophication.

Some sewage is not treated at all. It passes through a long pipe into the sea. Sometimes the tide carries the sewage back towards the beach. This is a health hazard for swimmers.

Most air pollution is caused by burning fossil fuels (coal, oil and natural gas) in power stations, factories, vehicle engines and in our homes. The main gases produced from burning fossil fuels are sulphur dioxide, nitrogen oxides, carbon dioxide and carbon monoxide. Some of these gases contribute to the greenhouse effect and to acid rain. These gases are light in weight and may be carried high into the atmosphere by warm air currents. They can be carried far from the place where they were made.

Water is used for many industrial processes. Factories and power stations are often built close to rivers and seas so that water is available. This water is returned to the river but it often contains chemicals or is warm. This higher temperature encourages eutrophication.

Massive areas of tropical rainforest are being cleared for timber and to provide land for agriculture. The plants in these areas would have used carbon dioxide gas in photosynthesis. Their destruction leads to increased levels of carbon dioxide.

Chlorofluorocarbons (CFCs) are found in aerosols and refrigerators. They break down the protective ozone layer in the atmosphere. This allows an increase in harmful ultraviolet rays to reach the ground.

BIOLOGY

▶ *Individuals, farmers, conservationists, industrialists and governments all have a role in managing the environment. List ways they could do this.*

## Surviving pollution

Some plants and animals have characteristics or adaptations which allow them to live in polluted areas.

▶ *There are two forms of the peppered moth, one is light coloured and the other dark. During the daytime they both rest on trees. They are both eaten by thrushes whilst they are resting. Suggest why the light form is mostly found in rural areas and the dark form in industrialised areas.*

▶ *Explain why this colour adaptation is a useful adaptation for survival.*

⬛ Peppered moths.

## Summary

- All organisms need to obtain from their environment the things they require to keep them alive.
- Organisms must compete with members of their own species (intraspecific competition) and of other species (interspecific competition) to obtain the resources they need.
- Organisms adapt and develop features (anatomical and behavioural) which will make them successful in their natural habitat.
- Habitats can change over a period of time; this is known as succession. Eventually a stable ecosystem, called a climax community, may be formed.
- Successful organisms survive and breed. Unsuccessful organisms die.
- The more resources available in a habitat, the more organisms will survive and breed and population size can increase.
- When a population grows the resources they need may decrease, which prevents further population growth.
- When several populations live in the same habitat one species (the prey) may be eaten by another species (the predator). This predator–prey relationship affects the population sizes of the two species.
- The human population of the Earth is increasing rapidly. This is because improvements in nutrition, health care and sanitation have led to a decrease in infant mortality and an increase in life expectancy.
- Human population growth is not the same in all areas of the world; growth is greater in developing countries compared with the more industrialised areas of the world. In some cultures birth control is used to control population increase.
- Increasing amounts of foods are needed to feed humans. The techniques used for agriculture have a large impact on the environment.
- The greater the size of the human population the more resources it requires. This has led to greater impact on the environment, particularly land clearance and pollution of land, air and water.
- There is increasing concern about environmental damage and the eventual resulting problems for humans. More thought is being given to management and conservation of habitats. Some people feel there is a 'duty of care' to ensure that the Earth is maintained in the best condition possible for future generations and to avoid cruelty to other species.

# Revision Questions

**1** Explain the difference between a community and a population. Give one example of each.

**2** Match the terms and descriptions below:

| Term | Description |
|------|-------------|
| Ecosystem | The place where an organism lives. |
| Habitat | Non-living, physical things in an environment. |
| Adaptation | Living things in an environment. |
| Biotic factors | All the living and non-living things interacting in a particular habitat. |
| Abiotic factors | A feature in body structure, physiology or behaviour which helps an organism to survive in its habitat. |

**3** Study the graphs below:

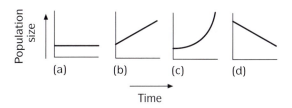

**a** Which graph shows the change in the human population of the world over the last 500 years?

**b** State *three* factors which can cause:
  *i* an increase in human population size
  *ii* a decrease in human population size.

**4**

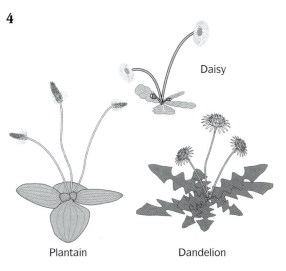

Dandelions, plantain and daisy are often found growing amongst the mown grass of garden lawns and playing fields.

**a** Give *two* reasons why these plants are well adapted to grow in this habitat.

**b** Name the resources which they compete for.

**5 a** Explain the term pollutant.

**b** Name *four* pollutants. For each one state how it is produced and the effects it has on organisms and the environment.

**6 a** Sparrows and other small birds often visit garden bird tables. How are they adapted for eating seeds, flying and perching?

**b** Suggest how kestrels are adapted to prey on small birds.

**7** Following a woodland fire a gradual succession of changes take place.

**a** What pioneer plants would you expect to see first?

**b** How would these colonising plants get there?

**c** What type of climax community would be formed?

**8**

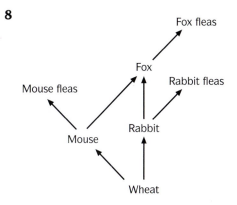

**a** For the community shown in the diagram give one example of:
  *i* interspecific competition
  *ii* intraspecific competition.

**b** If the number of rabbits increase name the animals whose number might:
  *i* decrease
  *ii* increase.

**9** Explain the difference between renewable and non-renewable resources. Give *one* example of each.

**10 a** Why are power stations always sited near water?
 **b** How might they affect organisms in the water?
 **c** Explain how fossil fuel power stations are involved in acid rain production.
 **d** What damage can be caused by acid rain?

**11 a** Explain what is meant by the term *pesticide*.
 **b** State *three* advantages of using pesticides.
 **c** Small quantities of pesticide have been found in Antarctic penguins. Suggest how it got there.
 **d** What do you think would be the ideal properties of a pesticide?

**12** Adult limpets live on rocks on the seashore. When the tide is out they are exposed to air, when the tide is in they are covered by sea water. List the environmental factors which affect the limpets and suggest the effect of each factor.

**13** Name some of the reasons that habitats are being destroyed.

**14 a** Why are hedges useful to wild animals?
 **b** Suggest *two* ways in which hedges could be useful to farmers.
 **c** Explain why farmers have often removed hedges in the past.

**15** An ecologist wanted to compare the ground living animals in a wood with those in an adjacent field. She placed 20 pitfall traps in the wood and 20 in the field. The animals which were trapped were identified, counted and recorded in a table before being released.
 **a** What is an *ecologist*?
 **b** Why were the same number of pitfall traps placed in the wood and in the field?

| Type of animal | Number of animals caught | |
| --- | --- | --- |
| | In the wood | In the field |
| Centipedes | 3 | 0 |
| Millipedes | 4 | 0 |
| Beetles | 24 | 12 |
| Woodlice | 27 | 3 |
| Ants | 0 | 6 |
| Spiders | 19 | 5 |
| Total number of animal types | 5 | 4 |
| Total number of animals | 77 | 26 |

 **c** Draw a bar chart(s) to show the number of each type of animal caught in the two habitats.
 **d** Which is the most commonly found animal in
  *i* the wood
  *ii* the field?
 **e** Suggest why there are both more types of animal and a greater total number of animals in the wood than the field.
 **f** In which habitat would you expect to find the greatest number of birds? Explain your answer.
  The ecologist used the capture-recapture technique to estimate the total size of the beetle populations in the two habitats.

| Number of beetles captured | Habitat | |
| --- | --- | --- |
| | Wood | Field |
| In the first sample | 24 | 12 |
| In the second sample | 23 | 10 |
| Marked beetles in the second sample | 5 | 2 |

 **g** Use the Lincoln index to estimate the size of each population.
 **h** How could the accuracy of this estimation be increased?
 **i** What assumptions have to be made when using the capture-recapture technique?

# Energy flows

No matter how active or lazy you are, you need energy to keep your body alive and moving. All this energy originally comes from the Sun, but just lying in the Sun will not keep you alive because human body cells cannot use solar energy directly.

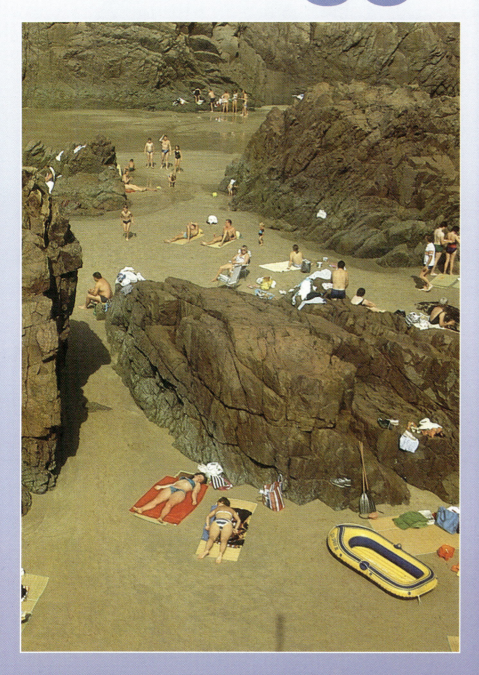

In this chapter you will investigate how the energy in sunlight can be captured and passed on to you.

# Review

All living things need nutrients and energy for respiration, growth, repair, movement, reproduction. They get these nutrients and energy from their food.

Before going any further, read this page and attempt the tasks. Write the answers in your notes.

A bramble bush is an important year-round source of food and shelter for many animals.

Chaffinch

Butterfly

Blackbird

Vole

Caterpillar

Field mouse

Snail

Stoat

🔺 A few of the animals which live in and around bramble bushes.

## CHECK FIFTEEN

*Using the information in the diagram answer the questions below.*

**1** Give examples of a
  **a** plant
  **b** predator
  **c** prey animal
  **d** herbivore
  **e** carnivore
  **f** producer
  **g** consumer

**2** Draw food chains which:
  **a** start with the bramble bush
  **b** end with a stoat

**3** A farmer sprays pesticide on a nearby field. Some of it accidentally reaches the bramble bush and kills the caterpillars. Suggest what the effect on this community might be.

# Food for plants

You may have read about photosynthesis in Chapter Twelve (Photosynthesis). Green plants can make their own energy-containing chemicals using simple chemicals from the air and soil. Plants are able to produce their own food so they are called **producers**.

▶ *To produce food, plants need energy. Where does this energy come from?*

Although vast amounts of energy from the Sun reach the Earth, the plants use only a very small amount of it for photosynthesis.

The glucose produced during photosynthesis can be used immediately to give the plant energy to stay alive. Any excess can be converted to other substances needed by the plant for growth and reproduction, for example, protein to produce new leaves and seeds. If the glucose is not needed immediately for energy or growth and reproduction, it can be converted to **starch** or **lipid** (usually oils). These can be stored in the plant cells so they are easily available for future use.

Other energy-rich compounds may be stored in specialised areas of the plant.

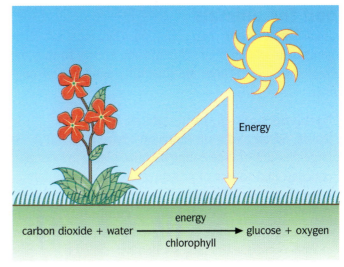

carbon dioxide + water $\xrightarrow[\text{chlorophyll}]{\text{energy}}$ glucose + oxygen

▲ Summary of photosynthesis.

## Food for seeds

Seeds released from the parent plant will be carried or will fall on to new ground. They use their stored food as a source of energy for germination and to grow leaves and roots. Then they can produce their own food.

▶ *Seeds often contain large quantities of oil. Why is this useful to us?*

## Food storage organs

During the winter the leaves of some plants die back completely, so the plants must rely on food they have stored underground to survive the winter and grow new parts above ground when the weather improves. Food storage organs are swollen because they contain the excess food produced during the summer.

Even after all the work some plants do to make and store energy and other nutrients they do not get to use them . . . they are eaten by animals.

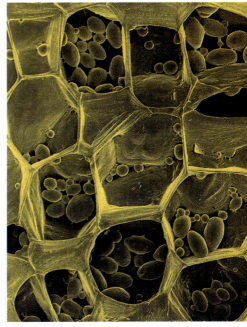

▲ Photograph of a slice through a potato magnified 170 times, showing starch grains in their cellular compartments.

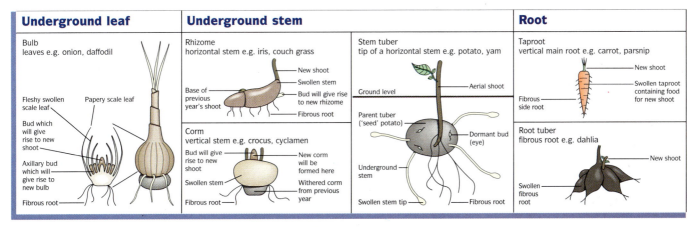

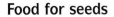
▲ Food storage organs in plants.

BIOLOGY

## Food for animals

Animals cannot make their own food. They must eat other organisms to obtain their nutrients and energy so they are called consumers. There are four different types of consumer:

▲ Life on an African plain.

- **Herbivores** eat only plant material, for example, leaves, nectar and fruit. Herbivores have to spend a large amount of time eating because plants are not a concentrated source of protein and they also contain a large proportion of cellulose which is difficult to digest. To help them digest plant material **ruminants**, such as cattle and sheep, have special stomachs with several chambers. Inside the largest chamber, called the **rumen**, are large numbers of bacteria which break down the cellulose in plant cell walls.
- **Carnivores** eat other animals. Meat is a good source of protein and energy so carnivores do not need to spend as much time eating as herbivores.
- **Omnivores** eat both plants and animals.
- **Parasites** live and feed on or inside another living organism called its **host**.

▸ *Write down examples of any herbivores, carnivores and omnivores you can see in the photograph of animals living on Africa's plains.*

Some animals eat only a few types of food, such as aphids (greenfly) which only suck plant sap. Others may be able to eat many types of food, as we do.

▸ *Why might it be an advantage to eat many types of food?*

## Feeding relationships

Plants and animals often show special features which help them get the food they need. For example, foxgloves can make food using sunlight and produce long flowers for reproduction. Butterflies have a long 'tongue' to reach into long flowers for nectar. Blue tits have a beak which can catch and eat butterflies.

These feeding relationships allow nutrients and energy to be transferred from one organism to another. The stages in these relationships are called **trophic** (feeding) levels.

## Food chains

Simple feeding relationships can be described in various ways. Consider the situation in which grass is eaten by a rabbit and then the rabbit is eaten by a fox.

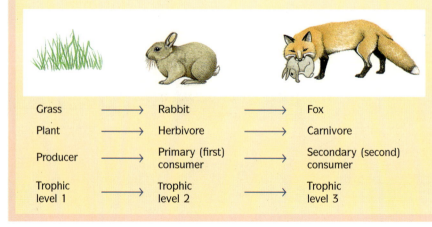

| Grass | → | Rabbit | → | Fox |
| Plant | | Herbivore | | Carnivore |
| Producer | → | Primary (first) consumer | → | Secondary (second) consumer |
| Trophic level 1 | → | Trophic level 2 | → | Trophic level 3 |

▲ A food chain.

The arrows in a food chain show the direction in which nutrients and energy are passed to the next organism and from one trophic level to the next. In this case the rabbit gets its food by eating grass and the fox by eating the rabbit.

▶ *Rearrange the following organisms into a food chain. Label the chain as fully as you can to show trophic levels, producer and so on.*

*owl   oak tree   shrew   beetle*

▶ *Give an example of a food chain with five trophic levels.*

It would not be surprising if you found the last question difficult because most food chains are short and they rarely have more than five organisms in them. The reason for this is that consumers do not usually eat the whole of their food source. For example, rabbits do not eat the grass roots, so food is wasted as it is passed along the food chain and there is not enough left to support many other consumers.

## Marine food chains

Food chains in the sea can have many levels. Marine plants (often small floating algae) cover a very large area so they can capture large amounts of energy. Many different consumers can be supported by this energy.

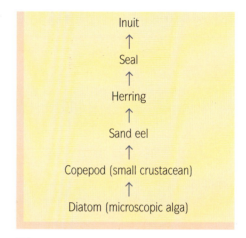
▲ A marine food chain.

## Decomposers and detritivores

A more realistic way to show a food chain would be to include **decomposers** and **detritivores**. These organisms break down dead plants and animals and animal wastes, releasing chemicals back into the environment. This makes the chemicals available to be used again by other organisms.

Although decomposers and detritivores have a vital role in recycling nutrients they are not usually shown on food chains.

▶ *What would happen to animal wastes and dead plants and animals if there were no decomposers?*

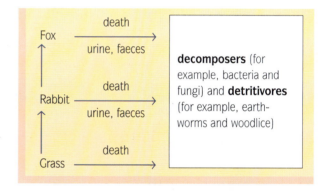

# Food webs

▶ *Look again at the food chain: grass → rabbit → fox*
*What would happen if all the rabbits in the area caught the disease myxomatosis and died?*

If an animal's only source of food is removed it will die. In real life an organism often eats more than one type of food.

If all the possible food chains in an ecosystem are combined a **food web** is produced, in which each organism is only shown once.

Food webs make it easier to see how the organisms in an ecosystem depend on each other for food.

▶ *Study the simple food web shown here.*

**a** *The fox and the hawk are top carnivores. What do you think this term means?*

**b** *Explain what might happen if the young oak trees were chopped down.*

▲ Rabbits eat different foods.

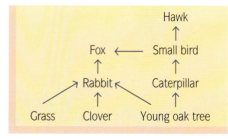
▲ A food web.

A food web can be very useful to show the relationships of the plants and animals in a particular place. All the living organisms and the area in which they live together is called an ecosystem. You may read about ecosystems in Chapter Fourteen (Adaptation and competition). Understanding the food web in an ecosystem can help you predict the possible effects of changing the conditions the organisms live in.

## Feeding relationships

Investigate feeding relationships by setting up an aquarium. You may be given a worksheet to help you with this investigation.

By observing the types of food eaten by each species that you add to the aquarium you could draw food chains, or perhaps a food web.

## Ecological pyramids

When studying the feeding relationships between organisms in an ecosystem it's not just the names that matter. We also need to know the numbers of organisms involved because this tells us how *much* food is available in a food chain or web. An easy way of showing these numbers is to use **pyramids of numbers**.

## Pyramids of numbers

These are used to represent information about the number of living organisms in a particular food chain.

▶ *Write down why:*
  **a** *the number of consumers decreases, and*
  **b** *the size of the consumers usually increases with each successive trophic level.*

Scientists represent each trophic level as a bar whose length is proportional to the number of organisms at that level. The producer is always shown as the lowest bar and the other bars are built on top.

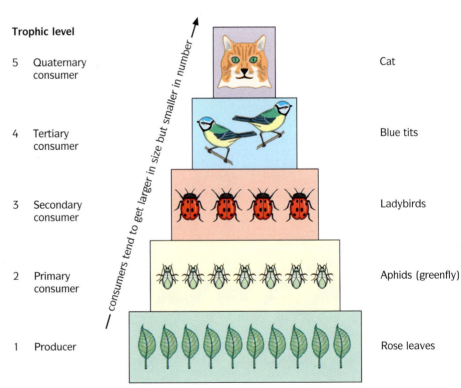

▲ Living organisms in a pyramid of numbers.

▶ *Use the information in the table to draw and label a pyramid of numbers. Try to draw it to scale.*

| Producer | Grass | 890 |
| Primary consumer | Grasshopper | 168 |
| Secondary consumer | Hedgehog | 12 |
| Tertiary consumer | Fox | 1 |

Pyramids of numbers sometimes look confusing because they do not have a *true* pyramid shape. In the earlier example, counting the rose bush as one organism, rather than counting all its leaves individually, the pyramid can be drawn as shown in the diagram.

Although the rose bush is only one producer it is large and contains lots of nutrients and energy, so it can support many animals.

▶ *Match the pyramids of numbers shown below to these food chains.*

  **1** *oak tree → caterpillar → small bird → owl*

  **2** *wheat seeds → mouse → cat*

  **3** *grass → rabbit → fox → fox flea*

  **4** *pond weed → tadpole → water beetle → pike*

  **5** *grass → rabbit → rabbit flea*

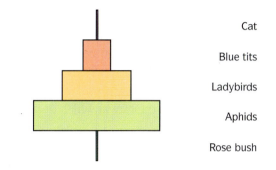

Cat
Blue tits
Ladybirds
Aphids
Rose bush

🔺 Pyramid of numbers counting individual organisms.

 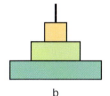  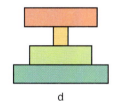 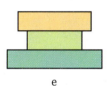

    a            b            c            d            e

▶ *Write down reasons for the unusual shape of pyramids c, d and e.*

The relative sizes of the organisms are important in influencing the shape of pyramids of numbers. One large individual plant can provide food for many animals and also many small parasites can feed from one large host.

▶ *Suggest other examples of food chains which will give unusual pyramid of numbers shapes. Sketch and label these pyramids.*

## Investigating ecosystems

Study a local ecosystem and use it to construct a pyramid of numbers. You need to select a particular food chain and count the number of each species involved. You may have studied methods of investigating ecosystems using a worksheet in Chapter Fourteen (Adaptation and competition).

## Pyramids of biomass

To overcome the problem of body size differences, scientists measure the **biomass** of each type of organism. This is the total mass of the organisms in each trophic level. Living organisms contain different amounts of water, so they are dried before weighing. Their **dry mass** gives a more accurate measurement of the nutrients which are available for the consumers in the next trophic level. To avoid having to kill the organisms by drying them completely, the live specimens can be weighed and their dry mass approximated from standard tables.

▶ *What is your dry mass? You are about two-thirds water so multiply your mass in kilograms by one-third (use 0.33) to find your dry mass.*

Pyramids of biomass usually give a typical pyramid shape because consumers need to eat more biomass than their own to allow for all the food which is wasted during transfer along the food chain.

Occasionally even pyramids of biomass have an unusual shape. This happens because the biomass measurements are made at a particular time and do not allow for the differences which might occur at various times of the year, especially in ecosystems where the climate changes during the year – for example, the variation in a beech tree during the summer and winter when the leaf numbers will vary greatly. Another factor which varies is the rate at which organisms reproduce.

▶ *When would the biomass of a beech be greatest?*

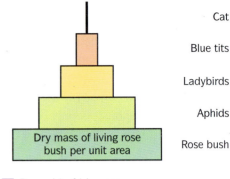

Cat
Blue tits
Ladybirds
Aphids
Rose bush

Dry mass of living rose bush per unit area

🔺 Pyramid of biomass.

🔺 A beech tree during the summer.      🔺 The same tree during the winter.

## Plankton and pyramids

Many marine (sea) food chains begin with microscopic organisms called **plankton** which lived near the surface of the sea.

**Phytoplankton** (plant plankton) are small plants which breed very quickly, particularly during the summer.

**Zooplankton** (animal plankton) breed more slowly than phytoplankton but live longer. Zooplankton consume phytoplankton.

When the pyramid of biomass was drawn it looked inverted (upside down).

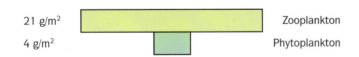

21 g/m²      Zooplankton
4 g/m²       Phytoplankton

🔺 'Inverted' pyramid of biomass.

🔺 Phytoplankton and zooplankton.

BIOLOGY

▶ *Why do phytoplankton breed most quickly during the summer?*

▶ *If the biomass was measured for the whole year would you expect the phytoplankton or the zooplankton to produce the most? Explain your answer.*

▶ *Suggest why the phytoplankton can produce enough biomass to support the zooplankton even though you cannot easily see this from the pyramid of biomass.*

In fact, although at this particular time of year the pyramid of biomass shows there is more biomass of zooplankton, there are always enough phytoplankton for the zooplankton to eat. This is because the phytoplankton are reproducing very quickly, so replacing the phytoplankton which have been eaten.

This study shows the importance of the time of year you choose to do an ecological study. The results obtained would be different depending on the time of year.

## Energy in the ecosystem

🔺 Desert.

🔺 Rainforest.

🔺 British meadow.

▶ *Study the ecosystems in the photographs. Which do you think would have the greatest energy transfer through its food chains?*

You probably chose an ecosystem which had lots of plants because these could capture the sunlight which reached them. But you could also have chosen the one which would have lots of sunshine, preferably all year round. The rainforest would have the greatest energy content. However, not all the sunlight which reaches a plant can be used for photosynthesis.

▶ *What happens to the Sun's energy which reaches a green leaf?*

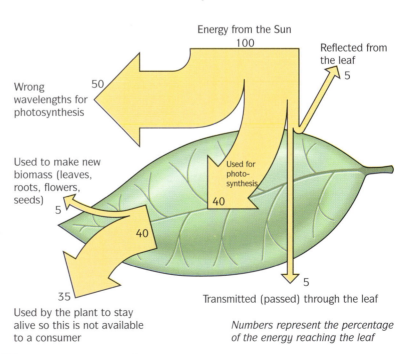

Energy from the Sun
100

Reflected from the leaf
5

Wrong wavelengths for photosynthesis
50

Used for photo-synthesis
40

Used to make new biomass (leaves, roots, flowers, seeds)
5

40

5
Transmitted (passed) through the leaf

35
Used by the plant to stay alive so this is not available to a consumer

*Numbers represent the percentage of the energy reaching the leaf*

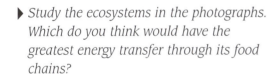
🔺 How a plant uses sunlight.

BIOLOGY

▶ *Some plants are better at capturing the energy in sunlight than others. Use the percentages given in the diagram to:*

  **a** *calculate the efficiency of the leaf in capturing the energy from sunlight:*

$$\text{Percentage efficiency of plant} = \frac{\text{total energy content of the plant}}{\text{total energy from the Sun}} \times 100$$

  **b** *How much of the energy reaching the leaf would be used by a herbivore which ate the leaf?*

## Energy capture

Only a small amount of the energy in the new biomass is passed along the chain as food for a consumer. For example, herbivores usually only eat certain parts of the plants, such as leaves, ignoring the other parts, such as the roots.

Similar losses of energy occur at all trophic levels of a food chain. For example, if you consume a beefburger you would expect it to contain flesh (red meat), but not the horns, skin or brain so the energy stored in these would be wasted or lost.

Even the biomass which is eaten is not used very efficiently by the consumer. Most of the energy is lost to the consumer before it can be used for growth.

▶ *Study the diagram.*

  **a** *Make a list of all the ways energy is lost from the consumer rather than being incorporated into new biomass.*

  **b** *Calculate the percentage of the energy taken in by the consumer which is used to make new biomass.*

  **c** *What types of biomass might the consumer make?*

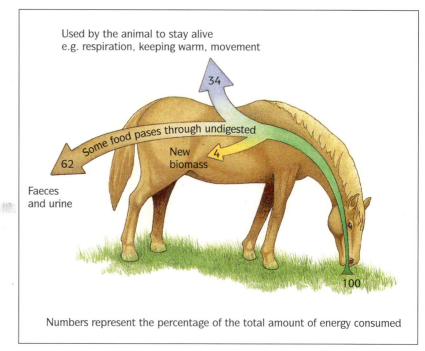

Numbers represent the percentage of the total amount of energy consumed

Used by the animal to stay alive e.g. respiration, keeping warm, movement — 34

Some food pases through undigested — 4

New biomass

62 — Faeces and urine

100

▲ To show what happens to the chemical energy from the plant leaves eaten by an animal.

## Pyramids of energy

The energy loss at each stage of the food chain means there is progressively less energy available for the consumers further along the chain. As a result **pyramids of energy** always have a true pyramid shape.

## Energy transfers and losses

The proportion of energy transferred between the trophic levels varies depending on the types of organisms. Typically an average of about 10 per cent of the available energy is passed from one trophic level to the next.

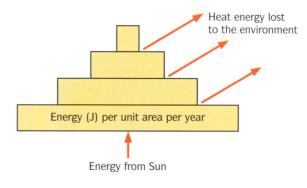

Heat energy lost to the environment

Energy (J) per unit area per year

Energy from Sun

▲ Pyramid of energy.

▶ *Using the information in the diagram and your earlier work on the relationship grass → rabbit → fox, suggest why food chains are short and may not include quaternary (fourth level) consumers.*

▶ *What eventually happens to all the lost energy?*

## Energy balance in ecosystems

The amount of energy entering an ecosystem and all the energy which is eventually lost as heat to the environment should be the same. This is difficult and time-consuming to investigate.

## Humans in food chains

Knowing about feeding relationships and ecological pyramids is useful when thinking about food production for humans.

We are part of many food chains and can be involved at any of the consumer trophic levels, as our digestive system is adapted for life as omnivores. For example:

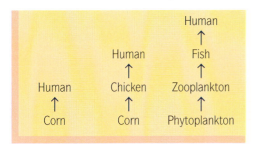

▶ *Write down some other food chains with humans as primary, secondary, tertiary and quaternary consumers.*

In the pyramid of numbers diagram **a** shows you that because of the energy losses along the food chain, a huge number of organisms is needed at the base of the pyramid to support just one human. If humans ate the producers directly, as in **b**, far less energy would be lost, so many more humans would have enough energy to live.

It would be much more energy efficient for us to eat plants directly rather than to feed plants to animals and then eat the animals – especially where farm animals are fed with grain which is fit for human consumption.

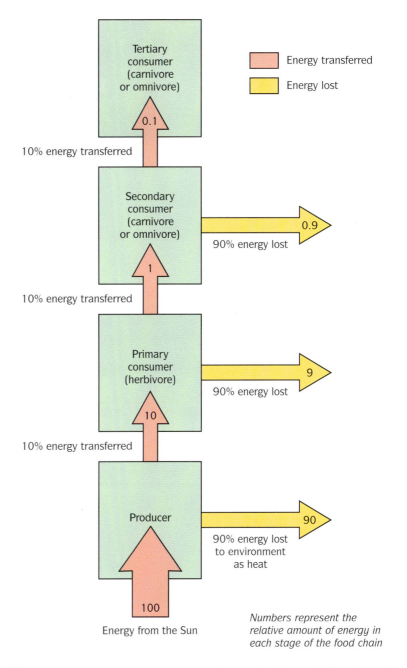

▲ A summary of how energy from the Sun may be lost as it flows through a food chain.

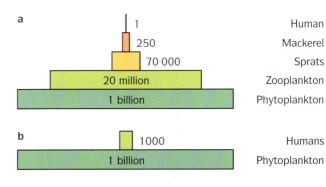

▲ Pyramids of numbers involving humans.

B I O L O G Y

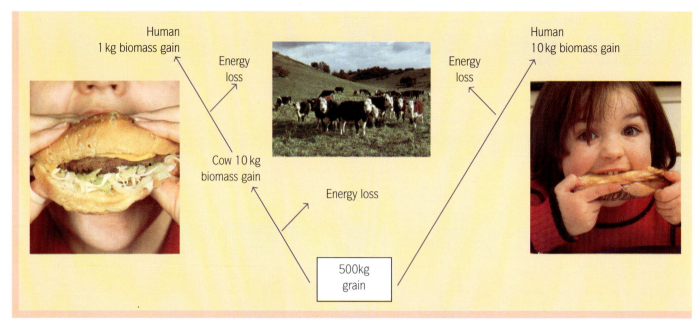

Human
1 kg biomass gain

Energy
loss

Cow 10 kg
biomass gain

Energy loss

Energy
loss

Human
10 kg biomass gain

500kg
grain

🔺 Less energy is lost during the short food chain, which results in greater gain of human biomass.

In 1798 Thomas Malthus predicted that human population would increase faster than food production and famine would occur.

As the world human population increases, and people live longer, larger amounts of food will be needed. One way of increasing the food supply is to keep food chains as short as possible by decreasing the quantity of meat which is consumed.

## Efficiency of agriculture

Farmers manage their farms to increase the efficiency of food production so that lots of energy-containing foods are available for human consumption. To do this they try to control the conditions in which the crops and animals grow. They also select species that have been bred to grow quickly.

For plant crops the farmer will sow the plants with enough space to grow and with as much sunlight as possible reaching their leaves. Herbicide use will kill weeds to stop them competing with the crop for sunlight and nutrients. Pesticide use will stop other organisms eating the crop before it is used by humans.

## Competition for resources

Investigate the effect of competition between plants for resources and find out how this affects their growth. One possible way of doing this would be to put different numbers of cress seeds into separate pots of the same size. Some pots would contain only a few seeds, giving a low density of plants. Other pots would contain many seeds, so they had to compete more for the resources in the pot. The 'crops' grown at different densities would be weighed to measure their yield (quantity). You could comment on how growing plants at different densities might affect their growth. You might be able to suggest how plant density would affect food production.

You may be given a worksheet to help you with this investigation.

## Control of crop damage

To prevent organisms competing with the cultivated plants and animals, farmers make use of *pesticides* – herbicides to kill plants, insecticides to kill insects and fungicides to kill fungi.

Some pesticides do not break down in the natural environment and are described as **persistent pesticides**, for instance the insecticide DDT. A persistent pesticide is absorbed into the plant through its roots or leaves. It then enters animals as they eat the plant. The chemicals cannot be broken down by the body so they accumulate (build up) in the cells. Eventually the concentration may become so high that the animal is poisoned. If the animal is eaten by a predator the chemical is passed along the food chain.

▶ *Explain why the further along a food chain an animal is, the more likely it is to have a high concentration of pesticide in its body.*

▶ *Suggest how an otter living by a river might be poisoned by insecticide.*

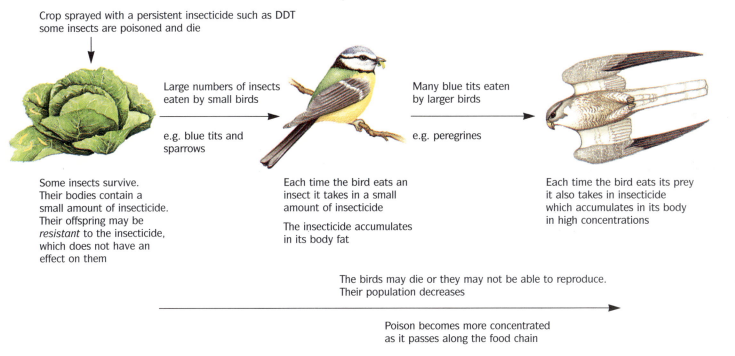

Crop sprayed with a persistent insecticide such as DDT some insects are poisoned and die

Large numbers of insects eaten by small birds

e.g. blue tits and sparrows

Many blue tits eaten by larger birds

e.g. peregrines

Some insects survive. Their bodies contain a small amount of insecticide. Their offspring may be *resistant* to the insecticide, which does not have an effect on them

Each time the bird eats an insect it takes in a small amount of insecticide

The insecticide accumulates in its body fat

Each time the bird eats its prey it also takes in insecticide which accumulates in its body in high concentrations

The birds may die or they may not be able to reproduce. Their population decreases

Poison becomes more concentrated as it passes along the food chain

🔺 Insecticide passing along a food chain.

## Factory farming

Some farmers may use factory-farming methods for meat production. The animals are kept warm and their movement restricted so that they do not use much energy and they gain weight more quickly. This allows them to produce meat cheaply, a major factor in consumer choice.

# Summary

- The energy needed by organisms comes from the Sun (solar energy).
- Solar energy is trapped by green plants (producers) during the process of photosynthesis.
- Some organisms (primary consumers – often herbivores) eat green plants to obtain their energy directly.
- Other organisms (secondary consumers – carnivores or omnivores) eat the primary consumers to obtain their energy.
- Trophic (feeding) relationships between the organisms in an environment can be shown as food chains and food webs.
- The organisms in food chains can be shown quantitatively using pyramids of numbers, biomass and energy.
- As nutrients pass along the stages of a food chain
  
  **a** the number of organisms often decreases
  
  **b** the biomass (living matter) decreases
  
  **c** the energy decreases.
- As the energy is passed from one organism to another, most is lost as heat from respiration and in faeces and urine.
- Agricultural techniques, such as using pesticides, herbicides and keeping animals indoors, are used to improve the efficiency of energy transfer to increase the food energy available for humans.
- By decreasing meat consumption and keeping food chains short, larger amounts of energy would be available for humans, and a larger world population could survive.

# Revision Questions

1 Why are plants called producers?

2 Consider the simple food chain below.
   dead leaves → worm → blackbird → hawk
   a Where does the energy first come from in this food chain?
   b Some energy is lost at each trophic level. Give one example of how this loss might happen.

3 Put the following groups of organisms in the correct order to form food chains, starting with the producer.
   a slug   lettuce   hedgehog
   b slug   grass snake   frog   cabbage
   c cabbage   thrush   caterpillar
   d spider   honeysuckle   bee   sparrow   cat
   e seagull   seaweed   crab   limpet
   f water flea   phytoplankton   perch   minnow
   g bank vole   blackberry   owl

4 This food web is from a garden ecosystem.

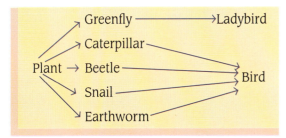

   a Complete these food chains using the information in the diagram.
      i plant → snail → _____
      ii _____ → earthworm → bird
   b Add another consumer and draw a food chain with five trophic levels.
   c The energy in a food chain can be used by decomposers when the plants and animals die. Name one type of organism that is a decomposer.

5 Which of the following food chains fits this pyramid of numbers?

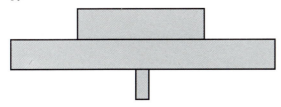

   a tree → squirrel → squirrel flea
   b grass → insects → bird
   c phytoplankton → zooplankton → sprat
   d tree → caterpillar → bird
   e grass → rabbit → stoat

6 Study the food web from the sea

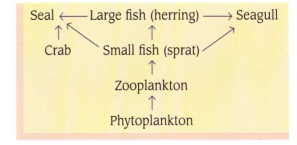

   a List:
      i the producers
      ii the primary consumers
      iii the secondary consumers
      iv the tertiary consumers
      v herbivores
      vi carnivores.

   b Write down two food chains that end in seagulls.
   c Write down a food chain which could end in humans.

7 a What is a pyramid of biomass?
   b Why can a pyramid of biomass be more useful than a pyramid of numbers?

8 Consider the information below about organisms in an estuary.
   ■ curlews feed on lugworms and bivalve molluscs that live in the mud
   ■ eel grass is the main rooted plant
   ■ lugworms and bivalve molluscs are filter feeders, living on the numerous small crustaceans and algae in the estuarine water
   ■ birds, such as dunlins, feed on the floating crustaceans
   ■ snails feed on the eel grass
   ■ fish feed on the free-floating algae
   ■ many overwintering birds, such as Brent geese, feed on the eel grass.
   Use this information to construct a food web.

**9 a** Use the information on the diagram below to calculate the percentage of food energy eaten by the sheep which is converted into meat.

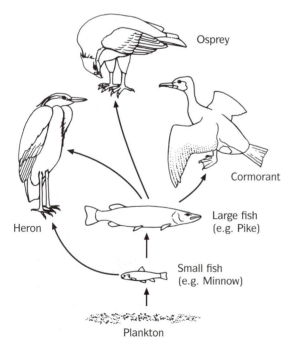

1055 kJ heat loss

195 kJ in new biomass

2000 kJ in faeces and urine

3250 kJ energy in food

**b** Why is the sheep so inefficient at converting grass into meat?

**c** Which of the following food chains is more efficient in providing food for humans?
  *i* grass → sheep → human
  *ii* soya bean → sheep → human
  *iii* soya bean → human
  Explain your choice.

**d** How could sheep farming be managed to improve production?

**10 a** Part of a food web for a freshwater lake.

Osprey

Cormorant

Large fish (e.g. Pike)

Heron

Small fish (e.g. Minnow)

Plankton

*i* Complete the boxes to show a simple food chain from the lake.

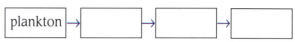

plankton →  □  →  □  →  □

*ii* Where does the energy first come from in this food web?
*iii* State *three* ways energy can be *lost* to the environment as it passes through the food web.

**b** Farmers use pesticides on their crops. They used to use DDT, a persistent pesticide, which is now banned in the United Kingdom.

| | |
|---|---|
| Cormorant | 26.40 |
| Heron | 3.57 |
| Minnow | 0.23 |
| Osprey | 13.80 |
| Pike | 1.33 |
| Plankton | 0.04 |

▲ Relative amounts of DDT found in the organisms in a food web in 1960.

*i* Why do farmers use pesticides on their crops?
*ii* Explain why the pike has a greater concentration of DDT than the minnow.
*iii* Explain why the cormorant has a greater concentration of DDT than the heron.
*iv* Describe *two* ways in which pesticides could enter a freshwater lake.
*v* Explain what is meant by a *persistent* pesticide.

**11** Describe how energy enters, passes through and is lost from a food chain of your choice.

# CHAPTER SIXTEEN

# Biology help

## Practice with investigations

This chapter is not the end. It contains helpful suggestions and hints which are designed to improve your science skills. It also contains a range of activities which might be used for homework or in class. Some of the work presented is based on real experimental work carried out by 15 year-olds. You might even be expected to mark some of the work as if you were the teacher.

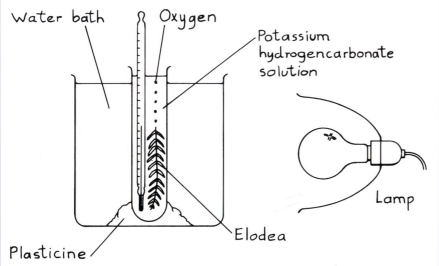

Water bath    Oxygen

Potassium hydrogencarbonate solution

Lamp

Plasticine

Elodea

# Light and photosynthesis

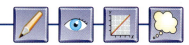

Anna carried out an experiment to see how altering the light affects the rate of photosynthesis. You might carry out this experiment yourself, or you could study Anna's work and answer the questions.

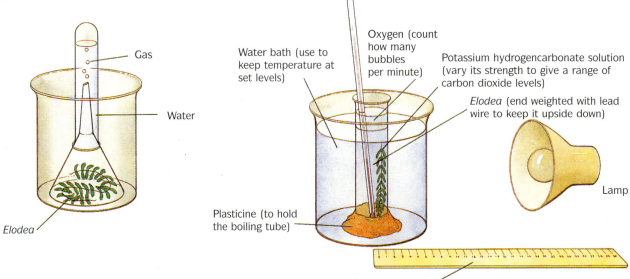

Gas

Water

*Elodea*

Water bath (use to keep temperature at set levels)

Oxygen (count how many bubbles per minute)

Potassium hydrogencarbonate solution (vary its strength to give a range of carbon dioxide levels)

*Elodea* (end weighted with lead wire to keep it upside down)

Plasticine (to hold the boiling tube)

Lamp

Ruler
(use to measure distance of light from *Elodea*, convert to light intensity using a light meter)

▲ This is the equipment that Anna used.

## Introduction

*Elodea* is a pondweed. A freshly-cut piece of stem gives off bubbles. These bubbles give you an indirect way of measuring the rate of photosynthesis. The higher the number of bubbles in a unit of time, the faster the rate of photosynthesis.

  I am going to alter the amount of light received by the plant and see how this affects the rate of bubbling.

## Hypothesis

I predict the stronger the light levels, the faster the rate of photosynthesis.

▸ *What scientific evidence could be used to support this prediction? Carry out the background research needed for this investigation and write notes suggesting how this prediction can be supported.*

▸ *Anna has not identified all the variables which might affect this experiment. Copy the table and complete each column as fully as possible.*

| Controlled | Independent | Dependent |
|---|---|---|
| | | |
| | | |
| | | |
| | | |
| | | |
| | | |

To investigate my prediction I am going to set up the apparatus as shown in the diagram. The nearer the light bulb, the brighter the light.

I predict that as the light gets nearer (and brighter) to the pondweed, the rate of photosynthesis will get faster.
I am going to record my results in this table.

| Distance from beaker (cm) | Number of bubbles in one minute |
|---|---|
| 1 | |
| 15 | |
| 25 | |
| 50 | |

🔺 Anna's results table.

▶ *How could this table be improved?*

## Results

▶ *Draw a line graph of Anna's results.*

▶ *What could Anna have done to make these results more useful and more reliable?*

| Distance from beaker (cm) | Number of bubbles in one minute |
|---|---|
| 1 | 32 |
| 15 | 24 |
| 25 | 20 |
| 50 | 20 |

🔺 Anna's results.

### Analysis

I think my prediction was correct. At 1 cm, the rate was the fastest at 32 bubbles per minute, nearly 50 per cent faster than at 50 cm. Light is needed for photosynthesis and so it is hardly surprising that the rate of photosynthesis is greatest when the light is nearest.

▶ *Before reading on, criticise the experiment, evaluating the results and the conclusions drawn from them.*

### Evaluation

I am worried about my results. I noticed that at 1 cm the beaker got quite warm. I would like to repeat this experiment and try to control the temperature. Perhaps I could keep the bulb at the same distance and use different sizes of slits to let different amounts of light through. I could try a different way too. I could heat up the beaker and keep the light the same distance. This would show me the effect of heat. That would be two variables to test. I think light is the most important though.

I talked through my results with my partner. If we were to do this again we would need more time. I would like to have done more readings for the bubbles. In particular, some readings at distances between the ones we used would have been useful. We did not really have enough readings to plot graphs, but we only realised that after we started to write up the experiment.

▶ *Do you agree with her evaluation? Is there anything she has missed?*

▶ *Your teacher might let you use a standard mark scheme to mark this piece of work. Which area is the best? If you were Anna's teacher what targets for improvement would you set for the next investigation?*

# Trampling damage

Adrian decided to investigate the effects of trampling on the school field.

## Introduction

The school field is covered with many kinds of plant, and not just grass. On closer inspection you can see many different types of plant; daisy, clover, dandelion, yarrow and plantain being the commonest. These will be affected in different ways by trampling. I expect that the most delicate plants will be the most affected, but I don't know what makes a plant delicate. I could do another investigation to find this out.

There are several ways to investigate this link: **quadrat analysis** is where you throw a 1 x 1 metre metal grid or **quadrat square** on to the field. This is divided further into one hundred smaller squares. Every time a plant occurs in one small square, you say it has 1 per cent cover, if it is in 50 squares, you say it has 50 per cent cover. You can also use a scale like **DAFORN** to record species.

D stands for Dominant, A for Abundant, F for Frequent, O for Occasional, R for Rare and N for None. This is useful when you have a list of plants to compare.

**Transects** are another method. A transect is a line. You stretch a line across the area you are studying and record the plants which touch the string every 10 centimetres. (We used this in a beach survey in Year 9 and I am going to use the same type of results table.)

▲ A quadrat square.

▶ *Like Adrian can you think of an investigation you have done in the past which could have been used to support one done this year?*

▶ *Have you ever evaluated an investigation and suggested doing a further experiment? Have you ever done that further experiment?*

▶ *Complete Adrian's introduction. He went on to describe what he thought were the most important features in plants resistant to trampling. Carry out some research to discover what might affect the ability of a plant to resist damage by trampling.*

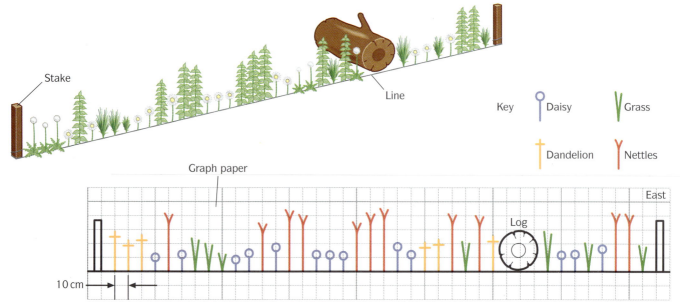

▲ Line transect.

B I O L O G Y

# Heat and vitamin C

▲ John and Kirsty investigating vitamin C.

John and Kirsty carried out an investigation to look at how heat affects the amount of vitamin C in a sample of greens.

## Introduction

John and Kirsty placed shredded cabbage in boiling water. They removed a sample of cabbage each minute and estimated its vitamin C content by grinding it up and seeing how much of it was needed to bleach a standard volume of a dye called DCPIP.

The greater the amount of vitamin C in the sample, the fewer the number of drops needed to bleach the dye.

## Analysis and evaluation

▶ *Plot these data on a graph. Which sample contains the most vitamin C? (Be careful!)*

▶ **a** *Is there a particular result that does not seem to fit?*
   **b** *What would you advise the student to do about strange results?*

▶ *Write down a hypothesis which you could now investigate based on this first experiment. (You might have to do some more research into vitamin C before you can do this.)*

## Results

| Time sample taken (minutes) | Number of drops needed to bleach DCPIP |
|---|---|
| Raw (0) | 6 |
| 1 | 7 |
| 2 | 7 |
| 3 | 6 |
| 4 | 8 |
| 5 | 9 |
| 6 | 10 |
| 7 | 12 |
| 8 | 11 |
| 9 | 13 |
| 10 | 20 |

# Estimating populations

▲ Estimating the number of woodlice in a population.

▸ *Read these notes taken from a student's practical file. Present the information in a more useful way.*

▸ *Substitute the data in this equation:*

$$\text{estimated population} = \frac{\text{number in sample 1} \times \text{number in sample 2}}{\text{number in sample 2 marked from sample 1}}$$

▸ *What is the estimated population of the area of hedgerow under study?*

▸ *Was this a fair test?*

▸ *Use this information to plan a second study on an animal of your choice. What variables might affect the distribution of your chosen animal?*

We collected 25 animals in 15 minutes. Each woodlouse was carefully marked on its underside and released. Two days later we repeated our search. This time we found 21 in 20 minutes. Nine were marked with ink from the first sample collected.

## Yeast and bread

Grace and Surendra decided to investigate the manufacture of bread. They discovered that adding yeast to the dough is a vital part of the process. Yeast respires anaerobically, producing gases and other chemicals. The gases make the dough rise. Other chemicals improve the flavour.

▸ *Research some of the background information for this investigation. You may read about this experiment in Chemistry, Chapter Eleven.*

They wondered about the best temperature for making the dough rise, and designed a simple experiment to collect the gas produced by the yeast. They collected the gas produced, and recorded its volume at regular intervals.

The group carried out this experiment twice, once at 25°C and once at 33°C.

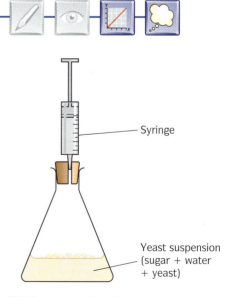

Syringe

Yeast suspension
(sugar + water
+ yeast)

▲ The production of gas by yeast.

BIOLOGY

## Results

▶ *Plot both sets of data on the same graph. Try to draw a smooth line connecting each set of points.*

▶ *Analyse and evaluate these results. What other experiments would you need to do before you can conclude that increasing the temperature of the yeast suspension increases the rate of reaction?*

| Time (h) | Volume of gas (cm³) | |
|---|---|---|
| | 25°C | 30°C |
| 0 | 12 | 12 |
| 4 | 24 | 27 |
| 8 | 30 | 54 |
| 20 | 108 | 220 |
| 24 | 150 | 258 |
| 29 | 225 | 261 |
| 44 | 240 | 225 |
| 53 | 220 | 118 |
| 68 | 42 | 18 |
| 72 | 0 | 0 |

🔺 Production of gas at 25°C and 33°C.

# Obtaining evidence

▶ *Make a large drawing of each cell shown below.*

▶ *Label each drawing as fully as possible.*

▶ *Estimate the size of the nucleus in each cell.*

> 1 m = 1000 mm
> 1 mm = 1000 μm

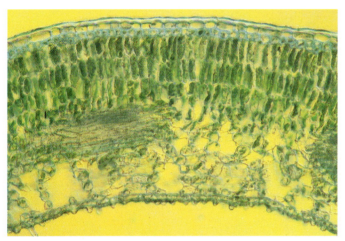

🔺 A photograph of a tobacco leaf cell magnified 120 times.

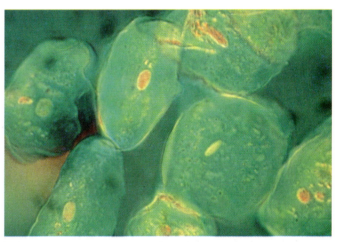

🔺 A photograph of an e cell magnified 600 times.

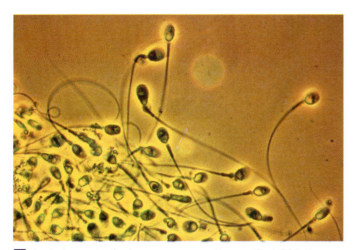

🔺 A photograph of a human sperm cell magnified 900 times.

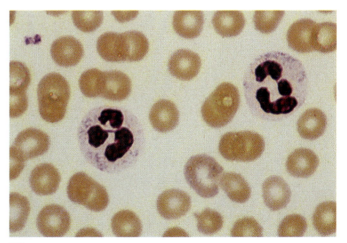

🔺 A photograph of blood cells magnified 3000 times.

# Classification

▶ *Use the classification chart below to list the main characteristics of each group.*

▶ *Choose a range of living things from the chart. Give the selection to a friend for him or her to produce an identification key. Check if the key works.*

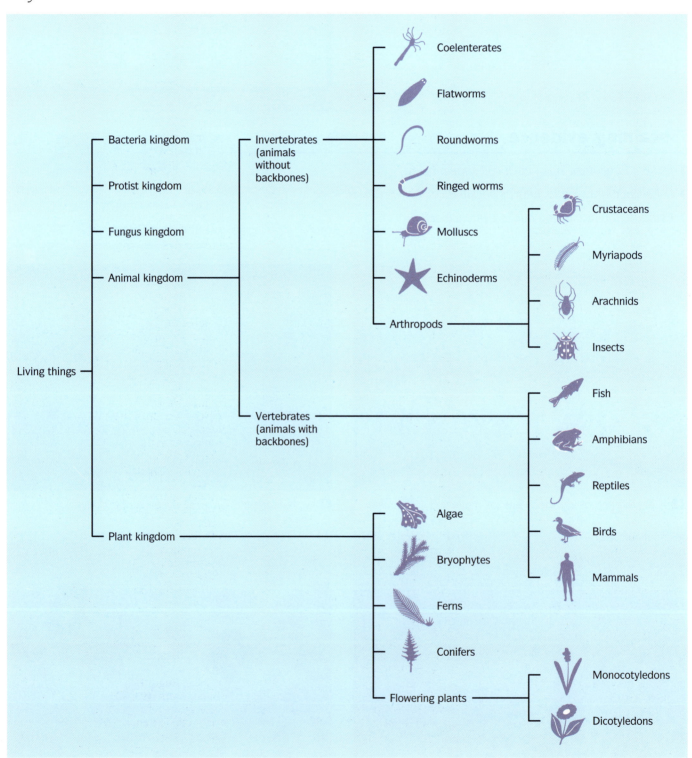

🔺 Classification of living things.

# Index

punctuated equilibrium 154
Punnett square 132
pyramids of biomass 227–9
pyramids of energy 230
pyramids of numbers 226–7, 231
pyrexia 116
pyrogens 116

quadrat analysis 240

radioactive isotopes 179
rainforest 217
recessive characteristics 131
rectum 53
recycling, elements 193
red blood cells 65
reflex pathways 82
reflexes 82, 83–4, 85
refraction 89
renograms 121–2
replication 135
reproduction 99–100, 128, 144
reproductive system 94
resistance, drugs 36
resources
    competition 232, 234
    human impact 216
respiration 16, 72–3
results 8, 9–10
resuscitation 63
retina 81, 87, 88
ribs 63
risk assessment 4, 7–8
rivers, nitrate pollution 201
rooting compounds 105
roots 104, 163
Rothamsted experimental station 202
rubbish 217
rubella 34–5
rubisco 184
rumen 224
ruminants 224

safety 4, 8
saliva 56
salivary glands 53
salt 48, 49
saturated fats 47
scale 19–20
scientific method 133
sclera 87
secondary sexual characteristics 99
secondary stimulus 85
seeds 223
selection, artificial 143, 144–5
semi-lunar valves 69
sensory neurones 82
sewage 217
sex cells 25, 128
sex chromosomes 129–30
sex hormones 99
shivering 113
shoots 102
skills 1–2

skin 31, 113–15
small intestine 53, 56, 58
smallpox 33
smog 216
smoking 38–9
snowshoe hare 214
social insects, chromosomes 130
sodium hydrogencarbonate 55, 56
soils 199
    structure 200
    testing 201
    water 161
solvents 41
somatotrophin 125
space 109–10
species 144
specific heat capacity 157
spectrum 180
sperm 128
sperm cells 14, 25
spherocytosis 66
spinal cord 78
stains 19
starch 57, 175, 177, 181, 223
statistics 1, 12
stomach 53, 54
stomata 11, 166–7
storage organs 223
strokes 86
succession 210–11
sugar 48, 49, 96
support, plants 160
surface area
    skin 114–15
    volume problem 66
survival of the fittest 153
sweating 114
sympathetic nervous system 84
synapses 82–3
synthesis 130
synthetic auxins 105

Taenia 211
tapeworms 211
teeth 48
temperature
    see also heat
    photosynthesis 183
    regulation 111–16
    skin 113–14
    vitamin C 241
    water 157
testes 95, 99
testosterone 99
thalamus 86
thermal imaging 112
thermoregulation 115–16
thesis 130
thrombocytes 38
thrombosis 70
thrombus 38
thyroid gland 95
tissue fluid 74
tissues 15, 74

trace elements 192
trachea 65
trampling damage 239–40
transects 240
transgenic animals 147
transpiration 5–8, 164, 166, 168
transpiration stream 169
transplants
    heart 74
    kidneys 118, 119–20, 141
    rejection 33
tricuspid valve 69
trophic levels 224
tubules 117
turgidity 160
Turner's syndrome 130

ulcers 55, 59
ultrasound scans 68, 100
unicellular organisms 16
unsaturated fats 47
ureters 117
urethra 117
urinary system 117
urination 117
urine 116, 117–18

vaccines 33–5
valves, heart 69, 70
variables 3, 6, 12
variation 127, 143, 144
veins 68, 70
ventilation rate 72
ventricles 68
Venus fly-trap 199
villi 58
vitamin C 23, 241
vitamins 46, 47
volume 66

Wallace, Alfred 147–8
waste 217
waste products 67, 116
water 46, 157–72
    cycle 159
    photosynthesis 178–9, 184
    ponds 191
weedkillers 105
weight 47–8
white blood cells 32
whitefly 214
wood 165
world population 215
wound tissue 105

X-rays 68, 70
xylem 160, 163, 165, 168

yeast 212, 242–3

zooplankton 228–9
zygote 128